Morality and the I
and Spy Fiction, 1880–1920

"A VERY SEEDY HARD FELT HAT."

Morality and the Law
in British Detective and Spy Fiction, 1880–1920

KATE MORRISON

McFarland & Company, Inc., Publishers
Jefferson, North Carolina

This book has undergone peer review.

Frontispiece: The opening scene of "The Adventure of the Blue Carbuncle" finds Holmes in deductive mode as he outlines the character and social standing of the owner of a hat delivered to him by the commissionaire, Peterson, along with a Christmas goose, both of which he came upon at the scene of a "garroting," or attempted murder, on his return home the previous evening along Tottenham Court Road (*Strand Magazine*, Vol. 3, 73. Artist: Sidney E. Paget. The Print Collector/Alamy Stock Photo).

LIBRARY OF CONGRESS CATALOGUING-IN-PUBLICATION DATA

Names: Morrison, Kate, 1952– author.
Title: Morality and the law in British detective
and spy fiction, 1880–1920 / Kate Morrison.
Description: Jefferson, North Carolina : McFarland & Company, Inc., Publishers, 2020. | Includes bibliographical references and index.
Identifiers: LCCN 2020016956 | ISBN 9781476677194 (paperback : acid free paper) ∞ ISBN 9781476639758 (ebook)
Subjects: LCSH: Detective and mystery stories, English—History and criticism. | Spy stories, English—History and criticism. | English fiction—19th century—History and criticism. | English fiction—20th century—History and criticism. | Crime in literature. | Law in literature. | Justice, Administration of, in literature. | Law and literature.
Classification: LCC PR830.D4 M67 2020 | DDC 823/.087209—dc2 3
LC record available at https://lccn.loc.gov/2020016956

BRITISH LIBRARY CATALOGUING DATA ARE AVAILABLE

ISBN (print) 978-1-4766-7719-4
ISBN (ebook) 978-1-4766-3975-8

Front cover illustration by Sidney Paget for the short story "The Adventure of the Reigate Squire" in *The Strand Magazine*, June 1893

Printed in the United States of America

McFarland & Company, Inc., Publishers
Box 611, Jefferson, North Carolina 28640
www.mcfarlandpub.com

For Sarah and Patrick O' Grady and
Heather and Sarah Morrison

Table of Contents

Abbreviations

The following short-form titles are used to refer to works that are cited frequently in the text.

Atonement: Schramm, Jan-Melissa. *Atonement and Self-Sacrifice in Nineteenth Century Narrative.* Cambridge: Cambridge University Press, 2012.

Bloody Murder: Symons, Julian. *Bloody Murder: From the Detective Story to the Crime Novel: A History.* Revised Second Edition. London: Pan, 1992.

Continent: Knight, Stephen T. *Continent of Mystery: A Thematic History of Australian Crime Fiction.* Melbourne: Melbourne University Press, 1997.

Conversation: Derrida, Jacques. *Deconstruction in a Nutshell: A Conversation with Jacques Derrida.* Edited and with a Commentary by John D. Caputo. New York: Fordham University Press, 1997.

Crime and Society: Emsley, Clive. *Crime and Society in England: 1750–1900.* Harlow: Pearson, 2005.

Crime Fiction: Kestner, Joseph A. *Crime Fiction: 1800–2000: Detection, Death, Diversity.* Basingstoke: Palgrave Macmillan, 2004.

Figure: Priestman, Martin. *Detective Fiction and Literature: The Figure on the Carpet.* New York: St. Martin's Press, 1991.

Form: Kestner, Joseph A. *Form and Ideology in Crime Fiction.* Bloomington: Indiana University Press, 1980.

Jurisprudence: Wacks, Raymond. *Understanding Jurisprudence: An Introduction to Legal Theory.* London: Oxford University Press, 2005.

Masculinities: Kestner, Joseph A. *Masculinities in British Adventure Fiction, 1880–1915.* Aldershot: Ashgate Publishing, 2010.

Memories: Conan Doyle, Arthur. *Memories and Adventures.* Cambridge: Cambridge University Press, 2012. Originally published in 1923.

Memory: Buchan, John. *Memory Hold-The Door.* London: Hodder and Stoughton, 1940.

Men of Blood: Wiener, Martin J. *Men of Blood: Violence, Manliness and Criminal Justice in Victorian England.* Cambridge: Cambridge University Press, 2004.

Abbreviations

Mystery: Cawelti, John G. *Mystery, Violence and Popular Culture: Essays.* Madison: University Press of Wisconsin, 2004.

Probable Cause: Panek, Leroy L. *Probable Cause: Crime Fiction in America.* Bowling Green, OH: Bowling Green State University Press, 1990.

Secrets: Kestner, Joseph A. *Secrets of Crime Fiction Classics: Detecting the Delights of 21 Enduring Stories.* Jefferson, NC: McFarland, 2014.

Sisters: Kestner, Joseph A. *Sherlock's Sisters: The British Female Detective 1864–1913.* Aldershot: Ashgate Publishing, 2003.

Special Branch: Panek, Leroy L. *The Special Branch: The British Spy Novel 1890–1980.* Bowling Green, OH: Bowling Green University Popular Press, 1981.

Spy Story: Cawelti, John G., and Bruce A. Rosenberg. *The Spy Story.* Chicago: University of Chicago Press, 1987.

Women Writers: Sussex, Lucy. *Women Writers and Detectives in Nineteenth Century Detective Fiction: The Mothers of the Mystery Genre.* London: Palgrave Macmillan, 2010.

Preface

In this exploration into the illegalities of fictional detectives and spies in crime and spy fiction from the past, my intention is to probe the motivations that trigger their actions, with a view to uncovering the ideological attitudes and moral codes of conduct that led to their attribution of heroic status. It examines the link between law and morality implicit in the texts, and questions the ethical choices of the detectives and spies in their response to crime by applying broad ethical concepts to the narratives. By scrutinizing their conduct, it reflects on whether their behavior is simply a reflection of the moral landscape of the time, or whether it embraces perennial values of justice and fairness that are universally recognized. This literary study presents a window of insight into the thoughts and experiences of those caught up in the conflict between justice and the law reflected through the lens of periodical writers from popular magazines, and it queries the interventions of the champions of justice who rally to their aid. Beginning with a study of Arthur Conan Doyle's Sherlock Holmes, it taps into a range of disciplines that enlighten our understanding of what topics engaged readers of popular magazines in the period from 1880 until 1920 and the rhetoric and discourse that influenced their attitudes to crime and moral viewpoints. In the work of nine prolific and popular writers whose work appeared in novel and short story form and who went on to achieve popular success, the book focuses on the anti-authoritarian challenges posed by literary detectives and spies that drew readers' approval. Most of the writers in this study contributed to the *Strand Magazine*, an organ of contemporary popular opinion that ran articles on social contemporary issues of concern, such as the series by George Sims. Writing as a flaneur exploring areas of London in 1904, his book *Off the Track in London* takes in the Royal Borough of Kensington, Camberwell and the Ghetto near Aldgate. It reveals popular anxiety over the impact of immigration on the nature and character of London whose boundaries expand to accommodate an influx of Jews from the Pale of Settlement and settlers from Eastern Europe (*Strand,* Vol. 27, 416).

1

Preface

In the course of research into the legal and cultural dimensions that surfaced in detective and spy narratives from the late Victorian through the Edwardian era and beyond, shifting climates of opinion served to reconstruct the hero in a new image. With the emergence of spy fiction in the late 1890s, the literary detective is remolded into a spy whose primary function is to rectify threats to national security instead of combatting domestic crime and righting judicial injustice. His transformation is accompanied by a more dubious relationship with ethical values in decision making where pragmatic reasoning for the greater good replaces an idealistic form of morality based on natural law. In the eyes of the pragmatist, truth is not absolute; therefore, spinning the facts for political gain normalizes the manipulation of veracity. Duty involves breaking the law because conformity to legal constraints jeopardizes the spy's ability to fulfill his role as defender of the realm: His actions are sanctioned by higher authority than that endowed in the common law, as Cawelti points out (Cawelti, *Spy Story*, 83). Evidence of this higher authority and permission to break the law is alive and well in the real world and can be read in The Intelligence Services Act of 1994, in which section seven provides a clause nicknamed the "James Bond Clause" in which spies are provided with legal amnesty for committing acts abroad that would otherwise be deemed crimes in the United Kingdom (Wadham, www.onlinelibrary.wiley.com).

Themes of flawed legal procedure and obstacles to justice recur in the stories that highlight the insurmountable difficulties for the common man to access or obtain basic justice. Despite major legislative reform of the justice system toward the end of the nineteenth and into the beginning of the twentieth century, such as the Criminal Evidence Act of 1898, The Poor Prisoners' Defence Act, 1903, and the Court of Criminal Appeal Act of 1907, gaps in the law such as the methods used to interrogate suspects and the admissibility of evidence remained. Clear resonances with the past are echoed in the legal fiction of contemporary crime and spy fiction where similar themes of domestic violence, miscarriages of justice and failure to prosecute white-collar crime, like fraud, reveal the inequities of the system. With its over-reliance on the vagaries of Magistrates' Courts, heavily biased in favoring wealthy and influential individuals in legal judgments, the lack of legal training of magistrates frequently resulted in unsound criminal convictions (Jenks, 67 and *The Secret Barrister*, 55). Through disruptive behavior that bypasses magistrates and the jury system alike, the detectives and spies in the stories challenge the credibility and power of legal institutions and the judgments they make by creating their own version of justice and implementing personal moral codes. Probing the relationship between crime fiction and the law, this study gives insight into the historical dramas, moral philosophical thinking and legal perspectives that influenced the attitudes of readers of the Victorian and Edwardian eras. Reflections from the past can also be read in current legal challenges, where the law struggles to keep abreast with contemporary technological change. Resorting to the use of outdated laws, such as the Vagrancy Act of 1824 to criminalize street sleepers and The Offences Against the Person Act of 1861 to prosecute cyclists, the reactionary nature of the law is exposed. As Oliver Wendell Holmes pointed out in his work *The Common Law*, 1881, "The history of what the law has been is necessary to the knowledge of what the law is" (37).

Given the abundance of crime writers from the 1890s to 1920s and their diversity, the choice of writers for this study was limited to those who contributed to popular magazines in Britain, mainly the *Strand, Ludgate* and *Windsor* magazines. With the arrival of the Golden Age of Detective Fiction just after the war, the profusion of British writers who defined a new style of murder mystery is outside the boundaries of this study. While recognizing the immense influence of successful American crime writers on detective fiction, from Edgar Allan Poe in the 1840s to Anna Katherine Green, Jacques Futrelle and the immensely popular hard-boiled detectives like Raymond Chandler and Dashiell Hammett in the 1920s and beyond, limited space prevents an in-depth discussion of their work but provides fertile ground for future research. As an interdisciplinary study, extensive analysis of each specialist area is advanced within the possible realms of the book; while providing enrichment through discourse on a variety of disciplines, space prohibits the same intensity of investigation for each field of study as that of a single subject investigation.

This book has been a long time in the making, and throughout its evolution and maturation, I have been very fortunate to benefit from the intellectual insights and advice of Professor John Gardner from Anglia Ruskin University, to whom I am deeply indebted. He nourished the belief that what started out as a thesis under his supervision was worthy of further investigation and publication and gave tirelessly of his time to edit and improve the work with inspiring appraisal and expertise. My grateful thanks go to Professor Rohan McWilliam for his detailed reviews, expert historical suggestions and specialist knowledge of Victorian popular fiction. For astute critique and advice on many aspects of the manuscript at thesis stage, I owe grateful thanks to Dr. John Coyle of Glasgow University and Dr. Elizabeth Ludlow of Anglia Ruskin University in Cambridge. I am also thankful to Professor Sarah Brown for her help in perceiving alternative readings of the texts and for her comments on issues raised in the book. I am grateful, too, for the support of the staff at Anglia Ruskin University who assisted my efforts in the course of this work.

Preface

My family has been regularly quizzed on their opinions on themes from the book, and I am thankful to them for their reflections and patient discourses, especially my daughters, Heather for her editorial expertise, and Sarah for her constructive observations—and to my wider family and friends for debating the questions of morality and legality endlessly.

Introduction

"Well, it is not for me to judge you," said Holmes, as the old man signed the statement which had been drawn out. "I pray that we may never be exposed to such temptation." "I pray not, sir. And what do you intend to do?" "In view of your health, nothing." ["Boscombe Valley," 252]

In the context of the story "The Boscombe Valley Mystery" from the collection *The Adventures of Sherlock Holmes* (1892) by Arthur Conan Doyle, the fictional detective Holmes takes the law into his own hands. Despite rescinding authority to adjudicate in the case, Holmes passes a secular form of judgment on the old man, John Turner, remitting the penalty to be paid for the crime of murder to a "higher court than the Assizes" (25). By absolving the old man and stepping beyond the boundaries of the law, Holmes assumes the executive prerogative of mercy and procures an alternative justice to that provided by the legal system. Holmes's actions in the story give expression to Derrida's argument that the law can be improved by deconstruction, as he reminds us, "Justice is not reducible to the law, to a given system of legal structures," but what gives us the momentum to improve and transform it (*Conversation*, 16). By dismantling it, Derrida argues, we expose its rigidity and need for reform, made manifest in Holmes's compassionate response to a dying man through his application of individual conscience-driven and superior justice (16). Holmes's response to the ultimate crime of murder illuminates the conflict between justice and mercy that is constantly evoked in crime fiction where the protagonist takes a different approach to human frailty and wrongdoing than that of the law. Part of the appeal of Sherlock Holmes in my early reading of his exploits was his confident negotiation of the legal system in his quest for justice, which always appeared as a more equitable one than that of the lawmakers. It raised questions of whether, and in what ways, his illegal behavior was replicated in that of other detective narratives of the time and what type of alternative justice his and their judgments endorse. Written in an age of utilitarian thinking and the debunking of natural law, it stimulates discourse about the ideological attitudes his actions and moral choices convey, and in what way they relate to the accepted norms and values of the reading public in the Victorian and Edwardian eras. Bending the law is an integral part of how the detective functions in classical crime fiction texts, and its perennial appeal can be read in the conduct of present-day heroes of crime and spy novels where the level of law-breaking by detectives, official police and spies intensifies dramatically.

The lawlessness and norm-violation practiced by Holmes in his pursuit of truth and justice confirms his status as a mythical champion of enduring appeal, confirmed in his rebranding as defender of the oppressed for the twenty-first century in a recent television series and Hollywood film adaptations of his exploits that ignited a new generation of Sherlockian fandom. His first appearance in print was in *Beeton's Christmas Annual* of 1887 in *A Study in Scarlet,* followed by a successful debut in the pages of the *Strand Magazine.* The July 1891 edition contained "A Scandal in Bohemia," setting a tradition of short story detective fiction that continued throughout the magazine's history and spawning a host of resourceful literary sleuths in a similar vein. Arthur Conan Doyle's creation of a hero who steps beyond the boundaries of the law by pursuing an individualized form of justice places his champion in the realms of criminality that highlight the disparity between justice and the law. This interdisciplinary work is an exploration of the ways Sherlock Holmes and his rival maverick literary detectives and spies manipulated the law by implementing their own codes of conduct to deliver a fairer form of justice than that of the judicial system. Examining their ethical approach to solving crime through an exploration of their conduct in each instance, it situates them broadly within one of the three main approaches to normative ethics: deontology, which emphasizes duties and rules; consequentialism, focusing on the consequences of actions; and virtue ethics that centers on virtues or moral character. It examines the work of nine prolific and popular writers whose fictional transmissions appeared in short story and novel form from 1880 until 1920 in popular entertainment magazines and newspapers, such as the *Strand Magazine, Windsor* and *Ludgate Magazine,* and who went on to achieve popular success, thus creating a shared connection and literary bond between them. Adding to insights on the relationship between crime fiction and law and justice, examined through the lens of critical legal theory and offered in the work of Maria Aristodemou, Fiona Macmillan and Patricia Tuitt in *Crime Fiction and the Law,* and others, this work addresses legal issues in a literary study of popular fiction. It encompasses a range of interdisciplinary analyses that enlighten sociological, historical and moral philosophical perspectives, including deliberation on what was ethically valued for individual happiness and the good of the community at the time of writing. In the light of a range of influences that created societal change, including the rise of professional society, evolving perceptions of crime, criminals and the law, and the impact of societal shifts from a religious to a secular morality, I engage with themes of gender, class and race, revealing the discrimination and marginalization endured by much of the population. In its dramatizations of life and death, pain and loss and the everyday dilemmas confronting people, crime fiction opens a window into the thorny legal and moral anxieties of the era that allow us to reimagine and reconsider our ideas of the past. Here, in close reading of selected texts, I identify the infringements on the law perpetrated by the literary detectives and spies and question the rationale underpinning their illegality. Exposing the multi-layered nuances and "voices" of the texts, this work goes some way toward filling the void of close reading accounts of crime fiction narratives that are not survey-based, nor an author study, alluded to by Stephen Knight in his work *Secrets of Crime Fiction Classics* (3). It is singular in unearthing specific sociological controversies of the time, providing an enhanced awareness of the historical roots and ancestry of crime fiction and allowing fresh insight into the past together with greater understanding of crime fiction. In his study *A Counter-History of Crime Fiction* (2007), Maurizio Ascari draws attention to the "sensational lineage" of detective fiction, indicating how "traditional accounts" of its development sought to distance it from its "sensational roots" by grounding its literary status on "scientific method," thus giving it respectability (1). Traces of the links between sensational literature and its association with crime and deviance are evidenced in the behavior of the literary detective whose tendency to "flout ordinary civil law or moral constraints" allows him to operate outside and above the law, despite his professing to defend it, as Charles Rzepka points out in *Detective Fiction: Cultural History of Literature* (47).

Contrary to critical opinion of the role of detective as defender of the status quo who acts as a normalizing force of policing power and disciplinary regulation on the minds of readers, I argue here for a disruptive role for the agents of justice: one that questions the credibility of legal institutions by challenging their power and authority and the judgments they implement. The behavior of literary detectives and spies exposes the flaws and inconsistencies of a judicial system which are antithetical to the principles of equitable justice, marginalize half the population, and are at variance with the society it seeks to represent. Functioning as a critique of the law, rather than its enforcer, as D.A. Millar maintains in his Foucauldian account *The Novel and the Police* (1988), detective fiction foregrounds obstructions to social justice. Examples include the marginalization of women through defective legislation like The Evidence Further Amendment Act of 1869 and the Matrimonial Causes Act of 1878, which failed to provide justice for women.

Introduction

Class discrimination is revealed in stories that run up against the iniquitous Habitual Criminals Act of 1869 and the Prevention of Crime Act of 1871, revealing how the poor are unfairly targeted in the criminal justice system. Issues of race emerge in the narratives producing the context for the introduction of the flawed 1905 Aliens Act, by which the country brought an end to the heady days of uncontrolled immigration. Subsequently leading to the harsher terms of the Aliens Restriction Act of 1914, the new legislation fed into racist and xenophobic tendencies. In my readings of detective and spy fiction, the relationship of the agents of justice with the legal system and authority clashes with its myopic view of justice, for they offer fairer alternatives that resonate with readers. Contrary to Julian Symons's assertion in *Bloody Murder* that "the detective story is strongly on the side of law and order" (10) offering "a reassuring world in which those who tried to disturb the established order were always discovered and punished," evidence indicates that the criminal frequently escapes justice, the detective often resorts to illegality to achieve his ends and the blurring of moral boundaries by detectives increases as the new century progresses (11). The illicit transactions conducted by crime fiction heroes filter into the realms of spy fiction where investigators become embroiled in international intrigue and where moral choices become blurred in the face of threats to nation and empire. Each of the chapters addresses predominant, contentious issues of the time and pinpoints aspects of the criminal justice system that run counter to the principles of justice. They trace the waning influence of morality on decision-making as detectives mutate into spies near the turn of the century. Motivated by legal pragmatism, in contrast to a former code of conduct aligned to virtue ethics that prioritized moral character, the actions of later agents of justice shift toward a functional, utilitarian approach, taken in the national interest.

The influence of the *Strand Magazine* in shaping the form of the detective short story with Sherlock Holmes, and its popularity, reflective of the tastes, ideology and opinions of its wide readership, makes it an ideal starting point for the investigation. Founded by George Newnes in 1891 on the success of his weekly paper *Tit-Bits*, it was the basis of literary success for a host of writers, including most of those in this study. Claiming to give "wholesome and harmless entertainment to hard-working people" and to be a family magazine, its appeal initially was mostly to the male population, according to one of its editors, Reginald Pound (*The Strand Magazine: 1891–1950*). With a wealth of material to choose from in the archive of neglected and canonical crime fiction writers of the time, my choice of texts is based on a mixture of canonical and non-canonical writers to give a wider perspective than the narrow confines of much previous criticism. Choice of authors reflects detectives and spies who originate from different backgrounds, professional and amateur, working class and aristocratic, male and female, beginning with Arthur Conan Doyle's Sherlock Holmes and followed by those who operate alongside him in his career. It probes the work of Arthur Morrison, J.E.P. Muddock, Richard Marsh, Fergus Hume, Catherine Louisa Pirkis, John Buchan, and Erskine Childers in relation to their fictional detectives and spies. Although the selection represents a fragment of all that is available, I selected stories that focus on socio-cultural, historical, criminological and legal themes, evidenced in newspapers and media accounts of the time and in cases tried at the Old Bailey. Since the literary heritage of these authors was shaped by the influence of mass circulation periodicals and newspapers, their drive for commercial success and wide readership directs the topics and attitudes they adopt. The issues that emerge in the stories reveal the disjunction between popular notions of justice and reality, the inherent flaws in the construction and formal application of legal rules and the absence of laws to challenge newer forms of criminality associated with industrial and corporate crime. In the age of discovery and invention in the fields of science and technology providing the backdrop to the stories, we witness shifting attitudes to cultural ideology in terms of gender, class, race and crime.

The predominant role played by Conan Doyle in the development of crime fiction, with his short story legend, Sherlock Holmes, lies in his conception of a hero immediately accessible to readers. The long list of legal transgressions Holmes commits, which would see a lesser man sentenced to a lengthy, prison sentence, if not life, includes allowing murderers to escape justice, failing to prevent an assassination, and breaking and entering on a regular basis. In judgment decisions in the five detective stories under review, his innate moral code of conduct, evocative of Aristotle's theory of excellent character and conduct, redirects the judicial process to reflect a more personalized and even-handed judgment. The stories I have chosen for analysis in Chapter 1 exemplify Holmes's attitude to gender, race and class in "A Case of Identity" (1891), "The Adventure of the Speckled Band" (1892), "The Adventure of the Blue Carbuncle" (1892) "The Adventure of the Abbey Grange" (1904) and "The Adventure of Charles Augustus Milverton" (1904). Foregrounding the legal status of women and the perils of the working class, the stories emphasize the marginal status of women, vulnerable to family exploitation and lack of redress in cases of blackmail and male violence. Prior to the earliest story in 1891, a raft of legislation aimed at improving the legal status of women in terms of property and marriage laws entered the statute book, but lack of agency in the legal and parliamentary system continued to create social injustice and exclusion for women and marginalized groups. Apart from

Introduction

the Factory and Workshop Act of 1895, which regulated working conditions for women and children, legislation to improve the plight of abused married women failed to reach the statute books until well into the next century and, notably, domestic violence remains an issue of grave concern even today. The ease with which the working-class may be criminalized can be read in the subtext of many of the stories, including "The Blue Carbuncle" (1892) in which Holmes condemns the police courts for arresting an innocent man on hearsay evidence and redresses the injustice by proving his innocence. He highlights the legal distortion in the treatment of ticket-of-leave men who are unfairly punished and often permanently, unjustly criminalized in society. Discourses of imperialism and racial stereotyping emerge in the narratives to reveal the dangers of perceptions of Orientalism and the atavistic nature of the aristocracy, exposed to its influence and gone to the bad.

The rise of professional society, based on the need for specialized training and expertise, provides the cultural context for Chapter 2 and comparison of the amateur detective with that of the professional detective in Arthur Morrison's Martin Hewitt and J.E.P. Muddock's Dick Donovan. Critical to this chapter is the work of Haia Shpayer-Makov, whose informative study of the history of police detection, *The Ascent of the Detectives: Police Sleuths in Victorian and Edwardian England* (2011), from its origins in 1842 to 1914, addresses the formative period of professionalization of the detective branch of the Metropolitan Police and Scotland Yard. The choice of Morrison's Martin Hewitt is based on his appearance in the *Strand Magazine* following the supposed death of Sherlock Holmes at the Reichenbach Falls in "The Final Problem," published in the December 1893 edition of the magazine. Morrison's fame as a writer of slum fiction novels, such as *Tales of Mean Streets* (1894), *A Child of the Jago* (1896), *To London Town* (1899) and *The Hole in the Wall* (1902), is well documented, and overshadows his skill as a writer of crime fiction. Hewitt is the antithesis of Holmes in many ways, except for his ready willingness to engage in lawbreaking when it suits his purposes, in a spirit of defiance of officialdom. As a self-made man who operates from an office in town rather than a comfortable home environment like Holmes at Baker Street, he relies on his hard-won reputation as an investigator to earn a living, and he develops a code of conduct in line with his professional stance and duty to his clients. Claiming to be a "law-abiding citizen," his actions belie his words as he regularly breaks and enters properties in the search for evidence, uses ensnaring techniques to flush out criminals and takes the law into his own hands by replacing courtroom procedure with his own form of justice. Highlighting the prevalence of middle-class crime in the suburbs, he focuses on the inability of the police to pierce the outward cloak of respectability of bourgeois criminals in their focus on lower class criminality. Bringing the influence of scientific intervention into the sphere of female crime and punishment, he redefines the offense of child abduction in a rehabilitative approach to justice. The Lunacy Act of 1890 and the Children's Charter are under review in "The Case of Mr. Geldard's Elopement" and "The Affair of Mrs. Seton's Child," both published in 1896, that provide a contrasting account of the professional approach to detection. The stories draw attention to the importance of skill and efficiency for the professional detective in achieving successful outcomes to the resolution of problems.

Sharing the professional ethic of Chapter 2, the writer and journalist J.E.P. Muddock is included as an early contributor to the *Strand Magazine* who was extremely popular and prolific in his fictional output. He made his entry into the magazine prior to Arthur Conan Doyle with his article entitled "A Night at the Grande Chartreuse" in the February 1891 edition of the magazine (Vol. 1, 268–276). Generally considered inferior in literary terms, Muddock's writing bears close affinity with Gaboriau and the earlier Casebook tradition of detective fiction, exemplified by the work of William Russell in *Autobiography of an English Detective by Waters* (1863) and James McLevy in *The Edinburgh Detective,* a series published in the 1860s. His characterization of Dick Donovan, the detective whose name he often adopts as a pseudonym in the stories under review, "The Riddle of Beaver Hill" and "A Railway Mystery," both published in 1896, is evocative of the Bow Street Runners, who were able to use their professional skills to augment their earnings from bounty-hunting, as Lucy Sussex points out in *Women Writers* (21). Muddock's detective, Dick Donovan, is remarkable in the study for his strict adherence to the letter of the law in response to crime, placing law and order over justice and compassion in a code of conduct far removed from that of Holmes. Heavily influenced by the French approach to detection, Muddock's work is worthy of study because he provides a link between the predominant reading material of working-class readers in popular magazines and that of more middle-class readership. Muddock's technique and style of writing, like that of Freeman Wills Croft in his Inspector French stories in the 1920s, prefigures the later form of detective fiction embodied in police procedurals. In an era where the pseudoscience of criminal anthropology shaped public perceptions of the nature of the criminal in line with the views of criminologist Cesare Lombroso, and in which "physiognomy and phrenology turned the body into a signifier of crime," as Ascari explains, the recidivist criminal posed a physically identifiable danger to society (Ascari, 146).

Chapter 3 is an appraisal of fictional female detectives, both amateur and professional. Notable for their arrival on the literary scene long before

Introduction

their acceptance in the real world of criminal investigation, the distinctive role of female detectives as agents of justice introduces a vibrant, new perspective on the search for truth and the unearthing of crime in the era. Unlike Kathleen Gregory Klein in *The Woman Detectives: Gender and Genre* (1995) who believes the authors of such protagonists engage in an "undercutting of the woman in one or both her roles," I argue for her depiction as an innovative experimentation in gender challenge, who stimulated debate over the changing nature of female identity (Klein, 5). In terms of lawbreaking, the transgressions of female detectives in this book stand shoulder to shoulder in the hierarchy of criminality with previous fictional detectives in the study. The unorthodox and retaliatory approach to detection and the punishment of wrongdoers is clearly illustrated in Richard Marsh's Gypsy protagonist, Judith Lee, and her counterpart, Fergus Hume's Hagar Stanley, who construe yet another vision of discretionary justice when they compensate for official police failure to capture Jack the Ripper. By contrast, the third female detective under review, Catherine Louisa Pirkis's Loveday Brooke, provides an early example of a professional detective who, in her New Woman role of income provider and independent woman, confounds traditional expectations of the "Angel in the House" in her adventure "The Murder at Troyte's Hill" (1893). Before creating his female detective, Richard Marsh was famous for his horror story, *The Beetle* (1897), and made regular appearances in the *Strand*. His embodiment of the female sleuth, Judith Lee, is symbolic of the attributes of the "New and Modern Woman" who redefines the feminine mystique with quasi-supernatural abilities to lip-read at a distance, inspiring dread amongst the criminal classes and wrongdoers. Using her lip-reading skills in "Conscience," one of the stories under examination in the study, she discovers a serial killer operating on the railway system and incites him to commit suicide—a response to the lack of security felt by women in the public transport system. Demonstrating the fusion of detective and spy fiction, she morphs into a secret agent in later adventures, using her skill in jiu-jitsu to fend off violent encounters, which become the norm as she confronts anarchists and defeats fraudsters in the pursuit of equitable justice. As Joseph Kestner suggests, operating in the "province of men rather than women, the female detective is gender-bending in terms of patriarchal constructions of the feminine, since she is a woman empowered primarily through rationality" (*Sisters,* 229). Judith Lee achieves a reversal of power by laying hold of it and redirecting it toward society.

Renowned for his self-publication of *The Mystery of a Hansom Cab* (1886), for which he achieved a runaway success, Fergus Hume is less well known for his creation of the female detective, Hagar Stanley (1898). My choice of Hagar complements that of Judith Lee, since her Gypsy background gives her marginal status like that of Lee, yet situates her in a working class environment. Gypsies presented an intriguing problem for the Victorians, who on the one hand romanticized their nomadic lifestyle and status as noble savages, while simultaneously prosecuting them for vagrancy under the Vagrancy Act of 1824. Hagar, a Gypsy protagonist "of considerable spirit," in Michele Slung's estimation, runs a pawnshop in Lambeth where her clients originate from the seamier side of London, presenting physical dangers seldom experienced by women (Slung, 361). In "The Seventh Customer and the Mandarin" we learn how, steeped in potential criminality, Hagar receives what often turn out to be stolen goods in her pawnshop and can be seen to turn a blind eye to low-level criminality. "Prior to the Moneylender's Act, 1900, largely aimed at the misdemeanors of Jewish moneylenders and small female moneylenders, they were considered by many to provide a useful service for short-term borrowing to alleviate poverty caused by insecure employment conditions" (O'Connell, 137). Despite her marginal status in society, when she encounters injustice in "The Eighth Customer and the Pair of Boots," she engages in investigative probes with the official police and assumes the role of interrogator of an aristocratic suspect in a murder inquiry in the story. Like Judith Lee, her female counterpart in this chapter, her approach to justice is retributive, akin to that seen in the Old Testament, and corresponds to the treatment she may expect as a marginalized member of the community. Alongside Hagar Stanley and Judith Lee, the presentation of Catherine Louisa Pirkis's sleuth, Loveday Brooke, presents a balanced approach to gender authorship of fictional female detectives and contrasts her approach to criminality in portrayal of the issues encountered by a New Woman professional investigator in "The Murder at Troyte's Hill" (1893). Created by a neglected writer whose work offers valuable insights from a female perspective, her investigator is a self-reliant, independent detective, highly esteemed by her employer, Ebenezer Dyer, for her "clear shrewd brain" and common sense. Operating undercover in different guises in many of the stories, she faces down danger and challenges gender stereotypes through her assertive approach to problems. Her presentation as an average, fairly nondescript individual contrasts sharply with the glamorized versions of female detectives prevalent at the time. She tackles prejudices associated with physical appearance in an era underscored by the ubiquity of Cesare Lombroso's theory of anthropological criminology, based on the premise of corporeal defects as representative of atavism, as Christopher Pittard points out in *Purity and Contamination in Late Victorian Detective Fiction*.

The allure of the modern spy in fiction in the UK owes its reputation, to

Introduction

some extent, to the emergence of a climate of apprehension and anxiety on the domestic and international fronts, sparked by brutal Fenian campaigns of violence and fears of invasion. James Fenimore Cooper's *The Spy* (1821) was an early example of the spy genre in the United States, which ignited the public imagination by creating the image of the spy as hero, in contrast to previous characterizations as criminal informant. Most notable was Eugene-Francois Vidocq, an ex-convict who headed the French detective police from 1812 and published his memoirs in 1828, which highlighted the use of clandestine surveillance and invasive techniques for the apprehension of criminals; his methods ran counter to English sensibilities and were viewed with disdain. In Chapter 4, each of the protagonists in the study is recast as spy to illustrate how issues of popular concern are dramatized in fictional texts that fuse detective and spy narratives, indicative of what Ascari calls "hybrid zones" where genres mingle (xii). Emerging alongside Invasion literature, first established in works like George Tomkyns Chesney's *Battle of Dorking* (1871), William Le Queux's *The Great War in England in 1897* (1894) and E. Phillips Oppenheim's *Mr. Sabin* (1898), the spy materializes as a champion of freedom rather than a figure to be despised. His methods in dispelling unease demonstrate greater willingness to step beyond the bounds of legality when national interests are put at risk. As characters adopt the role of spy-cum-detective in the stories under review, the theme of enemy agents operating clandestinely surfaces regularly alongside the theft of secret documents and traitors who are compromised in one way or another. Confronting enemies of the state prompts a reevaluation of moral codes and values where the virtues of honesty, empathy and compassion are superseded by deception, guile and detachment. In "The Adventure of the Second Stain" (1904) and "His Last Bow: The War Service of Sherlock Holmes" (1917), set at the outset of war, Holmes's ethical approach fluctuates in the face of threats to king and country when he is remodeled as spy. Martin Hewitt's adventure "The Admiralty Code" (1903) is, likewise, based on the theft of admiralty codes by a foreign agent that could prompt the onset of war and highlights the importance of secrecy in maintaining the upper hand in weapons technology. Called upon to act in the interests of the Admiralty, he is retained under special license to investigate the theft and bring the perpetrator to justice. In "The Strange Story of Some State Papers," the detective Dick Donovan takes on the job of spy when he is called upon by the Austrian ambassador to the Court of St James's to recover a secret draft treaty between Austria and Britain that had been stolen. Following on from the male protagonists, the female detective, Judith Lee, emerges as a convincing secret agent in "Two Words" (1916) when she embarks on a late-night adventure to confront a German agent who has acquired secret documents critical to national security. Her ability to confound the aristocratic Prussian officer she encounters reveals a steely professionalism that hints at prior experience and training in cloak and dagger techniques. Each of the stories in this chapter shows the fluidity of the genre of detective fiction as it mutates into spy fiction and demonstrates the extent to which morality and legality are clouded by "national vulnerabilities and fears," a topic ably explored in David Stafford's The *Silent Game: The Real World of Imaginary Spies* (ix). Patriotism, loyalty and threats to empire provide ample justification for illegality and establish the rationale for espionage.

The final chapter earmarking the bridge between detective and spy explores the lawbreaking behavior of Erskine Childers's accidental spies, Davies and Carruthers, in *The Riddle of the Sands* (1903), alongside John Buchan's Richard Hannay in *The Thirty-Nine Steps* (1915). With the rise of militarism in the lead-up to the First World War, this chapter adds to our understanding of the way in which detectives morphed into spies, creating their own version of legality and morality in the process. Caught up in international intrigue, Davies and Carruthers contravene the territorial sovereignty of Germany by spying in her waters and lying to the local police about their reasons for being there. Seeking to protect the national interests, they engage in duplicity and suspend their normal ethical code to prevent potential harm to England's future. The theme of military heroes and adventurous amateur spies persists in the character of John Buchan's Richard Hannay and his encounter with "The Black Stone" in *The Thirty-Nine Steps* (1915). Hannay, the reluctant amateur spy, reflects on his lawbreaking at one point in the narrative, charging himself with being "an unholy liar, a shameless imposter and a highwayman with a marked taste for expensive motor-cars" (Buchan, 51). He is pleased that as yet he is not a murderer, and a night in the open air appeases his conscience over his lawless behavior. In the epilogue to this study, the illegality of detectives and spies reaches its peak in the fashioning of the hero as an individual with, or without, group affiliations, inclined toward vigilante justice as a means of resolving crime. Edgar Wallace's *Four Just Men* (1905) and H.C. McNeile's *Bulldog Drummond* (1920) epitomize rough justice taken outside legal constraints. Depicted as defender of the realm, Bulldog Drummond advances a forerunner for James Bond, with his effortless suave charm, disregard for personal danger and blasé approach to legality. McNeile is notable for the creation of a fictional hero who, like Holmes, endured for generations, and inspired the characterization of leading men for cinema and television. Emblematic of empowerment of the many rather than individual heroics which counted for little, as demonstrated in the trenches in the face of mechanized warfare, Drummond's fierce brand of retributive justice stands in stark con-

Introduction

trast to that of Holmes at the outset of the study. In his depiction of the war-hardened veteran who battles vicious foreigners bent on the destruction of England and espouses the dictum that might is right in the struggle for survival, he shapes a prototype for future, steely-eyed protagonists.

"The law to break the law can be compelling," as Jonathan Kertzer points out in his study *Poetic Justice and Legal Fictions*, and, as the theme of this interdisciplinary study of transgressive literary agents of justice who challenge the forces of law and order to achieve justice, its ramifications are wide reaching (13). In the literary arena of popular culture, rejection of conformist behavior represents a challenge to the status quo made manifest in an attitude of defiance toward authority and regulatory institutions; its enactment presents "a domain of resistance" to existing hegemonies, as Joke Hermes points out (3). This work extends the boundaries of criticism through its engagement with the writings of forgotten and neglected authors, whose work achieved success and popularity in its day. Here I argue against the reductive view of literary detectives as puppets acting to uphold institutional values and the maintenance of law and order. Instead, they represent a narrative ability to identify the weaknesses of a partisan judicial system, which they hold to account through satiric discourse, disparagement and shrewd circumvention of its rules and procedures. Although in the end, elements of the law appear to be upheld in the stories in response to crime, the fictional detectives I examine engage in radical deviations from legality to achieve their ends and are, finally and reluctantly, congratulated by the official forces of law and order for their far-sighted interventions and despite using forbidden methods in tackling crime. This suggests that they too believe in alternative forms of justice, yet are constrained in solving crime by complex rules and regulations and subjection to inefficient legal procedures. In the contextual climate of the times in which the stories were written, the demise of natural law and its affinity with the divine saw its replacement with a system of ethics designed for "achieving the greatest good for the greatest number" in utilitarian legal positivism. Detective fiction narratives reflect the search for another form of reality, which re-establishes the links between religion and morality. They invoke a more compassionate form of justice toward those caught up in the expanding arena of the law: one that is in harmony with everyday human interactions, failings and emotions. Countering the harshness of scientific advances with a renewed morality in the early detective stories, the gentlemanly code of conduct, based on truthfulness and integrity, recedes in spy fiction as the decades wore on, yet can still be read in the "Golden Age" detective stories of Agatha Christie and others in the 1920s and '30s. Mindful of interpretation as a selective process involving speculation and cultural influence, my reading of the texts in this work is guided by the many theoretical and critical works available to consult in a range of fields apart from detective fiction, such as sociology, the philosophy of law, legal theory and criminology, amongst others. Steve Uglow's comment, "There are few, if any, offenses on our statute book that have not been tolerated at one time or another in society," raises questions over the nature of illegality and the types of crime explored in the pages of crime fiction. Surfacing in an era of industrialization and technological advance, the absence of legislation relating to modern crime, such as company fraud, is indicative of skewed judicial processes that unfairly targeted marginalized groups of the population (22). Crime fiction has been designated the most popular form of fiction in the UK, and global interest in it is demonstrated in the continued success of new interpretations of the role of detective that appear in print and media forms worldwide, giving great validity to its critical review and debate.

1

Justice According to Holmes

Conan Doyle's Amateur Detective

In 1903 the contentious arrest by Staffordshire police and prosecution of George Edalji, a young Parsee solicitor, aroused public indignation and caused a furor among his colleagues in the legal fraternity. They claimed the horrendous crimes with which he was charged were completely beyond his nature and that the justice system had wrongly indicted an innocent man. Accused of murderous attacks on animals, he was, nevertheless, sentenced to seven years penal servitude following a botched police investigation based on unreliable evidence and dubious testimony, conducted in a hostile atmosphere, and mooted as racially discriminatory in the police hierarchy. His conviction prompted an eminent judge, solicitors and barristers to procure 10,000 signatures from members of the public demanding a reprieve from the Home Office, subsequently ignored. Stumbling on an article in a small newspaper, *The Umpire*, in 1906, Arthur Conan Doyle was gripped by the unfortunate circumstances surrounding the case and used his celebrity to raise its profile further in the public consciousness. Convinced Edalji had suffered a miscarriage of justice, he set about investigating, in Sherlockian fashion, the details of the allegations and publishing his findings in an effort to rectify what he described as an appalling tragedy. Edalji was finally released three years into his sentence without explanation or receiving the benefit of a declaration of innocence. It became clear that since there was no avenue for appeal against sentencing and conviction in the judicial system once a sentence was handed down, and although he was presumed innocent, no compensation or apology would be offered to Edalji for his wrongful incarceration.

Much has been written about Conan Doyle's life and works, but less effort has been devoted to his interest and lifelong passion for achieving justice for those he believed to be wrongly accused of crimes and for improving what he saw to be the flaws of the legal system. His interventions on behalf of those accused of crimes were not restricted to Edalji, but included a range of cases, including that of Oscar Slater, wrongly imprisoned in 1908 for murdering

Morality and the Law in British Detective and Spy Fiction

Marion Gilchrist in Glasgow, and later reprieved, and mediations on behalf of Roger Casement that fell on deaf ears when he was executed for treason in 1916. Animated by recognition of the need to question and challenge unfair judicial process and decisions, Conan Doyle took issue with institutional prejudice and racism and sought to deliver justice where none was to be had through campaigns, personal petitions and the power of celebrity. Praised by George Meredith and James Barrie for his courage in tackling injustice, he emerged in the minds of some as the incarnation of the "English conscience," in Pierre Nordon's words (122). Through his work on behalf of Edalji and in the wake of the wrongful imprisonment of Adolf Beck in a case of mistaken identity in 1904, he exposed a range of gaps and flaws in the legal process. His exertions contributed to the foundation for the creation of the Court of Criminal Appeal, finally established in 1907 to prevent similar abuses and miscarriages of justice. Up to this point, evidence was not tested and frequently resulted in the handing down of harsh punishment where the verdict could not be challenged. Proving that public opinion matters in the creation of a fairer society, his crusades helped precipitate steps in legal reform. Like authors such as Charles Dickens, Wilkie Collins, Thomas Hardy and Anthony Trollope, amongst others, his writing, especially in the Sherlock Holmes canon, probes the complex moral and legal quandaries facing people who confront the rigidity of a partisan legal system, whose interpretation of the facts differs considerably from their own experiences. The circumstances that arise in the narratives of the Sherlockian canon and the resolutions achieved by the fictional detective, Sherlock Holmes, confront the vagaries of the law in a way that resonates soundly with his readership and endorses his defiance of the rule of law.

In his response to criminality, Sherlock Holmes puts the law itself on trial and questions its ability to reflect justice. By both ignoring the law and ridiculing its inability to offer substantive justice, he exposes its shortcomings and inadequacies. In this first chapter, I examine the liminality of Arthur Conan Doyle's amateur detective, Sherlock Holmes, in dispensing judgments through close reading of a selection of stories within the canon that focus on his response to crime relating to gender, class and race. Aware of the discriminatory nature and practices of the judicial system, Holmes acts as judge and jury, implementing his own code of justice in response to the circumstances of each story by exacting revenge, exonerating criminals and allowing others to escape justice. Drawing on issues and concerns raised in the texts and on Holmes's response to crime in particular cases, a picture emerges of the values and attitudes he communicates in his conduct toward women, family, racial identity and class loyalties. Shaped in the image of Aristotle's virtuous character, with an inclination to do the right thing through reasoned actions, he embodies the virtues of courage, wisdom and prudence, cultivating them through practice in ways that are beneficial to himself and others (Boone, 34). In parallel with the drama and theatrics of each story, ideologies of gender, ethnicity and social hierarchy fluctuate in the narratives, throwing up interesting deviations from ideological norms of behavior and identity. The less than "Angel in the House" characterization of women, the recidivist criminal able and willing to reform and the unionized working-class tradesman defying the pecking order of class status, appear in the stories as varied and mobile prototypes of the shifting parameters of class and gender emerging in the last decade of the nineteenth century.

The stories under review begin with an examination of the depiction of the status of women in society with reference to family relationships in "A Case of Identity" (1891). First published in the September 1891 issue of the *Strand Magazine* before publication in 1892 along with eleven other short stories in the collection titled *The Adventures of Sherlock Holmes*, it recounts the plight of Mary Sutherland, a young working woman abandoned by her suitor on the threshold of marriage. Her working-class roots prove no barrier to earning a living as a single woman in an office role rather than working in service or a factory. Yet despite her access to public space and experience, her sexual naiveté and prescribed feminine identity remain intact and prevent her full assumption of the benefits of impending modernism. The story sheds light on defects in legislation affecting women, such as the Evidence Further Amendment Act of 1869, intended to make provision for jilted brides who brought "Breach of Promise" claims for damages.

Written the following year and published in the March 1892 edition of the *Strand Magazine*, "The Adventure of the Speckled Band," Conan Doyle's favorite story, is replete with themes of dark motivation and cruelty by a tyrannical stepfather, Dr. Grimesby Roylott, evocative of sensation and Gothic fiction. Its powerful castigation of upper-class criminality provides a critique of the debauched behavior of the indolent wealthy whose excesses and self-indulgence lead to the demise of their estates and corruption of family life. The precariousness of existence in such households for unmarried, female members of the family is clearly depicted. Despite the improvements of The Married Women's Property Act of 1882, "the most important change in the legal status of women in the nineteenth century," according to Shanley, lack of economic or social self-determination before marriage often meant an uncertain future and submission to despotic fathers (103). Family inheritance is at the root of threats of violence and the prospect of imminent death for Helen Stoner when her stepfather returns from the East, contaminated by foreign influence, made apparent in his use of opium. Interwoven in the narrative are threads of class disparagement, gendered violence and racial discourse, set in a hostile quasi-tropical environment. In the context of the rise of eugenics, a term coined by Francis Galton, the prospect of atavism was much debated and can be read in Roylott's behavior. Galton's theory that body measurements were the main indicators in the "scientific study of criminal and racial types," along with his belief that "people of color, women and the poor" were thereby the "dictates of nature," confirmed racial, class and gender prejudices in the minds of many Victorians (Seitler, 71). In the story, the official inquiry's questionable finding of accidental death brings into question the role of police and that of lay magistrates in deciding which deaths should be properly investigated and how to proceed when a case of unexplained death occurs. The Justices of the Peace Act governing the behavior of magistrates had been enacted in 1371, making its provisions totally inadequate for the modern age. The Act survives along with other outdated statutes, including the forbidding of the wearing of armor in Parliament and the illegality of being drunk "on any licensed premises," which is covered by the Licensing Act of 1872; it is clear there are still some anachronistic laws in existence in our legal system.

"The Adventure of the Abbey Grange" (1904) reflects the injustice of the legal system in its treatment of both abused women and the poor who have no means of defense at trial. Uncovering the plight of a woman who suffers at the hands of a drunken husband, the story also exposes the discrimination of a legal process that denies agency to poor defendants accused of crimes, who are forbidden to speak for themselves yet are unable to afford the representation of a lawyer. Prior to the Criminal Evidence Act of 1898, a defendant was barred from giving evidence on his own behalf, which prejudiced the outcome of trials for the poor who could not afford expensive lawyers to provide a convincing defense. Insufficient curbs on domestic violence and the law's incompetence in dealing with it in a consistent way ensured its continuance. For the victims of domestic violence, the Matrimonial Causes Act of 1878 "had opened the door a crack" to allow an abused wife to leave a marriage by granting judicial separation, but its uneven application and the failure of conservative, subjective magistrates to grant separation meant the return of most applicants to domestic ill-treatment (Shanley, 183). A personal vexation for Arthur Conan Doyle, the outdated provisions of the Divorce and Matrimonial Causes Act of 1857 also comes under fire. In the story, Holmes is compelled to interfere with formal legal procedure to secure redress where the law cannot in a case of self-defense to save a suspect from the noose.

Questioning how Holmes responds to crime in relation to the criminal's status in society, "The Adventure of the Blue Carbuncle" (1892) factors in class tension and offers comment on the inadequacy of the use of circumstantial evidence to gain conviction for a crime. The context of the story echoes concerns expressed by Ticket-of-Leave men to Henry Mayhew in London when he convened a meeting with them. In his account, described in *London Labour and the London Poor* (18, 430), they protest the difficulties they face trying to earn an honest livelihood on release from prison, trusted by no one. Simulating the iniquitous provisions of the 1871 Prevention of Crime Act, the story dramatizes the conviction of an innocent man on account of past offenses, enough to place him in the dock. According to Helen Johnston in *Victorian Convicts: 100 Criminal Lives* (2016), the Act altered the nature of justice for the accused (36). Since the new burden of proof "required reasonable grounds for believing in the innocence of the accused rather than whether the latter could prove it," the biased judgments of middle-class magistrates, often class and race-based, skewed justice and regularly condemned the innocent to lengthy prison sentences, reflected in the real-life Oscar Slater case (Johnston, 36).

In the final story under review, "The Adventure of Charles Augustus Milverton" (1904), a wealthy female assassin escapes hanging when Holmes delivers his own brand of justice at the expense of a working-class servant and raises the possibility of class-inflected bias in his own judgments. The repercussions of blackmail involving crimes against the reputation, highlighted in the story, were severe, yet no effective legislation to counter the problem existed until 1895, as J.G. Murphy points out (6). Such literary narratives as those in the Holmes canon drove the need for a mediating champion like Sherlock Holmes to balance the scales of justice in favor of the innocent and the oppressed. By examining the representation of class interactions and tensions mirrored through the middle-class lens of the Holmesian canon, I will unfold the contrasting images of upper, middle and working-class criminality and interrogate Holmes's extralegal response, including perverting the course of justice, burglary, deception and aiding and abetting murderers to escape formal justice.

In the age of emerging modernism in which the stories were written and in which science and law were culturally dominant, women's sexuality was a contentious issue, often reflected in the media's reporting of cases involving sexual crimes. With W.T. Stead's "Maiden Tribute of Modern Babylon," published in the *Pall Mall Gazette* in July 1885, the Cleveland Street Scandal of 1889, alluding to royal collusion in sentence-rigging, and the notorious divorce trial of Lady Gertrude and Lord Colin Campbell in 1886 appearing in sensationalized accounts in newspapers, sexual impropriety was a staple item in the news. For those with limited or non-existent access to justice, recourse to the fictional remedies of an amateur detective like Sherlock Holmes offers an imaginary palliative to the realities of the legal system. Holmes's appeal embraces growing numbers of working-class readers, freshly primed with newly acquired levels of literacy, whose arrival encouraged writers to include more complimentary portrayals and orchestrate alignment with their sympathies. Spanning a period of forty years, including the last two decades of Queen Victoria's reign, the Edwardian era and a decade of the reign of George V, the selected stories highlight contentious legal and cultural issues that emerged at a time when the profound changes of industrialization furnished society with a "wholly new temper and texture," as Poplawski explains (519). Rapid progress in science and technology provides context to the stories that permit Holmes to challenge judicial power. In the process, he casts doubt on its ability to keep pace with societal change and questions whether it provides equal access to justice. Holmes's willingness to defy the law indicates he views it as unjust and inadequate in many respects. By exploring his behavior and attitudes in the stories and questioning his justification for infringing the legal process in cases involving the treatment of gender, class and race, my aim is to shed light on contemporary attitudes on access to justice and the problematic issues that arose in everyday life. Threads of a distinctive personal form of morality imbue his actions in a positive light that resonates with readers to this day.

"A Case of Identity" (1891)

The value of respectability linked to marriage and morality in the Victorian psyche was a powerful behavior modifier in determining identity and social status. Without the security of marriage and the economic means to support an illegitimate child, a woman was edged into poverty and placed on the margins of society where she was generally viewed with contempt and disrespected by those around her. A contemporary issue of differing public opinion, "Breach of Promise" of marriage hovers in the background of "A Case of Identity," where the plot is driven by a distorted family relationship between a young woman and her duplicitous stepfather and mother. It is a tale of family tyranny and intrigue featuring an absconding suitor, liable to legal action for "Breach of Promise" and fraudulent attempts to swindle her out of her inheritance. In the wake of Gilbert and Sullivan's comic opera "*Trial by Jury*," a satirical take on a breach of promise of marriage lawsuit, first performed in May 1875, the limitations of the 1869 Evidence Further Amendment Act can be fully understood in the failure to

24

find a just outcome for the unsuspecting victim of the deception. Illustrating the significant role of the media in promoting public consciousness of perceived criminal threats to society and the central role of women in its generation, the story begins with Holmes comfortably seated by the fireside reflecting on his wish to "gently remove the roofs and peep in at the queer things which are going on" (Conan Doyle, 236). His comments mirror popular public interest in other people's lives, evidenced today in the popularity of social media and real-life television dramas like *Big Brother* (Conan Doyle, 236). Watson, who is reading the police reports in the newspaper and whose sense of propriety is outraged by the sensationalist accounts therein, contradicts Holmes's sense of boredom, and complains that "the cases which come to light in the papers are, as a rule, bald enough and vulgar enough," and he rails against the scandalous, titillating details of accounts as "realism pushed to extreme limits" (Conan Doyle, 236). Acknowledging the fictional nature of many of the press accounts, Holmes comments on an article entitled "A Husband's Cruelty to His Wife," which he mockingly disparages as "crude" in its usual referencing of "the other woman, the drink, the push, the blow," denouncing it as overblown rhetoric and its details as "perfectly familiar to me" (236). Refuting the allegations of cruelty, Holmes asserts that contrary to the report, the husband "was a teetotaler, there was no other woman," and the abuse related to nothing more than his hurling his false teeth at his wife, rather than the embellished version presented in the press (236). His response echoes, to some extent, the accepted view of a nagging wife projected by Edward Cox, "a serjeant-at-law" and author of a leading textbook of the day, *Principles of Punishment,* in which he projects the view that "wife-beating was often provoked by a shrill and shrewish wife and that a blow to such a woman was almost in the nature of self-defence" (Shanley, 171). From his remarks, we may infer that Holmes seems to accept moderate physical chastisement of a wife, if circumstances dictate.

The main character in the story, Miss Mary Sutherland, is a woman of independent means who has recently been jilted by her fiancé, Mr. Hosmer Angel, an elusive and shadowy individual whom she has recently met. Her background circumstances have led her to the decision that whilst she remains living at home, she will give financial control of both her income of one hundred pounds per year and the interest on her inheritance, left to her in trust until her marriage, to her mother and young stepfather, Mr. Windibank, who use it to fund their lifestyles. Meanwhile, she lives frugally on her own earnings of sixty pounds per year as a typist, work indicative of a widening range of employment roles available to women, revealing her status within the respectable working class and evidence of emerging themes of modernity in the stories. Her own father had been a plumber in the Tottenham Court Road who built up his business, lifting his family into the entrepreneurial ranks of society. With the possibility of a change in her marital status looming, her mother and stepfather conspire to ensure that she remain at home, so that they continue to benefit from her largesse without the interference of a husband. As the beneficiary of a reasonable income, combined with her earned income and the bequest held in trust until her marriage, Miss Sutherland will be a wealthy woman in her own right once married, but the loss of her financial input will have a serious impact on her mother and Mr. Windibank's living arrangements. The terms of the Married Women's Property Act of 1882, which Shanley labels "the single most important change in the legal status of women in the nineteenth century," improved the position of women, but it was not until the Act of 1884 that the rules of coverture were removed, allowing women to have feme sole status and acquire an individual identity in law; considering her economic welfare, the future looks promising for Miss Sutherland (Shanley, 103). Devising a plan to maintain control of her money and ensure she never marries, Windibank disguises himself as Hosmer Angel and assumes the role of her suitor, securing an engagement very quickly after their first walk together. Miss Sutherland has developed a deep attachment to this quiet idiosyncratic man whom she describes thus:

> He would rather walk with me in the evening than in the daylight, for he said that he hated to be conspicuous. Very retiring and gentlemanly he was. Even his voice was gentle. He'd had the quinsy and swollen glands when he was young, he told me, and it had left him with a weak throat and hesitating, whispering fashion of speech. He was always well-dressed, very neat and plain, but his eyes were weak, just as mine are and he wore tinted glasses against the glare [238].

The description of a softly spoken suitor who is averse to daylight and is almost reclusive alerts us to the deception. However, Miss Sutherland is bewitched by his charms, and Hosmer Angel succeeds in gaining her trust, securing an oath of constancy at all costs before subsequently disappearing on the morning of a proposed wedding to be held at "St. Saviour's Near King's Cross" (238). The promise of engagement was considered a legally binding contract that had existed from medieval times and was now subject to the terms of the Evidence Further Amendment Act of 1869 due to the number of broken promises that ended in rape or desertion. It remained part of law until 1970, when it was finally removed from the Statute Book (Bates, 1).

Although the Act allowed women to recount their story from the witness box, it also maintained "that a successful claim must be supported by proof of an engagement other than the word of the plaintiff" (Bates, 36). This proof had to be of a "material standard" and was intended to "eliminate claims based on inference and fraud," as Denise Bates explains (36). Confirming the significance placed on breach of promise as a means of redress for deceived women, an article in the *Morning Post* of Saturday, January 31, 1891, relates how the Supreme Court of Judicature, Court of Appeal, resumed a case brought by Mr. Leslie Fraser Duncan, "late editor and proprietor of *The Matrimonial News* who contested the award of £10,000 damages made to Miss Gladys Knowles for 'breach of promise for marriage" (Issue 37014, 2). Mr. Duncan had enjoyed the benefits of a sexual relationship with the young Miss Knowles and, despite setting marriage dates on many occasions, he always "found a pretext for delay" (2). The judge, Lord Justice Bowen, delivered a verdict which reduced damages to £6,500 and scolded Miss Knowles's mother for allowing her daughter to associate with "an old man of seventy" (2). His view of Mr. Duncan was that "he was a villain of the deepest dye" (2). The reasons then for legal intervention in a case of breach of promise included the idea that a woman was more exposed to seduction on engagement and the possibility of loss of virginity, which would impair her future prospects of finding a husband. Socially, she would be viewed with apprehension for misplacement of her affections. Emotional damage was a further consideration. However, Bates points out, "By 1879 there were considerable misgivings among the middle classes about breach of promise claims" due to the number of fraudulent allegations being made and the ignominy of giving testimony in court (Bates, 38).

An analysis of the portrayal of Mary Sutherland, on the surface, reflects gender ideologies consistent with feminine attributes and identity prevalent at the time. Despite her independent working status and elements of self-assertion, she is characterized as unworldly and susceptible to exploitation due to her willingness to meet with Mr. Windibank without her stepfather's knowledge. Allusions to her lack of intelligence and emotional fragility demonstrate how women and men were believed to possess fundamentally different physical characteristics; furthermore, their mental capacities were also configured differently. According to Emsley in "Historical Background-Gender in the Proceedings" in the *Old Bailey Proceedings Online,* confining women's intellectual competence to a narrow field of engagement endorses patriarchal ideology in which "Men as the stronger sex were thought to be intelligent, courageous and determined. Women, on the other hand, governed by their emotions and their virtues, were expected to portray chastity, modesty, compassion and piety" (Emsley et al.). Miss Sutherland's entry into the narrative is described in gently mocking tones—her physical appearance likened to "a full-sailed merchantman" and reference to her nervous demeanor and "vacuous face" conjuring up a comical and slightly derisory image (237). Catching sight of her on the street outside his rooms in Baker Street, Watson remarks:

> Looking over his [Holmes] shoulder I saw that on the pavement opposite there stood a large woman with a heavy fur boa round her neck, and a large curling red feather in a broad-brimmed hat which was tilted in a coquettish Duchess of Devonshire fashion over her ear. From under this great panoply she peeped up in a nervous fashion at our windows, while her body oscillated backwards and forwards, and her fingers fidgeted with her glove buttons. Suddenly, with a plunge, as of a swimmer who leaves the bank, she hurried across the road, and we heard the sharp clang of the bell [237].

Having confided her financial and emotional circumstances to Holmes, Miss Sutherland confesses that on proposing marriage Mr. Angel made her "swear on the Testament" that no matter what happened, she would always be true to him and "even if something quite unforeseen occurred," he would claim his pledge sooner or later (239). In refusing to renege on her pledge of fidelity, the possibility of a sexual liaison between Miss Sutherland and Mr. Windibank provides more compelling evidence for her persistent loyalty to the missing fiancé. Fiercely defending him to Holmes, she declares that Mr. Angel's motives for leaving her cannot be financial, and explains, "Now if he had borrowed my money, or if he had married me and got my money settled on him, there might be some reason, but Hosmer was very independent about money and never would look at a shilling of mine" (239). Her devotion and implicit trust impress Watson, who remarks, "For all the preposterous hat and the vacuous face, there was something noble in the simple faith of our visitor which compelled respect" (239). His comment, characteristic of the common man, shows his approval that she has the requisite attributes of a truly feminine woman: virtue, kindness and vulnerability.

In the final denouement of the story Holmes, who has immediately recognized Mr. Windibank's ploy, summons him to Baker Street to confront him with his infamy. Mr. Windibank's first remarks are telling as he apologizes to Holmes and remarks:

> "I am sorry that Miss Sutherland has troubled you about this little matter, for I think it is far better not to wash linen of this sort in public. It was quite against my wishes that she came, but she is a very excitable, impulsive girl, as you may have noticed, and she is not easily controlled when she has made up her mind on a point" [241].

It is clear from his comments that Miss Sutherland betrays elements of the modern woman in her stubborn refusal to be entirely controlled by him and follows her own inclinations in matters that concern her. In spite of being abandoned at the altar, a cause of emotional trauma for most people, Miss Sutherland shows resolution and courage in determining to untangle the mystery herself. Her independent financial status, reflecting features of the New Woman, gives her the impetus to consult a detective against the wishes of her parents; washing her linen in public is a difficult decision for her, but one that she is willing to attempt.

When Holmes informs Mr. Windibank that he has identified him as the missing suitor, the villain offers no mitigation for his cruelty and retaliates instead by invoking immunity from prosecution in defiance of Holmes, and declares, "It—it's not actionable" (241). He had been careful to ensure his own safety from prosecution by typing his promissory letters, leaving no hand-written signature that could be used to convict him. Under the terms of the Evidence Further Amendment Act, as Ginger Frost indicates, the law speci-fied that "no breach-of-promise plaintiff" "shall recover a verdict unless his or her testimony shall be corroborated by some other material evidence in support of such promise" (Frost, 21). Windibank's cavalier attitude and lack of remorse for his vicious and abusive behavior infuriate Holmes, for he be-lieves him guilty of criminal intent to defraud, apart from the extensive social, emotional and financial damage he is willing to inflict on his stepdaughter. Holmes also realizes that the legal hurdle of a court procedure creates an insurmountable barrier to respectable women who might wish to pursue a claim for breach of promise. Agreeing that the case is not actionable, Holmes nevertheless castigates Windibank for his heinous behavior and is himself reprimanded in turn as Windibank retorts, "It may be so, or it may not, Mr. Holmes, but if you are so very sharp you ought to be sharp enough to know that it is you who are breaking the law, now, and not me. I have done nothing actionable from the first, but as long as you keep that door locked you lay yourself open to an action for assault and illegal constraint" (242). Incensed by Mr. Windibank's callousness, Holmes deplores the failure of justice and, threatening to flog him with a hunting crop, complains that whilst the law cannot touch him, "there never was a man who deserved punishment more" (242). Because Windibank has hijacked his stepdaughter's marriage prospects and sought to defraud her of her inheritance, Holmes considers him to have acted criminally and predicts his destiny on the gallows. His desire to resort to physical violence by whipping Windibank indicates the continued use of flogging for a wide range of crimes. In his 1914 work *The Law and the Poor,* Edward Parry informs us that flogging as a means of punishment was still being used for offenses such as "garrotting," violations of the Criminal Law Amendment Act such as procuring, and for "being an incorrigible rogue," of-fenses whose administration, he complains, "depend[s] on the taste and fancy of the presiding judge" (Parry, 210). His allegation that "the chances of a rich man being flogged for his wickedness on earth are about the same as those of the camel with an ambition to loop the needle" underscores his opinion of the class-based injustice of judicial authority, an injustice that Holmes seems ready to redress in his chastisement of Mr. Windibank (Parry, 212).

Despite his introductory dismissal of the press report on an abused spouse as fictitious, Holmes's behavior in this story alerts us to his sympathy for women who suffer emotional abuse at the hands of unscrupulous men and offers a critique of the sexual double standard that allows men to exploit vulnerable women by seeking to satisfy carnal desire, yet ruin their lives and reputations in the process. Holmes's personal code of conduct typifies a model of masculinity whose chivalric desire to protect women is indicative of Martin Wiener's view of male paternalism. In *Men of Blood* (2004), he suggests "the protection of women came to pose the question of the reconstruction of men" and "became a site of cultural contestation over the proper roles of and relations between the sexes" (Wiener, 6). By this account, Holmes models the acceptable role of the masculine protector of women. He exemplifies the morally upright individual mirroring what contemporary people valued as an ethical response to the situation. The story also illustrates an issue of grave concern to women, how their position of respectability in society can be readily undermined by exploitative practices endorsed by the sexual double standard. Although redress may be had through the Evidence Amendment Act of 1869, most respectable women would balk at the idea of sharing their indiscretions in a court of law and thus ruining any chance of a future engagement. Further insight into Holmes's character and his attitude toward women can be read in his decision to refrain from confiding the truth of the deceit to Miss Sutherland, preferring instead to keep her in blissful ignorance when he confides his reasons to Watson, "There is danger for him who taketh the tiger cub, and danger also for whoso snatches a delusion from a woman" (242). By concealing the fraud from Miss Sutherland, bearing in mind that her mother and stepfather were both party to it, he may leave Miss Sutherland exposed to future harm from her relatives. Given Victorian views of women's psyches prevalent in the era, Holmes constructs her understanding in terms of her biological configuration and believes her sanity to be at risk from learning the truth. As Andrew St. George points out, her "limitations were biologically defined"; her identity is thus "circumscribed" by society's image of her scope and capacity (100). Holmes chooses a paternalistic lie of omission intended to relieve her from further suffering in the manner outlined by William H. Simon in *Virtuous Lying: A Critique of Quasi-Categorical Moralism.* In it, he describes competing values, such as kindness and compassion, that need to be taken into account when lying or using deception (447). Despite some shades of worldliness in her portrayal, including her access to public spaces rather than domestic isolation, Miss Sutherland conforms to gendered Victorian identity in her resolve to remain constant to the vanished suitor. Yet by taking the initiative to consult Holmes and provide for her own welfare, she could, in my opinion, handle the truth of the affair.

"The Adventure of the Speckled Band" (1892)

> Oh, East is East, and West is West, and never the twain shall meet,
> Till Earth and Sky stand presently at God's great Judgment Seat;
> But there is neither East nor West, Border, nor Breed, nor Birth,
> When two strong men stand face to face, though they come from
> the ends of the earth! [Kipling, "The Ballad of East and West,"
> 1889].

David Gilmour notes that the initial response to Kipling's poem about the meeting of two men of equal courage from different races is often misread under a charge of racism. He contends instead that the poem conveys equality of class, race, nation and continent, where respect for individual difference is valued and honored (Gilmour, 89). Kipling's genius as a writer is uncontested, evidenced in his Nobel Prize for Literature in 1907, yet his attitude on race stirs controversy and dissent among critics to this day. Themes of race and national identity are pervasive in the writings of popular literature at the height of the British Empire toward the end of the century, where representations of the East reinforced cultural difference and the lawlessness that justified colonial intervention in Asia as a civilizing mission. Conflated in public consciousness with the evils of Orientalism and manifested in the unsavory presence of opium-dens in the cities, the links between Eastern criminality and decadent habits of opium use led to the rise of China phobia. Hostility toward Chinese workers burgeoned also in the United States, where the Chinese Exclusion Act of 1882 was enacted to "protect the good order of certain localities within the territory" (mtholyoke.edu). Antipathy toward Chinese people was later expressed in the behavior of Sax Rohmer's villainous Dr. Fu Manchu, labeled the Yellow Peril. In the age of aestheticism of Oscar Wilde's Dorian Gray and Sherlock Holmes, it is not only criminals who luxuriate in the pleasures of cocaine, but also the protagonist Gray and the fictional hero Holmes, who indulges in a seven percent solution on a regular basis. In *The Sign of the Four,* Arthur Conan Doyle's second story featuring Sherlock Holmes, we are introduced to Holmes's cocaine addiction:

> Sherlock Holmes took his bottle from the corner of the mantelpiece and his hypodermic syringe from its neat morocco case. With his long, white nervous fingers he

adjusted the delicate needle and rolled back his left shirt-cuff. For some little time his eyes rested thoughtfully upon the sinewy forearm and wrist, all dotted and scarred with innumerable puncture marks [Conan Doyle, 55].

His use of the drugs morphine and cocaine "three times a day for many months," which he finds "transcendentally stimulating and clarifying to the mind," brings rebuke from Watson, who views the habit with disdain. Despite the conspicuous horrors of opium-dens in squalid corners of city streets and the impact of stories of mental and physical decay outlined in stories such as Thomas De Quincey's *Confessions of an English Opium-Eater*, 1821, and Dickens's unfinished *The Mystery of Edwin Drood*, 1870, the caveats were not enough to restrict the use of opium in Victorian Britain. In an effort to curtail the use of the drug, the Pharmacy Act of 1868 restricted its sale to pharmacists and professionals, but the benefits of its use in the public estimation were felt to outweigh its pitfalls, and it continued to be an ingredient in a range of products. Prescribed as a temporary soothing remedy for the symptoms of toothache, colic, indigestion and sleeplessness, among others, it was very effective. However, since "the concept of addiction was not yet understood," as Sharon Ruston explains, and there was no restriction on the amount sold, it remained a favorite medical remedy (Ruston, British Library, May 2014).

Contrary to the exalted effect of opium experienced by Holmes, for Dr. Grimesby Roylott of Stoke Moran in "The Adventure of the Speckled Band," its use is linked to his contamination through exposure to pernicious Eastern influence (Conan Doyle, 55). "The last survivor of one of the oldest Saxon families in England," Dr. Roylott has recently returned from Calcutta transformed into the archetypal example of the lawless, wild and corrupted fallen man. Recast by his past association with the Orient, his decline from medical doctor, responsible for preserving life, to that of violent criminal, with intemperate habits and uncontrolled passions, fictionalizes popular perceptions of racial identity and demonstrates how these were influenced by imperialist ideology. As Douglas Kerr explains, fears of degeneration were linked to the Indian sub-continent in Victorian fiction, where returnees from the British Raj appeared to have been possessed by "the spirit of the place," unsettling their "racial loyalty" and leading them to barbarity, as seen in the characterization of Dr. Roylott (*Eastern Figures*, 122, 124). In parallel with "A Case of Identity," the theme of a wicked stepfather engaging in criminality by defrauding women of their property emerges in the story, alongside issues of gender and class. The story was first published in the February 1892 issue of the *Strand Magazine*, included as the eighth installment in a collection of twelve published the same year by Arthur Conan Doyle as *The Adventures of*

1. Justice According to Holmes

Sherlock Holmes. The narrative holds a special place in the canon because of how it was viewed by Conan Doyle himself, who was keen to keep Holmes alive to his readers and at the forefront of popular literature. He set up a reader's competition in the March 1927 edition of the *Strand Magazine* in which readers were invited to "list what they thought were the twelve best Sherlock Holmes short stories"—the winner who was able to list the selection closest to Conan Doyle's choices was to receive one hundred pounds and an autographed copy of *Memories and Adventures,* Conan Doyle's autobiography (Ashley, 238). Conan Doyle's first choice of "The Adventure of the Speckled Band" is no surprise, for it is one of the most intriguing of his stories. It is written in the locked room format of mystery detection, created by Edgar Allen Poe in his 1841 work "The Murders in the Rue Morgue" and defined by Julian Symons as one in which "nobody could have entered the room and there is no trace of a weapon" (30). It is set in 1883, a year before the passing of an important amendment to the Married Women's Property Act, whose importance lay in the alteration of a woman's status from that of a mere chattel to an independent and separate individual (Hamilton, 105). Under the terms of the Married Woman's Property Act of 1882, married women could keep all personal and real property acquired before and during marriage, giving them the same property rights as unmarried women. Historically, the law was not uniformly applied across class divisions: legally, a wealthy married woman, although she was classed as "feme covert," could set up a trust or settlement ensuring that on the death of a spouse, she could retain control of her property. Settlements usually provided for the children of the marriage on the death of the father. This situation appears to be echoed in "The Adventure of the Speckled Band," where a wealthy widow upon remarriage has bequeathed her entire fortune of "not less than a thousand a year" to her new husband, whilst her two children reside with him (Conan Doyle, 279). In the event of their marriage, "a certain annual sum should be allowed" to each of the daughters from this capital sum, a circumstance bound to cause difficulty on the death of the widow, given the criminal nature of her new husband (279).

The heroine of the story, Helen Stoner, arrives early one morning at Baker Street in "a considerable state of excitement" (278). Heavily veiled and dressed in black, she is ushered by Holmes to the fireplace to warm herself, for she is shivering, but she replies, "It is not cold that makes me shiver.... It is fear... It is terror" (278). Watson describes her arrival:

> She raised her veil as she spoke, and we could see that she was indeed in a pitiable state of agitation, her face all drawn and grey, with restless frightened eyes like those of a hunted animal. Her features and figure were those of a woman of thirty, but her hair was shot with premature grey, and her expression was weary and haggard [278].

33

Morality and the Law in British Detective and Spy Fiction

On his return from Calcutta, her stepfather, who ran a large medical practice in India, appears transformed by his experience of living there, rendering him susceptible to the influence of reckless passions. Incensed by burglaries of his house, he beat his native butler to death and narrowly escaped a capital sentence, sentenced instead to a long prison term. She tells Holmes that her stepfather has abandoned his attempt to set up a practice in London, likely due to the hurdles now in place with the professionalization of medicine. In order to practice in England, the Medical Act of 1858 required a would-be-practitioner to pass an examination allowing him to be placed on the Medical Register. Prior to this law, there was no regulated medical profession in Britain, and anyone could set up a practice. The introduction of a disciplinary code may have barred Roylott's registration with the Medical Register and prevented him from earning a living after his conviction for a felonious crime. From then on, he follows in the footsteps of his dissolute, aristocratic ancestors who had squandered the estate through gambling and waste by entering into a life of dissipation and degeneration. Construed as atavistic, Dr. Grimesby Roylott represents the contagion of opium to which he appears addicted, judging by his change of character and irrational mood swings. The fictional warning embodied in the narrative endorses the need for the civilizing influence of imperial control and political sovereignty over foreign territories in order to contain their influence. His passion for Indian animals and the native lifestyle he enjoyed in India is indulged when he attempts to recreate the jungle by sending for exotic pets, including a cheetah and a baboon that freely roam the estate. The evil characteristics he has acquired during his Oriental sojourn are presented as indolence and erratic violent behavior, which demonstrate Milligan's contention that "the characterisation of Eastern peoples as slothful and violent reinforced the power dynamics of Empire" and fostered the notion that returnees contaminated the English countryside with their corruption (Milligan, 6). Having lived in the "seductive environment" of India, where laws are lax and constraints are few, he loses his sense of civilization and returns to a beastly life ruled by bodily appetites, "a reverse of evolution" (Kerr, 125).

Helen Stoner describes to Holmes how her twin sister, who had been engaged to marry, had met her death under strange circumstances one night after reporting hearing a low whistling sound. No satisfactory cause of death could be found, as her room was inaccessible with the door locked; there was no visible trace of violence on her body. Two years have passed since her sister's death, and Miss Stoner, herself engaged to be married, hears the same low whistling sound in the silence of the night, making her fear for her life. During the interview between Miss Stoner and Holmes, further evidence of Dr. Roylott's barbarity emerges when Holmes notices "Five livid spots, the marks of four fingers and a thumb" imprinted on her wrist, evidence of physical abuse (281). Screening her bruises, Miss Stoner defends her stepfather saying, "He is a hard man … and perhaps he hardly knows his own strength" (281). Despite suffering physical abuse at the hands of her stepfather, her symbolic gesture of filial devotion and passivity in the face of violence conflicts with her presumption that he is responsible in some way for the death of her sister and is linked to her own perilous situation. Her vulnerable position reflects the social constraints imposed upon women who are isolated and devoid of assistance and signals the lack of legal support available to women at the time, especially in cases of family violence. Fear for her personal safety and exposure in terms of physical abuse is compounded by the knowledge that, as a single woman without the means of subsistence provided by her stepfather, Helen Stoner risks losing her livelihood if she chooses to leave; with nowhere to go and no money to support her, a career on the streets is the likeliest consequence. These conditions would be easily recognized as presenting a familiar theme to Conan Doyle's audience; Putney contends, "Doyle capitalizes on a contemporary topic to lend verisimilitude to stories rooted in real-life issues," confirming the prevalence of family tyranny in the era and evidence that the narrative is more true-to-life than it is given credit for (Putney, 48). A parallel may be drawn with the circumstances of the previous story where prospective economic loss on the marriage of his stepdaughter had driven the stepfather to devise an ingenious plot to maintain control of her wealth, albeit a less vicious one. Martin Wiener points out that there emerged toward the end of the century a growing awareness of "women's right to bodily security, against both beatings and coerced sex," a "civilizing" offensive which worked on public opinion to make it unacceptable and unmanly to inflict violence on women and children (*Men of Blood,* 34). The criminal aristocrat, Roylott, visits Holmes in his rooms in a temper, described thus:

> A large face, seared with a thousand wrinkles, burned yellow with the sun and marked with every evil passion, was turned from one to the other of us, while his deep-set, bile shot eyes, and his high thin fleshless nose gave him somewhat the resemblance to a fierce old bird of prey [282].

Roylott's presentation corresponds with the ideas of Cesare Lombroso, the Italian criminologist and psychiatrist, renowned for his publication *L'uomo Delinquente* (1876), whose popular theory of criminal anthropology was based on the notion of inherited criminality. Mary Gibson and Nicole Hahn Rafter, in their introduction to the work's translation, outline the parameters of his theory:

Morality and the Law in British Detective and Spy Fiction

[T]he born criminal, [is] a dangerous individual marked by what we call anomalies—physical and psychological abnormalities. For Lombroso, these anomalies resembled the traits of primitive peoples, animals and even plants, proving that the most dangerous criminals were atavistic throwbacks on the evolutionary scale.... He called his new theory "criminal anthropology" reflecting his desire to reorient legal thinking from philosophical debate about the nature of crime to an analysis of the characteristics of the criminal [Gibson and Hahn, 1].

His beliefs are echoed in an article written by Bernard Hollander, MD, for the *Strand Magazine*, published in the January 1908 edition, which posed the question "Can Criminals Be Cured by Surgical Operation?" He opines: "A man may be an idiot morally as well as intellectually.... As regards the anatomical marks of the typical criminal ... the Continental School of Criminal anthropologists have found that his skull is widest from ear to ear ... the ears sit very low, very much below the level of the eyes ... anatomically and psychologically, therefore, the born criminal presents the appearance of arrested development and resembles in many respects the lower animals" (Vol. 25, 94). Interestingly, despite the discrediting of Lombroso's theory, more than a decade later his views are still articulated in certain scientific circles. LeRoy Lad Panek in *Probable Cause* notes that an expert on the pseudo-science of phrenology in the 1880s, when asked his opinion on a range of head shapes, noted that they were all abnormal, but it transpired he had been shown "the heads of prominent individuals, including President Cleveland and George Vanderbilt" (47). Holmes consults the will of the deceased mother and discovers that Roylott will lose two hundred and fifty pounds from the estate for each of his daughters when they marry, confirming his belief that Helen Stoner is in danger. In the final showdown, Holmes travels to Stoke Moran, where he discovers that Roylott keeps a swamp adder in a safe in the room next to his daughter's bedroom. He sets it loose in the night so it can climb through the ventilator between the rooms, slide down the bell pull and onto the bed, in the hope that it will eventually sink its venomous teeth into his stepdaughter and cause her death. As the snake slithers gently down the rope, Holmes attacks it with his cane; it returns through the ventilator and back to Roylott's room where it attacks and kills him, its speckled body encircling his head.

Scrutiny of Holmes's role in the death of Roylott leads to a diminishing of the distinction between hero and villain. In his concluding remarks to Watson, he confesses, "Some of the blows of my cane came home and roused its snakish temper, so that it flew upon the first person it saw. In this way I am no doubt indirectly responsible for Dr. Grimesby Roylott's death, but I cannot say that it is likely to weigh very heavily upon my conscience" (287). Holmes's liminality is here verging on criminality as he accepts culpability for Roylott's death, but given the heinous nature of the rogue's behavior, Holmes's conscience is clear. In his opinion, providential punishment has been meted out, but in this assumption, he ignores his own role in manipulating events in the search for justice. In analyzing the reasons for his actions, we consider that he had several options before him, including capturing or shooting the snake, but he chooses to strike it knowing that it will "turn upon its master" and cause his death (287). Whether he reaches an impartial judgment is questionable, for he has been guided by personal antagonism based on the knowledge of Roylott's infamy. On the other hand, whilst it is difficult to gauge the extent of subjective emotion shown by Holmes, Watson informs us that he prided himself on his dispassionate and unbiased perspectives, so that his level of prejudice is likely to be minimal. Conan Doyle, a qualified medical doctor, was subject to the strict terms of the Medical Act. He has Holmes comment to Watson, "When a doctor does go wrong he is the first of criminals. He has nerve and he has knowledge. Palmer and Pritchard were the head of their profession" (Conan Doyle, 286). Alongside these poisoners, he may have in mind another: Dr. Thomas Neill Cream, the Lambeth Poisoner, whose evil exploits finally caught up with him in the same year as publication of the story.

Holmes's culpability for the death of Roylott is diminished in our eyes when we discover the outcome of the official enquiry into Roylott's death. Its conclusion that he "met his fate while indiscreetly playing with a dangerous pet" illustrates the inefficiency of judicial inquiries and to some extent exculpates Holmes (287). The system of inquiry into death under unusual circumstances required a member of the public to notify the coroner of evidence of foul play, which did not happen in this case. It is probable that Helen Stoner would prefer the details of her stepfather's relapse into primitivism to be concealed to prevent scandal. Conan Doyle's characterization of Helen Stoner illustrates Holmes's awareness of the inequalities of the judicial system that seriously disadvantaged women. Holmes's actions offer the consolation of assisted providence in the form of retributive justice. His attitude is summed up in the statement, "Violence does, in truth, recoil upon the violent, and the schemer falls into the pit which he digs for another" (287).

"The Adventure of the Abbey Grange" (1904)

The progress we have made in the criminal law in the last one hundred years is really remarkable. In very recent days we have at last allowed the prisoner to give his evidence of the matter he is charged with if he desires to do so. We have under certain restricted conditions, supplied him with legal assistance, and, best of all, there is at length a court of Criminal Appeal [Parry, E., 189].

The comments written in 1914 by Judge Edward Abbott Parry on legal reform note the importance of the creation of the Court of Criminal Appeal in providing a safety net for unsound verdicts that could be challenged with sight of new evidence. Such a possibility did not exist until its creation in 1907 following the Adolph Beck and George Edalji cases, and its recourse was absent from the legal statute books when "The Adventure of the Abbey Grange" was penned. An earlier enactment may have prevented Holmes from taking the law into his own hands in an apparent case of murder to assist an accused man. Despite progress in legal reform, a convergence of flaws in the judicial system in the Edwardian era surface in "The Adventure of the Abbey Grange," a story awash with problems of marital violence, gender disparity in the terms of the Divorce Act of 1857, lack of confidence in judicial decision-making and the gap in representational justice for an ordinary individual suspected of murder. By 1904 when the story was first published in the September edition of the *Strand Magazine,* the legal system had improved considerably from the time of "The Speckled Band." The Prisons Act of 1898, a momentous reform that introduced a more enlightened prison regime, was aimed at improving as well as punishing prisoners. Its inception marked the "beginnings of the modern penal system" and included the separation of young offenders from the main prison population (www.parliament.uk). An updated Larceny Act in 1901 prevented the fraudulent appropriation of property by agents in positions of confidence, a point not covered in law until then. The Summary Jurisdiction (Married Woman Act) of 1895 empowered magistrates to compel husbands to pay maintenance in cases of desertion, and the Infant Life Protection Act of 1897, designed to supervise more vigilantly the practice of baby-farming, helped alleviate previous injustice. Nevertheless, legislation continued to be steeped in inequalities and lagged behind industrial and commercial crime.

Collected as one of thirteen stories by George Newnes in a selection entitled *The Return of Sherlock Holmes,* released in 1905, "The Adventure of the Abbey Grange" describes the plight of a woman married to a titled, abusive and alcoholic husband that emphasizes the realities of violence suffered by women across the class divide. Ruskin's elevation of the status of the home to "the place of peace; the shelter from injury, terror, doubt and division" was denounced by feminists as the "sentimentalization of family life," which often led to greater violence when the woman did not conform to type (Shanley, 4). Escape options for abused women were even less accessible than today, and many stories of violence echo the experience of present-day gender assault. Before the Divorce Act of 1857, the only way to end a marriage (other than by ecclesiastical annulment) was by a Private Act of Parliament, an avenue unavailable to most women (Shanley, 9). The terms of the 1857 Divorce Act, although making provision for the protection of the property of deserted wives, were skewed in favor of the husband, for a divorce could only be procured by a woman "if he was physically cruel, incestuous or bestial in addition to being adulterous otherwise she would be 'guilty of desertion'"; meanwhile, he could cite adultery as the sole cause for divorce (Shanley, 9). Arthur Conan Doyle's championing of divorce law reform has been well documented and is addressed in Mike Ashley's *Adventures in the Strand* (2016). In a synopsis of Conon Doyle's advocacy for divorce reform, Ashley records his appointment as "chairman of a Royal Commission" on the subject and his participation in a parliamentary discussion in July 1917; Its remit was to draft a Matrimonial Causes Bill proposing that "a marriage be dissolved following a separation of three years"; unfortunately, their recommendations were ignored, and it was not until 1923 that terms for divorce were gradually improved (Ashley, 228).

In "The Adventure of the Abbey Grange," focus on domestic violence and the urgent need for reform of outdated divorce laws are central to the narrative, and in contrast to periodical reports of working-class spousal abuse, the prevalence of wifely abuse in upper-class settings is revealed. Holmes's opening remarks, "We are moving in high life, Watson, crackling paper, monogram, coat-of-arms, picturesque address," indicate that despite the grandeur of the setting, violence and bloodshed are familiar domestic scenarios in both upper and lower-class homes (Conan Doyle, 527). Demonstrating that Holmes and Scotland Yard at this stage have a sympathetic working relationship, and as an indication of the respect in which Holmes is held by the official police force, Inspector Stanley Hopkins sends for him to ask his opinion on the brutal murder of Sir Eustace Brakenstall that has taken place at the Abbey Grange. The official view of circumstances taken by Inspector Hopkins gives credence to Lady Brakenstall's account of events, and he welcomes Holmes and Watson:

> I'm very glad you have come, Mr. Holmes. And you too, Dr. Watson! But, indeed, if I had my time over again I should not have troubled you, for since the lady has come to herself she has given so clear an account of the affair that there is not much left for us to do. You remember that Lewisham gang of burglars? [527].

Blame for the murder has been fastened on a father and two sons, the Randalls, known to have committed a robbery recently in the neighborhood. Initially, Holmes, too, is impressed with the account given by Lady Brakenstall, who presents a picture of injured feminine beauty tinged with spirit when she narrates the events leading to her husband's death. Evidence of physical abuse is exposed by the "plum-colored swelling" above her eye and "two vivid red spots" on her arm (528). Any expectation of hysteria and emotional trauma, consistent with the customary gender depiction of women in distress, is confounded by her composure, prompting Watson, ever appreciative of an attractive woman, to applaud her poise and remark that "her quick observant gaze" showed that neither her wits nor her courage had been shaken by her terrible experience (528). She explains that her short marriage has been an unhappy one, dominated by the tyranny of Sir Eustace who was a "confirmed drunkard," and she continues to fulminate against her perceived captivity in a destructive and harmful marriage, declaring:

> To be with such a man for an hour is unpleasant. Can you imagine what it means to be tied to him for day and night? It is a sacrilege, a crime, villainy to hold that such a marriage is binding. I say that these monstrous laws of yours will bring a curse upon the land. Heaven will not let such wickedness endure. [528].

Her words echo, to some extent, the opinions of Frances Power Cobbe, who was instrumental in the passage of the Matrimonial Causes Act of 1878, which "allowed a wife beaten by her husband to apply for a separation order from a local magistrates court" (Shanley, 158). In her use of language analogous of "master and slave" to characterize her relationship with her husband, Lady Brakenstall evokes the same metaphor used in Cobbe's essay, "Wife Torture in England" published in 1878 (Hamilton, 442). She fabricates a version of events entailing the arrival of three burglars who assaulted her, tied her to a chair and then attacked and murdered her husband with the poker, before making off with the silver, convincing both Holmes and Watson of her innocence. Holmes's initial unquestioning acceptance of her version of events is evidence of his ideological views on class where a woman in her position would never engage in deceit. Holmes and Watson comfort her as she narrates the events leading up to the tragedy. In its presentation of the abusive, alcoholic husband, the story gives readers a familiar pattern of disorderly, aggressive behavior directed against a woman, and they would sympathize with her situation. Holmes, who has uncovered several clues discounting Lady Brakenstall's version of events, discovers that the silver has been deposited in the pond and advises Inspector Hopkins that the story could be a "blind," offering him a chance to solve the mystery. It is clear that Lady Brakenstall's mendacity is unexpected. Her departure from the norms of female behavior is attributed to her upbringing in the freer, less conventional atmosphere of South Australia where a less restrictive code of conduct, devoid of concern for respectability, exists (528). The perfection of religious fervor and honesty expected of an English woman is replaced by the image of one who is able to lie convincingly and temporarily deceive Holmes about the circumstances of her husband's death. This, despite Holmes's assertion in "A Study in Scarlet" that "deceit was an impossibility in the case of one trained to observation and analysis" (Conan Doyle, 17).

Sir Eustace Brackenstall's assailant turns out to be Captain Jack Croker, a former acquaintance of Lady Brakenstall's from before her marriage, who, having heard of the abuse she has suffered at the hands of her brutal husband from her maid, Theresa Wright, is anxious for her safety and aggrieved that "[t]his drunken hound … should dare to raise his hand to her whose boots he was not worthy to lick" (535). He visits Lady Brakenstall late one evening before his departure for Australia. In his desire to protect her from her husband's drunken assault with a stick, he becomes involved in a fight in which the abuser meets his end when Captain Croker "went through him as if he were a rotten pumpkin" (535). Croker could argue self-defense, if such an option were open to him and given credence by a jury, but the ability to engage a decent barrister to represent him in a criminal court would be well beyond his means. Although the Poor Prisoners Defense Act of 1903 provided counsel for the accused, Edward Parry explains that "it is not the same quality of legal defense that a rich prisoner can obtain for money" and cites the case of a Scotsman who offered five pounds to his counsel to be seated rather than further incriminate his client (197). Taking the law into his own hands, Holmes conducts enquiries into the background of Captain Croker by consulting his employers. Assured of the captain's integrity, he is satisfied that he is dealing with a man of excellent character and reputation whose primary motive of self-defense is strengthened by his desire to protect Lady Brackenstall from a violent husband. Captain Croker is at Holmes's mercy as he assumes judicial authority in deciding the outcome of the case. The reader is alerted to Croker's precarious legal predicament, as Holmes is about to inform Scotland Yard of his findings that will instigate a warrant for his arrest. On deliberation, Holmes revises his position and declares to Watson, "I couldn't do it, Watson… Once that warrant was made out nothing on earth would save him," expressing his belief that the law would find Croker guilty of murder and condemn him to death without any recourse to the mitigating circumstances and the possibility of an unjust verdict (Conan Doyle, 533). Self-defense was a verdict rarely used, and a charge of manslaughter, defined as "an unlawful killing without premeditation or malice," was the customary charge. It was not until 1907 "in response to the miscarriage of justice in the case of Adolph Beck and the likely miscarriages in the trials of George Edalji, and the alleged poisoner, Florence Maybrick" that a Court of Criminal Appeal was established, according to John Hostettler (251). Holmes and Watson act illegally when they assume the role of judge and jury, conceal the true facts of the affair from the police and shelter a suspected murderer from criminal prosecution. Holmes outlines his rationale for justice:

> Well, it is a great responsibility that I take upon myself.... See here, Captain Croker, we'll do this in due form of law. You are the prisoner. Watson, you are a British jury, and I never met a man who was more eminently fitted to represent one. I am the judge. Now, gentlemen of the jury, you have heard the evidence. Do you find the prisoner guilty or not guilty? [535].

In response to the not guilty verdict uttered by Watson, Holmes replies "*Vox Populi: Vox Dei*" and acquits Captain Croker, ordering him to remain overseas for a year (535). Scrutiny of Holmes's motivation and conduct show that he detects disparities in the legal system that prompt him to adopt measures to achieve a more equitable form of justice. Having identified the clash of principles between justice and the rigidity of the legal system that would see Croker hang or sentenced to a lengthy prison term, he is directed by conscience and, acting upon his own moral judgment, implements an individualized code that accommodates the specific circumstances of the case. In this instance, he makes his own laws determined by his belief in his superior moral intelligence, integrity and ability to reason and adjudicate equitably. As readers, we are led to empathize with Holmes's intervention and resolution and applaud his good intentions, acquiescing in his illegality because his reasons appear rational and his moral stance acceptable as the right thing to do. Our compliance is solicited when he observes, "Once or twice in my career I feel that I have done more real harm by my discovery of the criminal than ever he had done by his crime.... I had rather play tricks with the law of England than with my own conscience" (533).

In this story, Holmes supports the rights of women by castigating male violence, and in this he advances the cause of women's emancipation and empowerment (*Men of Blood*: 35).

"The Adventure of the Blue Carbuncle" (1892)

In Watson's comment in "A Case of Identity" on the scandalous nature of press coverage of crime when he loftily declares how rude and vulgar they are in sensationalizing crime, it is clear that, nevertheless, both he and Holmes regularly scour the pages of the newspapers for evidence of crime and deviance. Constant referencing of them in the canon as a primary source of information validates their status as culturally significant in shaping public perceptions of the nature of criminality. Holmes uses the pages to place advertisements and root out criminals in several stories within the canon, and he and Watson frequently comment on the manners and morals of those caught up in the legal system whose transgressions are exposed for public consumption. The constant flow of information and extensive crime reporting from media outlets, combined with the Victorian fascination for crime, its mysteries and solutions, fueled the growth of detective fiction. Ideological representation of the dangerous classes, often depicted in Victorian literature and media as those whose pernicious lifestyles and lack of self-discipline lead to rampant lawlessness, are vividly depicted in the slum fiction works of Arthur Morrison and journalist exposés, such as George Sims's book on London slum housing entitled *How the Poor Live* (1883). The nature and threat of criminality were fashioned in an age of scientific and technological advances that led to an altered vision based on social Darwinism. An increase in social mobility shifted the boundaries of power and authority, which were redrawn to validate an entrepreneurial and professional middle-class whose powerful voices declared outrage at the specter of encroaching lawlessness generated by an expanding urban sprawl and stoked by perceived criminal elements from the lower classes of society. Class tension and hostility simmered in a cultural environment that saw the portrayal of criminals as a separate class perched on the borders of society. Poverty and criminality were fused to create a criminal identity of "other" as opposite and different—the impoverished working class at the lowest end of society's hierarchy. Rowbotham notes that "the burgeoning working-class quarters of urban Britain were seen as the natural environment of the criminal," a perception bound to foment class anxiety and hostility (Rowbotham and Stevenson, 4). Representation of class interactions and tensions are clearly mirrored in the collision of upper, middle and working-class characters in "The Blue Carbuncle" (1892) and "The Adventure of Charles Augustus Milverton" (1904). In these stories Conan Doyle provides contrasting pictures of criminality where Holmes and Watson immerse themselves in illegal activities, such as perverting the course of justice and burglary, actions which prove law-breaking is not solely restricted to the lower classes of society. Holmes's response to crime in the stories reveals how and to what extent his class perceptions influence his judgments and challenge his integrity and, consequently, his ability to act as an impartial agent of justice.

Morality and the Law in British Detective and Spy Fiction

"The Adventure of The Blue Carbuncle" is the seventh story in a series of twelve assembled in the collection entitled *The Adventures of Sherlock Holmes* and was first released in a monthly version of the *Strand Magazine* in January 1892. Its presentation of the theft of a priceless jewel embraces character images molded from archetypal examples of working-class criminality alongside that of an aspiring middle-class entrepreneur, Breckinridge, a stall proprietor in Covent Garden. Theft was the most common category of crime tried at the Old Bailey during the nineteenth century and was considered a felony. Due to the vast number of thefts associated with servants convicted of robbing their masters, a specific offense was created in 1823 following an Act of Parliament, which provided for the "further and more adequate punishments of servants convicted of this offense," as Clive Emsley et al. in "Crimes Tried at the Old Bailey" inform (*OBP*). An updated version of the Larceny Act of 1827 consolidated the provisions related to larceny in the Larceny Act of 1861, which remained in place until 1901. The opening scene of "The Blue Carbuncle" finds Holmes in a deductive mood as he outlines the character and social standing of the owner of a hat delivered to him by the commissionaire, Peterson, along with a Christmas goose. He came upon both at the scene of a "garroting," or attempted murder, on his return home the previous evening along Tottenham Court Road. Holmes's instruction to Peterson to enjoy the consumption of the goose results in the discovery within its "crop" of a valuable gemstone belonging to the Countess of Morcar, who recently reported its theft from the Hotel Cosmopolitan. James Ryder, the upper-attendant who works at the hotel, accuses John Horner, a plumber, of stealing the carbuncle. Evidence against the plumber is purely circumstantial and based solely on the testimony of this one witness. Despite Horner's protestations of innocence and obvious distress at being committed to the Assizes because of a previous conviction, the evidence is believed to be sufficiently strong. The magistrate dealing with the case refuses to hear Horner's version of events because his earlier offense permanently stained his character, and he is duly imprisoned in Pentonville prison, the first modern prison in England opened in 1842, which was the subject of Dickens's satire in *David Copperfield*.

The story presents a critique of the Habitual Criminal's Act of 1869 and the Prevention of Crime Act 1871, both of which were conceived to "tighten control over criminals after their release from prison" (Shpayer-Makov, 37). The impact of the acts was to impose heavy administrative duties on official police forces due to the generation of paperwork involved in the maintenance of "more systematic records of convicted persons" (37). In line with the terms of the 1824 Vagrancy Act, the regulations targeted the poor and unjustly discriminated against them. Helen Johnston describes the provisions of the acts as "far reaching" and "open to interpretation," as she explains:

> [O]ffenders discovered by the police and thought to be obtaining a livelihood by dishonest means, about to commit or aid in committing a crime, waiting for the opportunity to commit or aid in committing a crime, or being unable to account for their presence could find themselves guilty of an offense and subject to a maximum of one year's imprisonment, with or without hard labour [Johnston, 35].

Added to these punitive conditions was the stipulation that once arrested on suspicion of an offense, a suspect had to prove his innocence to the court, an assumption of guilt rather than innocence. In Clive Emsley's view, "Most of those prosecuted in criminal courts came from the poorer sections of society," and the discourse of class became more central to the analysis and perception of crime (*Crime and Society*, 57). Criminality was seen as essentially a class problem, confirmed in the arrest of the fictionalized Horner. On hearing the circumstances surrounding the arrest of John Horner for the crime, Holmes snorts derisively, "Hum! So much for the police court!" (272). His poor opinion of the courts concurs with that of Anthony Guest, a writer in the July 1891 issue of the *Strand,* who decries the speed with which justice is dispensed as the magistrates "pride themselves on getting through the greatest number of cases in the shortest time possible, calling it 'absurd'" (85). He adds: "Whenever the police make a charge against any individual, they at once jump to the conclusion that he is guilty, and there is nothing they desire so much as a conviction" (85). The misuse of basic circumstantial evidence to secure convictions, as evidenced in the narrative of "The Blue Carbuncle," permeates the work of many Victorian writers and is central to the narratives of detective fiction writers of the era, including that of Arthur Morrison, J.E. Preston Muddock and those whose work forms part of this study.

We gain a glimpse of Holmes's attitude toward those in varying socio-economic groups in his response to their criminality. His first investigative class encounter is with Henry Baker, the owner of the misplaced hat, who comes under Holmes's initial scrutiny as the possible miscreant responsible for the theft of the jewel. Entering Holmes's apartment, Henry Baker exudes an air of exaggerated respectability in his mannerly address and courteous behavior toward Holmes, indicative of his once middle-class connections. His mannerisms reflect his middle-class roots, consistent with his previous status in society, that of a middle-class professional. Having fallen on hard times, a condition associated with "moral retrogression" through alcoholism, his pursuits and dress are now determined by his altered position, including his subscription to a "goose club," a commonly accepted way for working-class families to save for an otherwise unaffordable Christmas dinner. Evidence of poverty is linked to his address, where candles rather than gas lamps are used to light the household and to his inability to afford a new hat. Watson is mildly mocking of the appearance of the hat, for "it was cracked, exceedingly dusty and spotted in several places, although there seemed to have been some attempt to hide the discolored patches by smearing them with ink" (271). His middle-class snobbery comes to the fore in remarks about Baker's demeanor, as he condescendingly observes, "With a comical pomposity of manner he bowed solemnly to both of us and strode off upon his way" (274). Holmes, on the other hand, once he has ascertained Baker's innocence, refrains from comment on Baker's altered financial circumstances and, instead, expresses a generosity of spirit by gifting the newly purchased goose in place of the one he has lost.

The search for the thief brings Holmes to Covent Garden Market, a hive of working-class enterprise, and to his confrontation with the salesman, Breckinridge, a bristling, successful trader who registers little respect for middle-class etiquette. His tone of speech and bearing convey his unwillingness to adopt respectful deference to middle-class customers like Holmes, since a thriving business and entrepreneurial spirit place him above the need for obsequiousness. He seethes with resentment and hostility in his contretemps with Holmes, whom he suspects of accusing him of criminality in acquiring the geese, an understandable attitude considering the penalties imposed by the courts for theft.

Breckinridge complains of the fuss being made over the sale of the geese as Holmes is not the first to enquire about its provenance and defiantly declares that he won't disclose the information Holmes seeks—the source of the geese—responding, "Well, then, I shan't tell you. So now!" (274). Holmes replies:

> "Well, I have no connection with any other people making enquiries … if you won't tell us the bet is off, that is all. But I am always ready to back my opinion on a matter or fowls, and I have a fiver on it that the bird I ate is country bred" [274].

Holmes negotiates the discourse in a way that underlines his insight and understanding of the working-class psyche, allowing him to regain control of the situation and achieve his purpose whilst simultaneously deflating an inflammatory state of affairs. Holmes's use of psychology to read Breckinridge signals his preconceived notions of class conduct, confirmed in his assertion, "When you see a man with whiskers of that cut and the 'pink'un' protruding out of his pocket, you can always draw him by a bet" (275). As a subscriber to *The Sporting Times,* which is printed on pink paper and visible in Breckinridge's pocket, Holmes immediately conflates working-class men with an addiction to gambling. Thus, his omniscience identifies the nature of the hostile threat and provides a means of resolution. A similar approach to working-class partiality to gambling is made in John Buchan's *The Thirty-Nine Steps* when Richard Hannay offers the milkman money for his hat and jacket to fulfill his commitment to a bet.

James Ryder, the real jewel thief, embodies the idea of simmering criminality when he emerges as a nervous "little rat-faced fellow" who faints when confronted by Holmes (275). His character portrayal as a combination of effete emotional instability and physical peculiarity linked to degeneracy is further illustration of Britain's fascination with the new science of criminal anthropology that had filtered in from Europe. A Darwinian perspective is thus invoked to corroborate the "prejudices of gender" and class, to use Emsley's phrase (*Crime and Society*, 97). Ryder's outward appearance is described in terms of feeble and unhealthy attributes, which "seemed literally to embody the very physical and moral deficiencies undermining the standing of the nation," ably described by Judith Rowbotham and Kim Stevenson in their 2005 study *Criminal Conversations: Victorian Crime, Social Panic and Moral Outrage* (16). His portrayal evokes Henry Maudsley's image of criminality associated with evil ancestral influence where no amount of care will prevent those afflicted "from being vicious or criminal, or becoming insane" (*Crime and Society*, 77). Ryder, however, was able to confound the claim that his end was determined by ancestry, as he managed to elude the destiny shaping his ends due to the intervention by Sherlock Holmes. Holmes shows compassion in response to Ryder's appeal for mercy, as he throws himself down upon the rug and pleads:

> "For God's sake, have mercy.... Think of my father! Of my mother! It would break their hearts. I never went wrong before! I never will again. I swear it. I'll swear it on a bible. Oh, don't bring it into court! For Christ's sake, don't!" [276].

Having heard the sequence of events leading to the theft of the carbuncle, Holmes throws open the door and orders, "No more words. Get out!" (276). A reader's typical reaction to Holmes's humane response is sympathy and approval of his merciful judgment in awarding the criminal a second chance to reform and live a more law-abiding life. In the nature of his response, the middle-class reader vicariously enjoys a "sense of superiority" over the lower-class criminal, and the discourse serves to alleviate the fear of crime by providing "rhetoric of reassurance against the criminal," as Emsley suggests (*Crime and Society*, 175). Other readings could reveal a construction of Holmes's own powerful identity and his willingness to establish himself as a pre-eminent authority, ready to dispense justice more mercifully than the legal system dictates, an executive prerogative reserved for the monarch. Equally, his discretionary justice fails to account for the harm inflicted on John Horner, who was wrongly accused of theft and detained in prison, for he receives no redress for his incarceration. Whether it springs from an act of altruism or class superiority, Holmes's decision to allow Ryder to go free, acknowledged as an act of criminality on his part, is, in his view, mitigated when he declares, "I am not retained by the police to supply their deficiencies," a clear indication of his lack of confidence in their ability to solve the mystery (277). Further questions arise about Holmes's easy willingness to incriminate himself in order to redeem a confessed crook. In agreeing that he is "commuting a felony," it is apparent that Holmes is willing to show mercy where the law would not in an instance where, in his opinion, justice would not be served (277). His moral wisdom is based on a system of values and principles that overrides laws and customs. It demonstrates his capacity to distinguish the morally salient features of a given situation and his willingness to provide justice outside the legal system.

"The Adventure of Charles Augustus Milverton" (1904)

The offense of blackmail makes a regular appearance in nineteenth century literature. From Edgar Allan Poe's *The Purloined Letter*, 1845, to Dickens's *Bleak House* of 1852 and Mary Elizabeth Braddon's *Lady Audley's Secret* of 1862, threats of exposure of secrets in an age of burgeoning press coverage make sensational reading. W.H.D. Winder explains that the offense of blackmail did not exist until 1840 and was incorporated into the Larceny Acts of 1861, and, as a crime against the reputation, it was considered a form of robbery (24). As Jenks points out, the difference lies in the fact that "by the exercise of mental, rather than physical terrorism, it compels the victim, for fear of losing his position in society, to comply with the most outrageous demands," usually financial or criminal (236). Revenge taken for the ruinous effects of blackmail dictates the outcome of "The Adventure of Charles Augustus Milverton," one of thirteen stories released in 1904 and set in 1899. The story forms part of the collection entitled *The Return of Sherlock Holmes* and is rumored, in Nicholas Basbanes's account, to be based upon the factual exploits of Charles Augustus Howell, an art dealer and friend of the Rossettis and John Ruskin who died nine years earlier in strange circumstances (Basbanes, 15). Elements of revenge appear in several stories within the canon, including *A Study in Scarlet* (1887) and "The Boscombe Valley Mystery" (1891) in which Holmes appears to condone blackmail by refusing to condemn those who use it as a means for achieving elusive justice. The story skillfully engages us in its presentation of class issues and conflict, focusing chiefly on the depiction of treachery, middle-class superiority and upper-class female susceptibility to extortion.

In this story, Holmes embarks upon a dangerous assignment at the request of Lady Eva Brackwell, a debutante who is engaged to marry into a highly respected titled family: his task is to secure compromising letters written by her to a young squire of previous acquaintance and acquired by the blackmailer, Milverton, from a faithless servant. The high level of criminal activity undertaken by Holmes in this story raises questions over his moral integrity and judgment and challenges the motivations for his means and delivery of justice. At the outset of the story, Holmes, acting on behalf of Lady Eva Brackwell, anticipates the arrival of Charles Augustus Milverton at Baker Street to discuss the return of the letters, a visit that inspires dread and repugnance from Holmes, whose analogous comparison of him to serpents as "slithery, gliding, venomous creatures" indicates his level of repulsion for the "king of all blackmailers" (485). His revulsion derives from the type of criminal he encounters in Milverton. Mayhew argued for two different types of criminal: the casual and the professional. By his reckoning, the first category committed crime from accidental causes, such as lust, malice, shame, cupidity, need or political prejudice. Milverton falls into the second category of professional criminal, defined as someone who objects to labor and prefers to plunder others (*Crime and* Society, 73). Unlike the casual criminal, who lives in a separate world and is thought to be addicted to dishonesty, Milverton, the model villain, positively relishes his role for the sense of power it endows, and he fulfills Holmes's notion of evil incarnate. Predatory and evil in his avid pursuit of upper-class indiscretions, he threatens to expose and ruin men and women for financial gain. Unlike many criminals, he does not emerge from working-class roots and is seen to mix easily with the aristocracy, suggesting decadent affiliations. He is described as bearing a resemblance to "Mr. Pickwick's benevolence in his appearance, marred only by the insincerity of the fixed smile and by the hard glitter of those restless and penetrating eyes," a description akin to that of the villain, "The Black Stone" in John Buchan's *The Thirty-Nine Steps*. Allusions to his "round, plump hairless face" and "plump little hand" symbolize his lack of manly virtues (Conan Doyle, 485). When Milverton refuses to part with the letters for anything less than his original demand of seven thousand pounds, Holmes is "grey with anger and mortification" and attempts to lock the door and physically seize them from him, but Milverton is prepared for assault with a revolver tucked into his inside pocket. He chides Holmes:

> I have been expecting you to do something original. This has been done so often, and what good has ever come from it? I assure you that I am armed to the teeth, and I am perfectly prepared to use my weapons knowing that the law will support me [487].

Legally, as Lawyer Fenton in Baring-Gould's account explains, Holmes is guilty of "unlawful detention" at this point, and, in trying to rob Milverton of the letters, he is guilty of the crime of larceny (Baring-Gould, 563). As Jenks explains, "False imprisonment is regarded as an assault even though no actual violence be used to the body of the prosecutor, e.g., where the accused merely turns the key of a door in the room in which the prosecutor is sitting" (Jenks, 208).

Frustrated by his lack of progress with the negotiation and his attempts to retrieve the letters, Holmes's morality becomes muddied in his subsequent actions when he disguises himself as a plumber in order to gain access to Milverton's house and deceptively engages himself to Milverton's housemaid in order to procure information relating to the whereabouts of the letters. His actions in misleading the housemaid into a fraudulent engagement expose him to a breach of promise action, similar to that mentioned in "A Case of Identity" under the 1869 Evidence Further Amendment Act. Chuckling to himself as he relates the narrative of his engagement to Watson, he is dismissive of the impact of his actions on the unsuspecting housemaid and of the irony of the situation. On the one hand, there is an aristocratic woman who became enmeshed in intrigue through her own actions, juxtaposed with someone from the working class who did nothing to deserve the role assigned to her. In a clear indication of the lower level of esteem in which she is held, Holmes justifies his duplicity in the following terms: "You can't help it, my dear Watson. You must play your cards as best you can when such a stake is on the table" (487). It could be that he is referring to the capture of Milverton as much as rescuing Lady Eva, but his response may also be read as implying that rank and privilege outweigh moral considerations in this instance. In his desire to come to a resolution, Holmes sacrifices the welfare of his lower-class fiancée, but not before assuring us she has another suitor for her hand. His actions are justified in his estimation for the purpose of preventing harm to future victims and for preserving the future happiness and reputation of his aristocratic client. Holmes in his disguise as a plumber assumes the artistry of the criminal by sliding easily into the role in his final pursuit of justice.

Acknowledging his level of criminality to Watson, Holmes confides his intention to burgle Milverton's house and retrieve Lady Brackwell's "imprudent sprightly" letters from the safe where he has stowed them. In answer to Watson's threat to report him to the police if he does not allow him to accompany him, Holmes agrees and responds:

> "Well, well, my dear fellow, be it so. We have shared the same room for some years, and it would be amusing if we ended by sharing the same cell. You know, Watson, I don't mind confessing to you that I have always had an idea that I would have made an entirely efficient criminal. This is the chance of a lifetime in that direction . . ." He took a neat little leather case out of a drawer, and opening it he exhibited a number of shining instruments. This is a first-class up-to-date burgling kit, with nickel-plated jemmy, diamond-tipped glass-cutter, adaptable keys, and every modern improvement, which the march of civilisation demands [488].

Holmes's confession that the thrill of burglary appeals to his sense of adventure may also be read as a desire to enter into the mind of the criminal and prove his ability to circumvent the law at will without being caught, testimony to his superior abilities. The fact that the stakes are high, if caught, adds to the frisson of excitement. Adopting the role of burglar, he dresses for the occasion "with black silk face coverings," and compares himself and Watson to "two of the most truculent figures in London" (488). Baring-Gould notes that "once Holmes removes the circle of glass from Milverton's door, he is guilty under section twenty-five of the Larceny Act which states: 'Every person who breaks and enters the dwelling house of another with intent to commit a felon therein … shall be guilty of burglary,'" which is a crime "triable at the assizes and quarter-sessions and is punishable by imprisonment for life" (Baring-Gould, 566). The fact that the offense is carried out at night differentiates it from housebreaking, which carries a lesser sentence of a maximum of fourteen years. From the severity of the punishment, it is clear that Holmes goes to extreme lengths to achieve his ends. His illegal act of burglary may be construed as retributive in the sense that he may feel that heinous criminals, like Milverton, ought to suffer hardship in some way. The moral decadence and dishonesty shown by the villain when he "methodically and at his leisure tortures the soul and wrings the nerves in order to add to his already swollen money-bags," causing severe distress and harm, is placed in the balance against Holmes and Watson's criminal act of burglary (485). Milverton may be seen to have surrendered his rights to legal protection from theft because of his own illegal acts. Holmes embarks on a retributive form of justice as an effective punishment and the only suitable course of action available to eradicate Milverton's corrupt, parasitic practices. In 1823 the offense of threatening with intent to extort was made punishable by transportation for life; however, Holmes admits at the outset

51

of the story, that technically there was nothing they could do about Milverton's blackmail since the secrets he procured related to actual events that had really occurred, a condition explained in Emsley et al.'s "Crimes Tried at the Old Bailey" (*OBP*).

In the final denouement, an upper-class female assassin arrives like an avenging angel seeking redress for the wrongs inflicted on her and others who have suffered loss at Milverton's hands. Disguised as a maidservant for the Countess D'Albert with letters to sell, she deceives her way into Milverton's presence, presenting an outward appearance that belies her criminality. Her portrayal contrasts with fictional depictions of the lower order of female criminal often mirrored as physically repugnant, simple-minded, deranged or diseased. The woman's final act of revenge in shooting Milverton is articulated in terms of her desire to procure justice for the death of her husband who suffered as a result of scandal initiated by Milverton. Her vengeance is sought, not only on her own behalf, but on that of all the women whose lives he had ruined. The act of retribution is savagely compounded when she grates her heel into his face in an act of extreme violence, which Holmes refuses to condemn or prevent. Watson verbalizes the justification for this reticence on Holmes's part, declaring, "…that it was no affair of ours; that justice had overtaken a villain; that we had our own duties and our own objects which were not to be lost sight of" (491). Holmes proceeds to empty the contents of the safe into the fire, an action liable to prosecution for malicious damage, before escaping with Watson over the garden wall. Watson, too, by kicking the restraining hand of the gardener as he struggles to climb the wall, is guilty of an offense under Offenses Against the Persons Act of 1861, for the gardener was assisting the law in trying to prevent Watson's escape from the scene of a crime. In the concluding stages of the story, Holmes indulges in a final act of criminality by withholding evidence of the nature of Milverton's murder from the police. His statement to Lestrade evidences his reasons: "Well, I am afraid I can't help you Lestrade…. The fact is that I knew this fellow Milverton, that I considered him one of the most dangerous men in London, and that I think there are certain crimes which the law cannot touch, and which therefore, justify private revenge" (Conan Doyle, 491). From this statement we are led to query the interchangeability of Holmes who echoes criminal behavior in his pursuit of justice. In this instance he faces a conflict between telling the truth and saving a life. Applying practical wisdom in line with an ethical virtue approach, he determines what is morally appropriate and just in the situation.

Conclusion

In the final analysis of Holmes's response to criminality in these stories, general acceptance of him as a morally steadfast character of virtuous conduct who acts in the interests of justice demonstrates the agreed universality of his ethical approach to resolving problems. In his use of discretionary powers, he follows in a tradition introduced at the time of the establishment of the New Police in 1829, when nominated citizens and law officers were granted authority under public order legislation (*Crime and Society,* 2). He assigns himself an adjudicating role in response to individual cases for the purpose of balancing the scales of justice in a way that harmonizes with his sense of what is right and just. Holmes's disdain for legal judgments and procedures based purely on rule-based precedents, the essence of common law practice, is evident in his decision-making. In particular he rails against the failure of the police to properly evaluate circumstantial evidence when they rely on hearsay and unreliable testimony to prosecute crime. Condemning the use of outdated and ineffectual laws that fail to protect the weakest members of society, he draws approbation. His well-intentioned and morally inspired interventions on behalf of the victims of crime in the spirit of outlawed heroes and his resolution of cases is mostly engineered through rational deduction, or induction, and occasional boxing bouts with adversaries. Julian Symons's assertion in *Bloody Murder* that the nature of the detective story of the time was like "a fairy tale" unconnected to reality is refuted in Arthur Conan Doyle's autobiography *Memories and Adventures,* where he remarks on the similarity between cases he has been called upon to investigate and those he had invented to showcase "the reasoning of Sherlock Holmes" (Symons, 13). Conan Doyle remarks that several times in his life he was approached by women searching for abandoned fiancés, evocative of "A Case of Identity." In one particular case in August 1909, the woman in question wrote to thank him for "an extraordinary escape" when she discovered, through Conan Doyle's efforts, how "unworthy he [the absconded suitor] was of her affections" (*Memories,* 132). In his pinpointing of the legal inequalities of women, ticket-of-leave men and legal lacunae that allowed the likes of Milverton to escape justice, he arouses feelings of pity for the victims and their sufferings and revulsion toward the criminal whose actions inflict pain and sorrow. The crime of sexual blackmail was rife in Britain in the eighteenth and nineteenth century, and the victims were often men accused of sodomy as Angus McLaren points out. The Labouchere Amendment to the Criminal Law Amendment Act of 1885, which "criminalized all indecency between males," heightened the inducement to blackmailers and the cost of being caught (McLaren, 11). In Baring-Gould's annotated volume of Sherlock Holmes adventures, Mr. Robert Keith Leavitt notes that of the thirty-seven definite felonies where the criminal was known to Sherlock Holmes, in fourteen of these, "he took the law into his own hands" to free the guilty person; in twenty-three cases the offender was taken to the police, and in seven, suicide, Acts of God or death at sea account for the criminal's end. In only four cases did the criminals escape justice entirely (467).

Professional Detectives

Morrison and Muddock's
Unofficial Justice

ARTHUR MORRISON (1863–1945):
MARTIN HEWITT

The art of burgling and housebreaking has positively developed into a fine art, and, although we do not admire members of the craft, yet every individual representative of it is undeniably interesting [*Strand Magazine,* Vol. 7, 1894, 273].

With his creation of the cult hero Sherlock Holmes, Arthur Conan Doyle captured the public imagination and maintained Holmes's powerful presence through years of burgeoning mass-market publications and the arrival of ingenious rivals. Heavily influenced by the aesthetic and decadent ideals ascribed to Oscar Wilde devotées, he invested his detective hero with attributes reflective of the audacity of bygone men of courage, tinged with traces of subversion and socially rebellious opinions. Adopting behavior that conflicts with Victorian ideals of masculinity and traditional views of morality, he is unafraid to challenge legality and is driven by the aesthetic experience of romance and danger. Proving the popularity of subversive behavior on the part of detectives and adventure heroes, and in parallel with the arrival of Holmes in 1887, the success in Britain of dime novels from America demonstrated the growing influence of the American publishing industry. The books featured characters such as Nick Carter, the most prolific of all dime novel detectives, and Allan Pinkerton; their exploits provided leisurely entertainment for travelers on the long commute from the burgeoning suburbs into London. Readily available from myriad stalls at railway stations, their ubiquity proved the appeal of disruptive agents of justice who step beyond the law in pursuit of justice. In her study *Dime Novels and the Roots of Detective Fiction,* Pamela

Morality and the Law in British Detective and Spy Fiction

Bedore notes that the earliest detective fiction and dime novels grew from the period that produced the Western's adventure formula, and their heroes embrace the "seeds of subversion" in a similar vein to that of Holmes (Bedore, 9). The French contribution to Arthur Conan Doyle's Sherlock Holmes came from Emile's Gaboriau's Monsieur Tabaret and Monsieur Lecoq, first available in English translation in 1887 as *The Widow Lerouge* and heavily influenced by Eugene Francois Vidocq's *Memoires*, replete with his use of illegal methods for the entrapment of criminals (Ashley, 41). Holmes was not the only lawbreaker in fiction at that time, and his illegality resonated with the readership of popular magazines. Proof of the appeal of transgressive heroes is confirmed in the success of E.W. Hornung's Raffles (1899), the gentleman thief whose illegal activities kindled a popular response equivalent to that of Holmes, Guy Boothby's Simon Carne (1897), Arthur Morrison's Dorrington Deed (1897) and Austin Freeman's Romney Pringle (1902). Later, Maurice Leblanc's Arsène Lupin, another gentleman thief, appeared in "The Arrest of Arsène Lupin" in the magazine *Je Sais Tout* in 1905. Arthur Conan Doyle's unique contribution lies in the conception of a short story form of detective fiction featuring a charismatic flawed hero, whose adventure begins and ends within the narrative space of one issue of each magazine. His innovation inspired a host of writers to emulate his success and achieve some measure of literary prosperity by evolving their own eccentric and gifted investigators.

The aim of this chapter is to provide a contrasting view of the behavior of two fictional professional detectives as distinct from amateurs like Holmes in how they approach legality and the way they interact with the criminal justice system in the stories they inhabit. It examines their ethical approach to solving crime through an exploration of their conduct in each instance and posits them broadly within one of the three main ethical approaches previously described: deontological, consequentialist or virtue ethical. The texts under scrutiny are viewed through the lens of Arthur Morrison's detective, Martin Hewitt, and J.E.P. Muddock's, Dick Donovan, whose backgrounds lie in different spheres of society from that of the more aristocratic Holmes. It explores their alternative routes to justice and the legal themes that emerge in the narratives within their historical contexts, including the impact of the rise of professional society and the influence of the New Woman in fiction. The rigid structure of the legal system and its standard procedure and regulation necessitates the intervention of an intermediating champion in the shape of a private detective who can resolve conflicts in a humane and sympathetic way. By engaging in detailed close reading of four stories taken from collections of works that appeared in the *Strand* and other popular magazines, a contrasting picture of their response to crime and the use of unlawful measures to achieve their ends emerges. It gives insight into what appealed to readers of the time and the ways in which a mythical character could resolve seemingly complex and obscure situations to the satisfaction of its audience. With the rise of new unionism, women's suffrage, fears of racial degeneration and the disintegration of Victorian values in the lead up to the First World War, the background to the stories seethes with political and social anxiety, providing opportunities for sensational raw material for subject-hungry writers like Morrison and Muddock.

A problem arose for the *Strand Magazine* upon Sherlock Holmes's supposed death at the Reichenbach Falls at the hands of Professor Moriarty in "The Final Problem" in the December 1893 issue of the magazine. Who could replace such a successful and iconic personality, one with the ability to step beyond the law and defy authority in a way that had found so much favor with an enthusiastic readership? The choice of Arthur Morrison's professional detective, Martin Hewitt, ensured the continuing success of the magazine. He appeared alongside writers such as Grant Allen, winner of an 1890 major writing competition for *Tit-Bits,* and later famed for his controversial novel *The Woman Who Did* (1895), and the translated works of foreign writers like Alexander Pushkin and Voltaire (Ashley, 29, 36, 39). Morrison's early forays into writing included freelance contributions to *Macmillan's* and *Tit-Bits* magazines before entry into the *Strand Magazine* with pieces such as "Zig-Zags at the Zoo." His slum fiction *Tales of Mean Streets* (1894), *A Child of the Jago* (1896), *To London Town* (1899) and *The Hole in the Wall* (1902) received critical praise and condemnation in equal measure for their use of Realism, an innovative approach to literary themes in a style evocative of the Naturalists Emile Zola and Honoré de Balzac. His dark and disturbing presentation of people living in the deprivation and squalor of London's worst slums, the consequence of urban growth and the mass arrival of agricultural workers from the country to the town, was appalling to readers in its terrifying insight into the lives and criminality of London's underclass. Far removed from the urban nightmare of the slums, Martin Hewitt, his fictional detective, occasionally reveals traces of familiarity with the form of criminality imbuing Morrison's slum fiction and emphasizes the hidden villainy of middle-class criminals who hide under the cloak of respectability. He is defined by his professional status and constrained by financial considerations and an occupational code of conduct that is geared to the most efficient and profitable use of personal resources. He stands in contrast to the amateur who dabbles with detection and is not reliant on its income. The professionalization of state institutions in the 1880s, including codes of conduct for the medical profession and civil service, is echoed in his profile. It sees his promotion from young clerk in the services of Messrs. Crellan, Hunt and Crellan, a notable solicitor's firm, to independent private detective in his own thriving business. His expertise in detection enables him to transcend class constraints and gain entry to all levels of society without question, unlike the official police, whose presence in middle-class homes is resented. In this, he typifies Trollope's description of a professional whereby "a gentleman, not born to inheritance of a gentleman's allowance of good things, might ingeniously obtain the same by way of education and profession" (Perkin, 85–86). Although Hewitt lacks the charismatic personality of Holmes, the plot-driven narratives provide insight into the ethical dilemmas of a professional detective.

"The Case of Mr. Geldard's Elopement" is a story written by Arthur Morrison, first published in the January 1896 edition of *The Windsor Magazine* before publication with five other stories in the collection entitled *The Adventures of Martin Hewitt*. In it, the detective Martin Hewitt encounters a woman faced with the prospect of desertion in a narrative iteration of the contemporary issue that propelled the Summary Jurisdiction (Married Women) Act of 1895. This act enabled deserted wives to seek maintenance for themselves and their children in the event of abandonment (Shanley, 175). The second Martin Hewitt adventure, "The Affair of Mrs. Seton's Child" (1896) from the same collection, also appeared in the *Windsor Magazine* and articulates the nature of adult attitudes to missing children in middle-class Victorian society. It sheds light on public attitudes to baby-farming and the problem of infant murder associated with it. The case of Amelia Dyer, a baby-farmer who also operated as a midwife, caused a media sensation at the time, when it emerged that she had murdered countless infants. Her death by hanging at Newgate Gaol in 1896, in the same year as publication of the story, raised the profile of the recently founded London Society for the Prevention of Cruelty to Children and strengthened its efforts to stem the tide of cases of infanticide prevalent in London, according to Allison Vale, her biographer, in *The Woman Who Murdered Babies for Money: The Story of Amelia Dyer* (2011). "The Affair of Mrs. Seton's Child" foregrounds the professionalism of the detective in his methodical approach to investigation and his less than chivalrous attitude to women of shrewish character who suspect their husbands of infidelity.

Martin Hewitt, symbolic of the era's self-made man, is a solid professional detective who is dependent for his livelihood on the acquisition of a reputation as a skilled operator in his field of expertise: detection. Outwardly, he is affable, conventional even, but his dogged determination and tenacity evoke Inspector Bucket of *Bleak House,* and his ability to rationalize owes credit to Poe's Chevalier Auguste Dupin. Like Dupin, his personality is lightly sketched, with the main focus centered on intricate puzzles in the stories. Despite the distinct character remodeling in Hewitt's portrayal of the hero detective, he successfully replaced Holmes as a substitute in the affections of the readers of the *Strand Magazine* from March to September 1894. Appearing in seven issues of the magazine, exquisitely illustrated by Sidney Paget, the stories were published in the same year in a collection entitled *Martin Hewitt: Investigator*. This was followed a year later by *Chronicles of Martin Hewitt*, which made its initial appearance in *The Windsor Magazine*. The popularity of the stories prompted a further collection, *The Adventures of Martin Hewitt*, published in 1896, with the final series, *The Red Triangle: Being Some Further Chronicles of Martin Hewitt, Investigator*, emerging seven years later in 1903 (Bleiler, xi). This final collection was notable for its foray into the embryonic genre of spy fiction and for its depiction of the arch-villain Mayes, whose evil actions arguably transcend those of Moriarty. Hewitt's cases combine original and ingenious plots with authentic working-class characterization and dialect, reminiscent of his own working-class background and knowledge of the East End of London, which he was at pains to disguise, according to Stan Newens. Like Conan Doyle, Morrison was influenced by Robert Louis Stevenson, and several of his cases echo themes explored in *The Strange Case of Dr. Jekyll and Mr. Hyde* (1886) almost a decade earlier: that of overt respectability masking innate criminality. Martin Priestman suggests that "[t]hough hardly works of explicit protest, the Hewitt stories repeatedly make the point that there are many most respectable persons living in good style in the suburbs whose chief business lies in financing such ventures as bank robbery and taking the chief share of the proceeds." This attitude reflects Morrison's appreciation of legal failings in addressing wealthy criminals rather than zealously pursuing lower-class offenders (*Figure on the Carpet*, 112). In choosing to situate the criminal as a visibly respectable and upright citizen, in contrast to the easily recognizable lower-class deviant with abnormal physiognomy who featured in much of the era's fiction, Morrison often focuses on white-collar crime and the ominous threat of ruined reputations, which were greatly feared. Investigation of financial crime, including embezzlement and fraud amongst other legal infractions, differentiate his cases from those of Holmes. Detecting the criminal for Hewitt requires a clear-headed approach to detection rather than the reflex reaction symbolized by "the official police" response, whose simplistic reading of clues at the crime scene fails the test of scientific scrutiny. His panoptic gaze is fine-tuned to filter the cloak of respectability or social standing and expose hypocrisy and corruption using scientific and professional methods. Hewitt's amanuensis, Brett, a journalist, explains that Hewitt was "on terms of pretty regular, and, indeed, friendly acquaintance-ship" with the official police, referring to Inspector Nettings on regular occasions, yet he supersedes them in inquiries and applies his own code of practice that is at variance with theirs, using illegal means to get results.

"The Case of Mr. Geldard's Elopement" (1896)

The scandal of an assumed illicit affair and desertion on the part of Mr. Geldard lie at the heart of "The Case of Mr. Geldard's Elopement," the second story in Arthur Morrison's collection of six detective stories, entitled *The Adventures of Martin Hewitt* (1896). Elopement and the ramifications of spousal desertion was an issue of contemporary feminine anxiety and a topic regularly represented in discourses in both the sensational and mainstream media publications of the day. Despite well-intentioned legislation to alleviate the problem of abandoned wives in 1895, the year prior to the story's publication, its provisions were inadequate and much of the population of the workhouse consisted of deserted wives right into Edwardian times (Gibson, 75). The Summary Jurisdiction (Married Women) Act of 1895 extended magistrates' power to order husbands to pay maintenance in the case of desertion or neglect; however, deserted and abused wives were unable to take advantage of its provisions as husbands frequently disappeared without a trace, leaving authorities unable to serve the court summons. The story opens with remarks from Brett, Hewitt's journalist amanuensis, on the proliferation of "matrimonial cases" undertaken by unscrupulous private inquiry offices who "manufactured a case from beginning to end," implying dishonest practices by private detectives motivated by greed (Morrison, 94). Like Pinkerton, Hewitt's belief is that divorce cases are scandalous and only fit for disreputable agents. Pinkerton's National Detective Agency, established in 1850 in Chicago, enshrines its "affirmation of values and protocols" for its operatives in a code of conduct that proclaimed "the birth of a noble profession" (www.pinkerton.com). Comprising seven distinct rules, its mandate to accept no bribes or reward money was amplified with the caution to refuse to accept divorce cases or cases that initiate scandals. Whilst conceding "matrimonial cases there were, and often of an interesting nature," Brett is less than sympathetic toward women who engage the services of detectives to check up on their husbands, believing them to be "actuated by mere unreasoning or fanciful jealousy" (94).

Mrs. Geldard, the mirror image of these dubious sentiments, is characterized as sharp-tongued and rancorous in her suspicion of her husband's infidelity with a maidservant. She charges Hewitt with setting a watch on her husband and declares, "I've endured this thing in silence long enough. I won't

have it" (94). Her negative presentation as a vocal, cantankerous and physically unattractive woman client who differs markedly from the conventional
portrayal of women clients in Conan Doyle's fiction and distances the reader's
moral sympathy from her toward a more cynical view of her position; outer
and inner ugliness in appearance are synonymous in her characterization.
Her presentation hints at the assertive and opinionated New Woman, whose
departure from the ideals of womanhood may have brought her misfortunes
upon herself as Hewitt rejects her "vague catalogue of sufferings" as an act of
disloyalty toward her husband and advises, "Come to an understanding with
your husband in a straightforward way as soon as you possibly can" (95). In
its portrayal of a respectable middle-class businessman who leaves his substantial suburban home each day to take up a fraudulent identity, the story
echoes Conan Doyle's "The Man with the Twisted Lip" (1891). In that case,
Mr. Neville St. Clair, a prosperous businessman, assumed the role of a beggar,
Hugh Boone, in London, a common form of fraud in Victorian England. As
with him, we are forewarned of covert criminality as Mrs. Geldard relates
how she follows her husband to his office, where he subsequently disappears,
leaving his empty office locked and the "entire suit of clothes" he had worn
when he left home on the morning of the previous day laid on a cupboard
shelf, along with scraps of a letter signed "Emma" (98). Despite his initial
refusal to act on her behalf, Hewitt, motivated by her persistence and his own
curiosity rather than compassion for her predicament, agrees to take the case.
Despite his initial waiving of a fee for consultation, his expectation is of remuneration at the end of his investigation once he agrees to act on her behalf.

On arrival at Geldard's office, Hewitt contrives to rid himself of Mrs.
Geldard to allow unhindered access to her husband's accounts book and
achieves this by directing her to the bank to secure information on her husband's bank account. He cautions, "You mustn't say you are employing me to
bring him back from an elopement. That will shut up the channel of information at once. Hostile enquiries they'll never answer, even by the smallest hint,
except after legal injunction" (100). She is thus engaged as co-conspirator in
his investigation. The precarious nature of a woman's economic reliance on
her husband's income becomes apparent as she is commissioned to find out
whether her husband has emptied the bank account, leaving her destitute.
However, as a counter to any sympathetic identification with the victim,
Mrs. Geldard informs him, "Thank heaven I've enough to live on of my own
without being dependent on a creature like him" (Morrison, 99). Thanks to
the Married Women's Property Act of 1882, a married woman could keep
all personal property, make a will without her husband's agreement and act
as "autonomous legal personages" rather than sustain the proscriptions of

coverture (Shanley, 104). Hewitt's small deception in his use of stealth as a method of investigation has criminal undertones. Shifting to the realms of dubious practice, we learn:

> As soon as she left Hewitt turned to the pedestal table and probed the keyhole of the locked drawer with the small stiletto attached to his penknife.
> "This seems to be a common sort of lock" he said. "I could probably open it with a bent nail…. Perhaps there is an easier way" [100].

His nonchalance and intimate familiarity with the use of clandestine practices for obtaining confidential information demonstrate scant affinity with the rule of law prohibiting trespass, and he could be accused of malicious damage. Writing in the *Strand Magazine* on "Crimes and Criminals," the author notes the popularity of the jimmy, akin to a stiletto, for burgling and as a means of gaining entry to safes, noting how they are symbolically labeled in order of size from "The Lord Mayor" to the "Alderman" and "Common Councilman," with the smaller jimmies being used for housebreaking. Interestingly, he advises, "there was positively no law" to prevent the manufacture of burgling tools (Vol.7, 1894, 273, 275).

By gaining unlawful access to the locked bureau drawer in her husband's office, Hewitt finds incriminating clues to Mr. Geldard's furtive behavior: receipts for a stable rental and a coded message from the mysterious Emma, complete with seventeen kisses, which he keeps hidden from Mrs. Geldard. Although his initial intention to help solve the mystery of Mr. Geldard's disappearance is carried out with a view to maximizing the wellbeing of Mrs. Geldard and yield positive results, a moral dilemma ensues between his professional duty to his client and the ethical duty to report unlawful goings-on. Convinced of illegal activity, we follow Hewitt to the stables, where he gains unlawful entry to the building:

> The doors were unusually well finished and close fitting and the lock was a good one, of the lever variety, and very difficult to pick. Hewitt examined the front of the building very carefully and then, after a visit to the entrance to the yard, to guard against early interruption returned and scrambled by projections and fastenings to the roof [103].

Once there, we learn that, like Holmes who makes use of illegal entry into suspect properties, he removes the putty and then the glass from the windowpane in the skylight, making him guilty of housebreaking, a serious crime and liable to indictment. Once inside the building, his discovery of old linoleum rolls and a cart confirm his belief of illegal activity, for "it was evident that it [the linoleum] had remained thus rolled and tied with cord in two places for a long period," suggesting its use was other than for sale

2. Professional Detectives

(103). Following the trail of evidence to Crouch End, where the maidservant Emma's uncle lives, he arrives at a genteel suburb and a large substantial villa maintained by Mr. Geldard under the fictitious name of Cookson and staffed by "one old woman, deaf as a post, for servant" (105). In the midst of stylish respectability, he uncovers an illegal still situated in the villa from which Mr. Geldard transports whiskey concealed in the rolls of linoleum, aided and abetted by Emma and her uncle, Mr. Trennatt. Further inquiry brings him up against Mrs. Geldard, who, having learned of the situation and satisfied of her husband's fidelity, now colludes in her husband's criminality by locking Hewitt in a tool shed. In the final denouement, Hewitt offers his opinions on the unraveling of the mystery of Mr. Geldard's disappearance and his uncovering of the criminal gang running an illegal whiskey distilling operation that was disguised as a legitimate and respectable business:

> Yes, it's a case of illicit distilling—and a big case, I fancy. I've wired to Somerset House, and no doubt men are on their way here now.... The whole thing is very clever and a most uncommonly big thing. If I know all about it—and I think I do—Geldard and his partners have been turning out untaxed spirit by the hundred gallons for a long time past [108].

A conflict between ethical and professional considerations arises when Hewitt deliberates on whether to report his findings to the police or allow Mr. Geldard to escape because his wife, Mrs. Geldard, had commissioned him to work on her behalf. He explains his rationale:

> But then I grew perplexed on a point of conduct. I was commissioned by Mrs. Geldard. It scarcely seemed the loyal thing to put my client's husband in gaol because of what I had learnt in course of work on her behalf. I decided to give him, and nobody else, a sporting chance. If I could possibly get at him in the time at my disposal, by himself, so that no accomplice should get the benefit of my warning, I would give him a plain hint to run; then he could take his chance [109].

Despite his professional dilemma, his overriding sense of the right thing to do under the circumstances is to maximize the welfare of the community over the individual rights of his client in a resolution focused on the consequences of his actions in a consequentialist approach. Therefore, he notifies Somerset House, Office of Revenue and Customs, of the unlawful activity.

Significantly, the illegitimate undertakings of Mr. Geldard and his gang take place in a respectable suburb and in full view of a policeman on patrol duty outside the large house. The policeman mistakenly interprets the meaning of the strange behavior of the residents of the house, observing to Hewitt, "That's a Mr. Fuller as lives there—and a rum 'un too." He incorrectly attributes the anomalies of the occupants' exploits to the idiosyncrasies of

63

middle-class residents; his working-class roots prohibit invasion of privacy of a middle-class home (105). His failure to probe the surface appearances of unconventional behavior bears testimony to his steadfast conviction that middle-class morality and reputation are beyond reproach. In this narrative, Hewitt questions the popular conception of the criminal mind as it is expressed in the newspapers and journals of the day by expanding its boundaries to embrace seemingly respectable middle-class men and women. We hear of the capture of Geldard and his criminal gang along with the seizure of the still and "subsequent raids on a number of obscure public houses in different parts of London" (Morrison, 110). Brett's witty comment, "Some of the public houses in question must have acquired a notoriety among the neighbors of frequent purchases of linoleum," concludes the narrative on a humorous note, a feature of several Morrison detective stories (110).

Hewitt's departure from legality in this story entails breaking and entering on three separate occasions, criminal damage to property, deception and the intent to pervert the course of justice in considering aiding and abetting Mr. Geldard's criminality by giving him "and nobody else, a sporting chance" to escape (109). His pattern of housebreaking for the purposes of retrieving evidence of criminality coincides with that of Holmes, the amateur detective. Considering the severity of punishment meted out to serial housebreakers in the era, evidenced in the records of *The Old Bailey Proceedings Online* and exemplified in the case of John Twyher, who was sentenced to seven years penal servitude in 1890 for "the theft of a clock and other articles" due to previous convictions, Hewitt's risk-taking seems exceptional (t18900303-234). Gatrell calls attention to the vagaries of the law in the 1880s whereby felonious wounding and burglary both shared liability to the maximum punishment of penal servitude for life and in which "the differentials became marked lower down the scale of offenses." Housebreaking carried a maximum of fourteen years penal servitude, for example, compared to only five years for malicious wounding; the inference here is that property is "of greater value than human life" (Gatrell, 296). The punishment Hewitt inflicts on the Geldards is for crimes he anticipates rather than anything concrete and verifiable by warrant, and his inner conviction of their guilt preempts any idea of the presumption of innocence. In this case, he disregards the aspects of the law that constrain his intuitive capacity for unearthing deviance and assigns himself the role of adjudicator invested with a higher moral authority. Like Holmes, he shows a public-spiritedness in tackling crime, but his comment on reporting Mr. Geldard to the police, "My duty was plain. As you know, I am a citizen first and an investigator after," places his professional status as secondary to his obligations as a member of the community (109). Since he operates without a warrant to search the premises and fails to notify the police of his suspicions, his criminality is more extensive than that of the Geldards, whose crime was considered a misdemeanor, in contrast to his crime of breaking and entering, a felony, not to mention his criminal damage to property.

Notably, in several other stories throughout the series, Hewitt is content to allow the criminal to escape, e.g., in "The Case of Mr. Foggatt" (1894), a locked-room murder mystery, published in the May 1894 edition of the *Strand Magazine*. In response to Brett's question about a murder, when asked, "Don't you propose to go into this further, then?" Hewitt replies, "I'm not a policeman," and refuses to follow up on the crime (Vol.7, 526). He often demonstrates a sense of humor in relation to helping the police with their inquiries exemplified in "The Case of the Dixon Torpedo" (1894). When asked for his advice on how to deal with the criminal, he responds, "Here's his stick—knock him downstairs with it, if you like" (Morrison, 29). Hewitt's actions bring to public notice his dissatisfaction with the era's legal constraints, which staunchly protect middle-class privacy from intrusion and create challenging conditions for the issuing of a warrant. Limitations on the power of entry and search into middle-class geographical spaces are critiqued in the inability of the law to address its failures. Mrs. Geldard exemplifies gender reconstruction reflective of the prejudices and biases of the story's recipient audience in the *Windsor Magazine*, with the aim of "acting as cultural modifiers in shaping opinions and influencing ideas" about her lack of womanliness (Rowbotham and Stevenson, xxii). Hewitt, in contrast to Holmes's chivalry, in this story remains aloof and unaffected by female emotional trauma, maintaining a disciplined focus on the measures needed to solve the mystery. His code of conduct bears some resemblance to that of the Pinkerton code in his initial reluctance to embark on a possibly scandalous divorce case and in his willingness to partner with law enforcement by informing on the villain. Embracing the notion of enforcing a moral imperative in financial behavior, he exposes those who engage in fraudulent activity, especially the middle classes, who have so far remained beyond the bounds of legal limits. Pinkerton was known to adhere to the requirement to keep clients apprised on an ongoing basis and for his opposition to "improper conduct" in gaining information, a charge that could be leveled against Hewitt ("History" Pinkerton Consulting and Investigations, Inc.). Morrison's familiarity with the privations and penury of life for the residents of the East End of London informed his views on criminality; he was aware that the working-class were often compelled to sidestep the legal framework of the law through dire economic necessity in the newly industrialized modern society, perhaps triggered by unemployment or illness, as evidenced in his own family. Since moral rationality for unlawful behavior was deemed to be inferior in poorer communities, to some extent their behavior could be explained and justified, but the middle classes, who live in comfort and style, suffer no such deprivation and have no evident extenuating circumstances to justify their crimes; their motivation is greed.

Morrison's narrative presents an underlying critique of a legal system heavily prejudiced against the working classes which fails to acknowledge criminality across the entire spectrum of society, including the middle classes. In his exposé of criminality, the Geldards are emblematic of middle-class hypocrisy and the fluidity of class status; their ability to descend easily into criminality and transgressive behavior calls for reflection and judgment on shifting cultural values. In his application of discrete justice in relation to crime, Hewitt's behavior, like that of Holmes and other fictional detectives, raises questions about their ability to be impartial and even-handed in the way they respond to crime. The notion of universal justice, central to equality, may be damaged by an individualized response, since only those who engage the services of the detective or capture his sympathy are the recipients of his configuration of right-minded justice. This particularity in applying justice creates conflict between the rights of the individual and those of the wider community; in choosing to address the needs of the individual, the rights of others are ignored. Synchronous to this private infraction of the legal process, the narrative exposes a range of themes that suggest moral ambiguities in the delivery of this fictionalized form of legitimacy by the detectives.

"The Affair of Mrs. Seton's Child" (1896)

"Alleged Kidnapping at Croydon," one of the articles featured in *The Morning Post* of Saturday July 28, 1894, was lengthier than many corresponding kidnapping reports in the media that year and was guaranteed to cause a stir (6). Its reference to the status of the accused kidnapper as a member of the middle classes, whose respectability was now in jeopardy, combined with the aristocratic connections of the suspect, ensured a sensational popular reception. The story from Croydon Borough Police Court relates to a child kidnapping that had taken place in the town a short time previously. Elizabeth Grosvenor, a respectable middle-class, middle-aged woman, stood charged with "stealing and detaining Arthur Bartrum, aged three and a half years, with intent to deprive the parents of the lawful possession of the said child" (6). At the hearing, her distress is palpable, as she hotly denounces the treatment she has received since her arrest, declaring that she has been "persecuted shamefully by a class of people who ... said I [was] not fit to get my living or to live as I have a right to" (6). In her defense, she refutes the allegations of wrongdoing, and instead, seeks sympathy from the court for her unhappy childless state. Justification for taking the child, which she maintains was given to her by a stranger, was based on her claim that since she was "alone in the world, without a friend since the Duchess of Sutherland's death" and was "passionately fond of children," she thought it would be a comfort to her. The child is represented as a commodity in an era where children are held to be the property of their parents and are treated accordingly. Exclusion of narrative representation from the child of his actual abduction experience in the newspaper report is notable because following an amendment to the Children's Charter of 1889, the first Act of Parliament for the prevention of cruelty to children and an amendment to the Act in 1894, they were allowed to give evidence in court and mental cruelty was recognized (the National Archives, www.legislation.gov.uk). However, in this instance, no one took advantage of this opportunity, and we hear instead about the outward appearance of the child rather than any possible inner turmoil he may have suffered. When questioned on the circumstances surrounding his reappearance after the abduction, a witness comments, "The child's appearance was altered to that of a girl. He had been well cared for and kept clean." In her opinion, despite his gender transformation, he was well nourished, his physical requirements were met and there were no obvious signs of abuse, the crucial factors in determining his wellbeing. Her affirmative remarks on the child's condition infer a quasi-acceptance of the negligible nature of the offense, as no apparent harm was inflicted on the child as a result of the encounter.

Popular views of criminality and justice, as Emsley, Gatrell, and Dolin suggest, are tied firmly to "historical context," which is made clear in public attitudes toward the crime of kidnapping (*Crime and Society*, 2). In an explicit demonstration of shifting boundaries of criminality, what was once considered a misdemeanor in the Victorian era becomes a much more serious crime in the judicial system by 1908 with the Children's Act. This legislation made sexual abuse within families a matter of state intervention and made provision for juvenile offenders, including restricted use of the birch (the National Archives, www.legislation.gov.uk). Whatever the truth of Miss Grosvenor's statement, and despite her emotional appeal and links to the aristocracy, the outcome of the Borough Police Court decision indicates her failure to convince the judge of the sincerity of her intentions, for she was committed for trial. Court proceedings from the Old Bailey of the era indicate a plethora of instances of child kidnap by both male and female abductors. Male child abductors did so for sexual exploitation and begging, but for female abductors, the object was either the theft of the children's clothing, or to make money through placing them for adoption; occasionally, the kidnapper sought the companionship of a child if they themselves were childless. Based on the length of sentences issued for the offense of child kidnap, in contrast to those for theft or burglary, and the brevity of most newspaper reports on their occurrence, popular perceptions of kidnapping may be confirmed in Adrian Gray's assertion that "Victorian society regarded crimes against property more seriously than crimes against the person" (Gray, 61).

Echoes of the circumstances of the aforementioned case appear in "The Affair of Mrs. Seton's Child," one of six stories from Arthur Morrison's 1896 Martin Hewitt collection, entitled *The Adventures of Martin Hewitt*. One of many original storylines pursued in his work, it underscores the originality of Morrison's plots and follows the pattern of a locked room mystery, where no obvious solution to the puzzle can be devised. Similarly based on the abduction of a two-year-old boy by a respectable middle-class woman, the outcome for the criminal, thanks to the intervention of the detective, Hewitt, differs dramatically to the judgments passed down for comparable offenses in the *Court Proceedings of The Old Bailey* of the era. Hewitt's manipulation of the legal system emerges toward the end of the story, where his compassion for a middle-class female kidnapper elicits a merciful response from him, as he shields her from prosecution. The reasons for his actions link her deviance to her sexuality, expressed as a form of temporary insanity rather than criminality. His attitude forms an expression of gendered stereotyping that testifies to Louise Hide's assertion that "women from across the class spectrum were believed to have a proclivity for mental instability due to the effects of their reproductive system" (Hide, 35). One of Hewitt's characteristic principles in response to criminality features in the story: his belief that criminal actions may not always require legal redress. In other words, he determines his own code of conduct in specific cases. In a clear demonstration of his preference for restorative rather than retributive justice in the story, he advocates the cooperation of the victim rather than sentencing and punishment for the offender. However, his ad hoc application of discretionary justice raises moral and ethical questions in this case, in particular, because one of the perpetrators evades prosecution despite what would appear to be valid reasons for legal action. In the story, Hewitt appropriates the role of merciful adjudicator of justice, thus supplanting both courtroom judge and the rightful owner of forgiveness, the aggrieved victim.

The story opens with Mrs. Seton in a state of distress consulting Martin Hewitt over the disappearance of her only child, Charley, from the morning room of their home, where he was last seen playing with a box of toys. Hewitt, in contrast to his response to Mrs. Geldard in the previous story, is moved by her grief as she begins to rise to greet him. He sympathetically lays his hand on her shoulder and comforts her, advising, "Pray don't disturb yourself, Mrs. Seton.... Mr. Raikes has told me something of your trouble, and perhaps when I know a little more I shall be able to offer you some advice" (234). The substance of Mrs. Seton's complaint elicits a consolatory reply from Hewitt, as he adds, "[I]t is important for you to maintain your strength and spirits as much as possible," affirming his view that the female psyche is fragile and in need of bolstering in times of anxiety (234). Hewitt initially accepts the absence of her husband from the scene without comment, and only later does he enquire into his whereabouts in the ensuing conversation:

"By the way, where was Mr. Seton yesterday when you missed the boy?"
"In the City, he has some important business in hand just now"
"And today?"
"He has gone to the City again. Of course he is sadly worried; but he saw that everything possible was done, and his business was very important" [246].

Cultural ideology is reflected in the depiction of Mrs. Seton and her acknowledgment of her gender role as prime overseer of the family's welfare in the separate sphere of home life; she models conventional hegemonic values, as she shoulders the burden of the child's disappearance alone. Mr. Seton, the breadwinner, continues to work to provide for his family in the public sphere, despite the disappearance of his only child. The story then proceeds in the tradition of a locked-room mystery in which the child has vanished from the premises and no visible trace of his abductors or the means of his kidnaping can be established. It transpires that he had been left alone while Mrs. Seton sent his nurse on an errand. On discovering his disappearance, Mrs. Seton contacts the police who "issue bills containing a description of the child and offering a reward": a regular procedure for locating missing children (Morrison, 238). The reward of twenty pounds is offered to the general public for any information leading to the return of the child: a seemingly small sum compared to the amounts offered for the return of stolen property, a situation later remarked upon in the narrative by a blackmailer and indicative of the child's lack of agency in society. Comparatively, in J.E. Preston Muddock's Dick Donovan story "The Mysterious Disappearance of Helen Atkinson" from his 1888 collection entitled *The Man-Hunter*, a reward of one hundred pounds is offered by the distraught middle-class family for the return of a missing daughter (Muddock, 177).

Investigations lead Hewitt to discover that the child had disappeared another time six weeks earlier, a fact that Mrs. Seton considers unimportant. In response to Hewitt's question about his disappearance, she replies, "But that was quite different. He strayed out at the front gate, and was brought back from the police station in the evening" by a Mrs. Clark, whose throat bore the marks of a scar, suggesting she once had her throat cut and whose name and address turn out to be false (244). The incongruence of Mrs. Clark's respectable outward appearance with the disfigurement of the wound on her throat forewarns the reader of unusual circumstances, for it would seem odd for a middle-class woman to be in a position where her throat has been cut. However, according to Joan Lock, "While some aspects of historic crimes may often appear familiar, others link them clearly to their time as she explains that although 'cut-throat murders … are unusual now … before the invention of the safety razor they were commonplace,'" signaling the possibility of such an attack on Mrs. Clark (Lock, 51). This detail, together with the lax security of the premises where Mrs. Seton lives, illuminates the mystery, and Hewitt's professionalism springs into action as he pursues the investigation in a systematic and businesslike way that is in tune with his professional code of conduct. His investigative duties entail detailed questioning of the servants; extensive fieldwork, where he tirelessly explores a range of clues; and time-consuming false trails of evidence and scrutiny of family background along with Mr. Seton's business interests. Hewitt differs from Holmes in his methods of investigation, relying on hard work and long hours to achieve results, which sometimes come to nothing. Like Pinkerton, he keeps his clients up to date with investigations whilst informing them "such professionalism costs money"; the message is "solving crime does not happen overnight and it is not cheap" (*Probable Cause,* 28). Unlike Holmes, whose infallibility locates him in the realms of myth, we hear from Brett, Hewitt's journalist amanuensis, of his fair number of failures; his imperfections ally him to the common man and to society's approbation for tenacity in the face of difficulty and industry as a means to success in business. The significance of reputation for Hewitt is highlighted in "The Stanway Cameo Mystery" (1894), where Brett rectifies misconceptions about a case that was publicly viewed as a failure and signals the damage that accrues to lack of success (Morrison, 30). As a preamble to events, he absolves Hewitt from incompetence and proceeds to set the record straight, submitting his redemptive testimony in the following statement: "Therefore no harm will be done in making the inner history of the case public; on the contrary, it will afford an opportunity of vindicating the professional reputation of Hewitt, who is supposed to have completely failed to make anything of the mystery surrounding the case" (30).

Despite his professional efforts to discover the whereabouts of the missing child, Hewitt arrives at an impasse in the investigation until serendipitous events in the shape of two anonymous letters, both written on the same paper and clearly from the same source, arrive at Mrs. Seton's home to move the plot forward. The first, in Hewitt's opinion obviously from a woman, assures Mrs. Seton of the child's safety. It reads:

> The writer observes that you are offering a reward for the recovery of your child. There is no necessity for this; Charley is quite safe, happy and in good hands. Pray do not instruct detectives or take any such steps just yet. The child is well and shall be returned to you. This I solemnly swear. His errand is one of mercy; pray, have patience [250].

Hewitt is baffled by the message and in what way the child could be instrumental in delivering mercy when a second message, clearly from a man in Hewitt's opinion, arrives with a contradictory tone:

> Madam, if you want your child you had better make an arrangement with Die. You fancy he has strayed, but as a matter of fact he has been stolen, and you little know by whom. You will never get him back except through me; you may rest assured of that. Are you prepared to pay me one hundred pounds (£100) and no questions asked? Your present reward, £20, is paltry; and you may finally bid good-bye to your child if you will not accept my terms [251].

Despite the danger posed to the child in the threatening letter and its request for a ransom, Hewitt disregards official police channels and offers to negotiate with the kidnapper by placing an advertisement in the press offering to meet him. After several days of inactivity in response to the request, providence resolves the situation when the child turns up in a similar way to his disappearance, materializing in the same place from whence he vanished. Despite Charley's return, Mr. Seton insists on unearthing the criminal to bring him to justice and asks Hewitt to continue investigating, telling him he wants to know why Charley was abducted. Since Charley is unable to give any information about his capture, Hewitt discovers the only anomaly in his appearance: a new pair of shoes, which he borrows for his investigation. Hewitt is led to a baby-linen shop where he learns of a Mrs. Butcher who takes babies to mind and of whom the proprietress insists that she knows nothing of her, adding, "nor do I want to" (263). The insalubrious practice of "baby-farming" that arises in the narrative was common practice in the era but was frowned upon by respectable members of the community like the proprietress. Emsley defines their role: "Baby-farmers were individuals, generally women, who for a fee would keep children in their own homes. In some instances, 'keeping appears to have been tacitly recognised as a synonym for allowing to die through lack of food and care, or even murdering'" (*Crime and Society*, 100).

The unraveling of the mystery occurs when Hewitt visits the police station and witnesses the confession of a middle-class drunkard who has handed himself in and admits to Charley's abduction. The inspector on duty is amused and treats his disclosure as the intoxicated ramblings of a drunk, then confines him to the police cell for the night. It emerges that, although he wrote the ransom note and is the brother of the woman who abducted the child, he was not personally involved in the abduction. Armed with this knowledge, Hewitt is finally able to confront the perpetrator, Mrs. Isitt, alias Mrs. Clark, with her crime. On learning of her exposure as the criminal, she crumples at Hewitt's harsh accusatory words as he declares that she has "been recognized" (273). Justification for her actions in abducting the child on two separate occasions is grounded in her compassion for her husband's mental state as he is incarcerated in an asylum; the child soothes his troubled soul. "My husband is a lunatic," she explains, and as a result of a brain tumor, "he rose from bed a maniac and killed our child, a little girl of six, whom he was devotedly attached to" (274). Having killed his child, he then tries to kill his wife, but she survives and faithfully dedicates herself to alleviating his suffering. In his visits to her husband, the child provides a substitute for his own child and relieves her husband's angst.

Whilst the narrative of Mrs. Isitt's admission of guilt is contrived to elicit the reader's sympathy for her predicament, her actions in stealing someone else's child initially temper the reader's acquiescence in her wrongdoing. In presenting an image of her as self-sacrificing and totally dedicated to alleviating her husband's misery, it engages our compassion by reminding us of "the scar on the side of her neck peeping above her high collar"; the narrative intention focuses on the sufferings she has already endured and should be considered in remittance of possible future punishment for her crime. (273). On the surface it appears that, harnessing the Christian principle of forgiveness in a society in transit from religious to secular beliefs, Hewitt responds mercifully and absolves Mrs. Isitt from culpability in accordance with his own moral conscience. In his decision, he is guided by his belief in her diminished responsibility in line with gendered perceptions of insanity. Lucia Zedner proposes that "the Victorians came to view female criminals as 'feeble-minded' or prisoners of their 'special bodily functions' (to use Maudsley's terms) and were thus moved out of the criminal justice sphere" (*Crime and Society*, 99). Of the abduction, Mrs. Isitt declares, "There was the temptation—the overwhelming temptation … [and] as I stood there I almost fell into the delusion of my poor mad husband" (279). By condoning her actions, Hewitt acknowledges the child's ability to bring redemptive spiritual and physical healing to the tormented father, thus entrenching patriarchal recognition of her wifely duties and allegiance to her husband. To alleviate reader apprehension and moral dubiety over Hewitt's decision to spare Mrs. Isitt from legal prosecution, we are told, "The woman's anguish was piteous to see." Hewitt had gained his point and was willing to spare her, signaling his desire to show mercy by exculpating her offense (273). The narrative escalation of mitigation on behalf of Mrs. Isitt emerges with her obvious remorse, which is followed by her concern for the unjust distress she inflicted on Mrs. Seton. The death of Mr. Isitt at the end of the story obviates the possibility of reoffending. Hewitt believes it to be in the best interests of everyone to ignore the law on this occasion and deliver a consequentialist outcome by sparing Mrs. Isitt. In this he assumes a "magisterial role," formally linked to monarchical privilege, by placing himself above the legal system, like Holmes. His demonstration of the power of pardon, described by Austin Sarat and Nasser Hussain in *Forgiveness, Justice and Mercy* is "Like all sovereign prerogatives, its essence is discretionary, its efficacy bound up to its very disregard of declared law" (6). However, in administering justice in this way, he takes upon himself the role of pardoner, for which he could be accused of moral usurpation (Sarat and Hussain, 5). To eliminate the imputation and uphold the moral high ground, Hewitt must consult the aggrieved party, the Seton family, who are rightly entitled to offer pardon or demand retribution in a court of law. On the other hand, in considering Hewitt's application of justice, since he does not represent the official police, his final private resolution of the case preempts the possibility of public exposure at a trial in a criminal court. Since the Seton family agrees not to prosecute Mrs. Isitt, at Hewitt's request, his response indicates that no good can be achieved by subjecting Mrs. Isitt to criminal procedures. In this scenario, Hewitt's actions show that rather than adopting the power of a sovereign with the prerogative of pardon, his ability to show mercy could be read as an attempt at a calibration and individuation necessary for justice to be done. Since conflicts often arise between justice and mercy in a courtroom setting, the particular circumstances, characters and historical context of the legal system justify his remedial intervention. In vindicating Mrs. Isitt, it is worth considering the real-life case of Elizabeth Grosvenor and those like her, charged with kidnapping, who ended up at the Old Bailey and whose fate would have been shared by Mrs. Isitt without Hewitt's act of clemency.

Evidence from trials in the period in the Old Bailey records indicates sentences for female abductors ranging from six weeks imprisonment to twelve months, with or without hard labor, depending on the circumstances of the offense. These sentences were often accompanied by a recommendation from the jury for mercy, which to some extent balances the scales of justice when considering Hewitt's behavior. Male offenders were treated more harshly, for as Emsley explains in "Historical Background—Gender in the Proceedings," by the early nineteenth century, as serious crime came to be masculinized, "Most crime committed by women was seen essentially as sexual rather than a criminal form of deviance...." (*OBP*). While Mrs. Isitt's circumstances could claim mitigating elements, Hewitt's failure to punish or report Mrs. Isitt's brother, Oliver Neale, for his threatening ransom demand is more ethically problematic. By ignoring his treachery in writing a threatening ransom note and failing to inform Mrs. Isitt of her brother's treachery, Hewitt could be accused of complicity. Although Oliver Neale apologizes for his drunken behavior, he has no recall of events, which does not entitle him to remission, as he may reoffend at a later date. In his violation of the law, with inebriation his only defense, a more equitable distribution of justice is called for. As Schramm observes, "[T]he essential point of punishment is to declare society's condemnation of criminal wrongdoing thereby encouraging the offender's repentance and reformation" (*Atonement*, 30). To this may be added the fact that it serves as a deterrent to future crime. Charley, the real victim of the abduction, appears unscathed from his ordeal in the story, but recognition of the vulnerability of children was gradually gaining ground.

Further light is shed on Hewitt's interactions and relationship with the police in "The Case of the Lever Key," a story involving stolen bonds where Hewitt advises his client, "I think the police should know, not because they can see further into the thing than I can ... but ... the police are armed with powers that are not at my disposal. They can get search warrants, stop people at ports and railway stations and arrest suspects" (Morrison, 49). In this he acknowledges the importance of institutional support from the police in the legal process to give closure to his cases. Notably, in "The Affair of the Tortoise" (1894), Hewitt makes a citizen's arrest without waiting for the police and hands the culprit over to the authorities himself. From his behavior, we may infer that in circumstances in which he feels the application of the rule of law may cause more harm than good, he appropriates the role of merciful adjudicator of justice, supplanting both courtroom judge and the rightful owner of forgiveness, the aggrieved victim. By ignoring an equitable distribution of punishment in a democratic system of justice, we could say he poses a challenge to the political and legal system dedicated to the principles of formal equality and respect for rules in Sarat and Hussain's words (Sarat and Hussain, 3). On the other hand, since the rule of law already pervades large swathes of private life, an individual resolution achieves greater fairness than an outcome governed by strict adherence to rules. It considers the emotional and human side of circumstances, in contrast to the law, which is only interested in facts and technicalities.

JOYCE E. PRESTON MUDDOCK
(1843–1934): DICK DONOVAN

Many successful literary careers were fashioned in the lavishly illustrated pages of the *Strand*, founded in 1891 by George Newnes "on the profits of *Tit-Bits*," a popular magazine geared to middle and working-class readers of all ages (Pound, 10). A marketing phenomenon in its day, the *Strand's* first edition sold three hundred thousand copies, perhaps surprising since, "Editorially, the magazine bore the marks of a hasty compilation rather than artful planning," as Reginald Pound explains (32). The early contributors to the magazine like J.E. Preston Muddock had no public reputation and were not "in any sense superior," and their work, from a literary standpoint, was "subordinate to that of more established writers" in Pound's estimation (32). Comments aside, the early writers of the magazine contributed significantly to its initial appeal, confirmed not only in its success but in the subsequent participation of prominent writers like H.G. Wells, P.G. Wodehouse, Jacques Futrelle, Rudyard Kipling and a host of well-known authors, who went on to grace its pages until its final edition in March 1950. The legacy of such acclaimed writers lives on in the strength of their familiarity and popularity to this day, but a different history has been written for the author of my next detective fiction case study: James Edward Preston Muddock, who used a variety of pseudonyms and interchangeable Christian names in his work, including that of his detective, Dick Donovan (1843–1934). Despite featuring in six editions in the early days of the magazine with tales of Dick Donovan, he failed to gain a foothold in the annals of literary history and has been relegated to obscurity, along with other writers of popular fiction. In his February 1891 debut in the second edition of the *Strand*, a month before Arthur Conan Doyle's anonymous article "The Voice of Science," Muddock's story "A Night at the Grande Chartreuse" appeared. It describes a night spent in the austere seclusion of the monastery in the company of the silent order of Carthusian monks who lived there. His article typifies love of travel and an affinity with travel writing that was later pursued in works such as *J.E.M. Guide to Davos-Platz* (1882), recently reprinted along with many of his detective and horror stories.

Muddock was a prolific writer and journalist who established his reputation in the popular press with a range of work encompassing science fiction, horror stories, detective fiction, thrillers, guidebooks and an autobiography entitled *Pages from an Adventurous Life* (1907). Although some of his earlier stories were lambasted in *The Athenaeum* of July 7, 1894, for grammatical inaccuracies and "wearisome adaptations from police reports," more positive comments appear in the same journal some years later. One critic comments, "Mr. Muddock's fiction has been in steady demand for many years, and he has added much to the public stock of harmless pleasure" (Kathryn L. Forsberg, Bio-Bibliography, 1977). Apart from occasional mention in analysis of crime fiction, appraisal of his work is scarce and varies from complimentary to derogatory and mostly limited to brief references. Peter Ridgeway Watt and Joseph Green are clearly impressed by Muddock, signaling approval in the statement, "The first major detective in English fiction after the debut of Holmes was Dick Donovan, who appeared in one hundred and fourteen short stories, published in ten collections between 1886 and 1896" (Watt and Green, 264). In their opinion, "Some of the Donovan stories are excellently done, employ scientific procedures and could rank with the less successful Holmes stories" (265). However, Sandra Kemp takes an opposing view in her publication *Edwardian Fiction: An Oxford Companion* (1997). She attributes his success to the ability to emulate more successful writers like Conan Doyle, and she dismisses his literary efforts as "feeble" and his fiction as "poor stuff" (Kemp, 103). Notably, the same has been said of Arthur Morrison's detective Martin Hewitt and many other detectives of the era, much of it more recently challenged.

Filling the gap of Homes stories between the June 1892 and the December edition of the *Strand,* Muddock provided four Dick Donovan stories in the series "Romances from a Detective Case-Book" beginning with "The Jewelled Skull" in the July edition. However, his style and tone of writing, character and plot failed to live up to the appeal of Holmes, and his detective tales were dropped from the magazine. Whatever the truth of his literary credentials, Muddock's work was undoubtedly popular; much of it was translated into several languages across different parts of the world, including the United States, Canada and Australia. Kathryn L. Forsberg, author of a Bio-Bibliography of his work, reports that he was particularly appreciated in the Scandinavian countries, a factor of interest in view of the current popularity of Nordic Noir and its corresponding use of a realistic style in the form of police procedural crime fiction. In his chapter on popular fiction in *The Cambridge Companion to Scottish Literature* (2012), David Goldie attributes Muddock's style to his drawing on a tradition of indigenous popular Scottish crime writing including the casebooks of two Edinburgh policemen, the real James McLevy, an Irishman whose memoirs were published in the 1850s and early 1860s, and the fictional James

2. Professional Detectives

McGowan, the creation of William Crawford Honeyman in the 1870s (191). Muddock, like Gaboriau, replicates elements from the casebook tradition where stories are realistic, devoid of sentimentality, and largely based on real-life scenarios.

Fresh from completing a history of Eugene Vidocq's life in 1895, Muddock's work entitled *Eugene Vidocq: Soldier, Thief, Spy, Detective* forms a retelling of Vidocq's own memoirs, published in Paris in 1828–1829, and its influence can be read in his detective characterizations. At the time of publication in England, Vidocq achieved great success with his Vidocq yarns, for they were fast-moving and racy, tracing his career from criminal to informant, then detective and finally as founder of the French Sûreté Nationale, the equivalent of England's Scotland Yard. Muddock was impressed by the efficiency of the French system of policing in reducing crime and its perseverance in the pursuit of criminals, traits which he instilled in his hero, Donovan. In the first story in the collection *Riddles Read,* "In the Shadow of Sudden Death," Donovan emerges as a student of Monsieur Eugene Fourbert, the chief superintendent of the Paris police, where he extols the virtues of the French system of policing, describing it as "infinitely better" than its English equivalent, particularly "The Detective Arm" of the service, which "seems to have been brought almost to perfection" (Donovan, 2). Donovan's views on criminality differ markedly from Morrison's professional detective, Martin Hewitt, and the amateur detective, Sherlock Holmes. As a professional detective, his attitude could be encapsulated in the Pinkerton rule never to compromise with criminals, articulated by his detective when he states, "Crime is in effect a guerrilla warfare against well-conducted society and the forces of law and order" and "Since crime is unlawful, any means of tackling it is justified," providing a rationale for his use of illegal practices in the tracking of offenders (Donovan, 2). Donovan's views on the efficiency of the French police system conflict with popular views of their methods at the time of the founding of the Metropolitan police and prevailing throughout the Victorian period. Despite this, his work had wide appeal, particularly resonating with working-class readers and revealing the diversity of public opinion on how to deal with crime. Where middle-class society was outraged at the idea of the introduction into England of a French system that endorsed espionage, the use of disguise and the role of criminals as policemen, the working class appeared to endorse its methods. *Riddles Read,* published in 1896 by Chatto and Windus, London, is a collection of eight stories written under Muddock's pseudonym, Dick Donovan, and featuring his protagonist, Dick Donovan, an official detective policeman, who occasionally works privately when his superior abilities are called upon. The introductory story to the collection, "In the

Shadow of Sudden Death," sets the tone for the ensuing adventures—a rigid application of the law on suspects at all costs by the detective Donovan in a deontological approach focusing on the criminal act that is inherently and immorally wrong. In contrast to Conan Doyle, and even to Morrison, Muddock's plots generally provide a realistic picture of the type of crime encountered in everyday life, with detailed descriptions of the gory scenes of death and destruction. The stories in *Riddles Read* contain elements of melodrama, fused with traces of *The Newgate Calendar* criminality. Resplendent with aphorisms such as "The evil-doer can never prosper," moralizing threads pervade the text (Donovan, 157). Although less well known than the previous story in the collection, "The Problem of Dead Wood Hall," Muddock's chronicle of "The Riddle of Beaver's Hill" presents a contrasting approach to the theme of child kidnapping to that of the previous story. It reveals an unforgiving approach to those suspected of crime. The importance given to Victorian respectability and morality in the story validates the power of social and moral norms over legal sanctions in society. For those who transgress, marginalization results. Unlike Holmes, who seldom mentions remuneration for his services, Muddock feels no disgrace in referencing his ability to secure financial recompense for his labors when working on private cases, which he does on many occasions. The stories under review, like those of Arthur Morrison, illustrate attitudes to the treatment of children and how criminal women were reconstructed medically as insane or unstable. Muddock's detective, Donovan, articulates a complex relationship with the official police force, paradoxical in his assurance of upholding the law by breaking it. In his professional capacity, he regularly upbraids his colleagues for their incompetence.

"The Riddle of Beaver's Hill" (1896)

"What a wild night that was; the 17 February 1868; a savage night truly and awful with the demoniacal fury of the warring elements. From somewhere in the frozen regions of the Northern Pole a hurricane had swept, bent on destruction, and in its giant might had so lashed the Atlantic that the ocean … broke into a maddened roar" [Donovan, 165].

"The Riddle of Beaver's Hill," sixth story in the collection of *Riddles Read,* is set almost thirty years in the past in 1868 and opens with Muddock's use of pathetic fallacy as a foreshadowing of disaster and the imminent death of the criminal by suicide (Donovan, 165). The story begins with the steamship *Roman Empire* battling its way through a fierce storm on its way to Liverpool, heavily laden with a cargo of sugar from the West Indies. Onboard,

2. Professional Detectives

Donovan, one of sixty passengers on the ship, witnesses a man's suicide at the height of the storm, as he plunges from the rails and "hurl[s] himself forth into the night of death," with "a cry of wild despair that went up to the watching stars" (168). Reverting to 1855, the story switches to Charles Garton Pennefather's return to England from India after a posting with the East India Company, corrupted, to some extent, with Oriental habits and decadence which are mirrored in his perceived lack of moral regulation and wayward habits (reminiscent of Arthur Conan Doyle's Thaddeus Sholto in the story *The Sign of the Four* [1890]). He purchases a property, Beaver's Hill in Southampton, and "tries to keep up his Anglo-Indian habits," including building a quasi-bungalow and hiring two Indian servants to attend to his needs (169). Described as "a fretful fuming sort of man ... of sour temper" who led a sort of "isolated life," he appeared not only eccentric but also disagreeable (170). His characterization evokes the transformation of an individual exposed to inferior values and asserts the superiority of the British way of life and its moral and legal authority over the primitive colonial. His characterization resembles that of Dr. Grimesby Roylott of "The Adventure of the Speckled Band," whose disposition similarly altered on his return from India (170). Douglas Kerr provides contextual background to the story in his assertion that the British thought of their society as "a culture of law" and their imperial activity as "bequeathing the rule of law to Asia." This law was morally as well as legally drawn and through it the East, in contrast, was defined as "essentially lawless, or subject to rival corrupt, decayed or barbaric customs and jurisdictions" (Kerr, 3). These corrupt moral practices are echoed in Mr. Pennefather's irregular behavior when he engages a housekeeper named Laura Shapcot, described as a childless widow whom he marries six months later "to the astonishment of his neighbors" (170). Four months later, she bears him a child, indicating that they had engaged in pre-marital sex. His disregard for external codes of morality arouses local hostility, and the response to this breach of sexual politics is articulated through "the horror of Mrs. Grundy," the local gossip, and the observation that the household was shunned, cynically described by Donovan in the words, "[T]he whole neighborhood, with a hypocritical uplifting of the eyes, exclaimed 'shocking'" (170). Despite Donovan's sarcasm, the importance he places on "the role of women as agents of moral regulation" in society, described by Alan Hunt in his social history of moral regulation in Britain, *Governing Morals* (1999), is iterated in his treatment of Mrs. Pennefather in the subsequent narrative, mirroring his own prejudice in the disapproval of her immorality in conceiving a child out of wedlock (Hunt, 2).

The disappearance of the child from his bedroom one evening occurs when the Pennefathers are on a trip to London, "mainly with the object of consulting an eminent specialist with reference to Mr. Pennefather's eyes," which were affected with blindness. Despite the offer of a substantial reward, no trace of the child can be found (171). A tribe of gypsies is thought to be responsible, and although they are exonerated from suspicion, the general consensus remains, "the gypsies on the common had a hand in it" (173). The main complaint against the initial inquiry into the child's disappearance was the time taken "between the discovery of the abduction and the police being informed of the crime," which meant the kidnappers had plenty of time to escape, leaving no trace (173). Subsequently, a letter arrives for Mr. Pennefather, which reads:

> Sir, you will no doubt be glad to learn that your child is well and happy. Since the day he was taken from you for a special object, he has been well taken care of and looked after: but the time has now come when he will be restored to you under certain conditions. The first of these is that you send a bank draft for the sum of five thousand pounds, drawn upon the Credit Lyonnais, Paris [174].

Echoes of evil intent are disclosed in the ransom letter and evoke the situation in "The Affair of Mrs. Seton's Child," where reassurance of the child's safety is juxtaposed with the threatening undertones that Mr. Pennefather would never again see his child. The Setons' offer of twenty pounds reward for the return of their abducted child in the previous story pales in comparison to the large amount demanded in this ransom note. Incensed by the demand, Mr. Pennefather refuses to pay and engages the official police who blunder through, missing clues and opportunities leading to their failure to find the child. Six months later, Mr. Pennefather is robbed and Donovan in his official capacity enters the investigation.

Donovan's role as detective places him above the uniformed branch of the police and equips him with superior skills of deduction rather than simply the physical requirements of catching and restraining criminals required of the police. Donovan concludes after investigation that whoever committed the burglary also abducted the child; he dismisses the members of the household as possible suspects after investigation, since they were all of good character. Finally, he surmises that the motive for stealing the child is one of "revengeful spite," and directs his attention to finding to whom the revenge is directed (179). In his first-person narrative, he rebukes the process of the law in scathing terms:

> There used to be an unwritten law that if a man insulted you, you must knock him down. But this is a risky proceeding in such a law-ridden, prosaic country, as ours is; and if one ventures to resort to such means of expressing his feelings, the chances are

he finds himself in the grip of a clumsy and stupid policeman, who hands him before some self-opinionated judge, only a little less clumsy and a degree less stupid than himself [181].

Considering his affiliation to the police service, his critique of the judicial system appears harsh and devoid of any loyalty to the forces of law and order. His sentiments are replicated, in part, in a series of articles for the *Strand Magazine* entitled "The State of the Law Courts," published in 1891 and disparaging aspects of the legal process. The author, Anthony Guest, in the fourth of the series "The Criminal Courts," published in July 1891, opens his report stating:

So far as its procedure is concerned, our criminal law has hardly changed since the time of the Conquest, and in the opinion of many lawyers, as well as laymen who have studied the matter, it is high time that some improvements were introduced [Vol. 2, 84–92].

In his conversations with the Pennefathers, Donovan discovers that Mr. Pennefather finds adjusting to life in England difficult and "expressed a strong objection to the strained conventionalism and narrow-mindedness of English society generally," a feeling with which Donovan has sympathy to some extent (183). He takes an instant dislike to Mrs. Pennefather, describing her as "sharp-tongued," "brusque and discourteous," evocative of Martin Hewitt's client, Mrs. Geldard (184). Questioning her about the disappearance of her child, he adopts a cold, unemotional approach, in contrast to the compassion received by Mrs. Seton and Mrs. Isitt in the previous story. Dismissing her testimony out of hand, he observes that "she was incapable of discussing the matter calmly and dispassionately" revealing his belief that her behavior has been less than respectable.

Pursuing the strands of the investigation to the West Indies, Donovan finally locates the criminal in the shape of a wastrel son of Mrs. Pennefather from a previous marriage, named Francis Fulton, whom she had kept secret from her new husband. Having arrested the suspect, Donovan charges him with having abducted the child and of having robbed Mr. Pennefather of his deeds and other documents, before transporting him back to England. Donovan puts Fulton in irons in case of escape, but he allows him on deck to take some air. On one of these occasions, the prisoner commits suicide at the height of the storm, prompting Donovan to remark, "and thus added to his many crimes the crime of self-slaughter" (199). Donovan, despite acknowledging the ill health of Fulton at the start of the voyage, pursues his rigid application of the law without fear or favor. The kidnapped child victim receives scant attention in the story, as we are finally informed that, having been taken to Paris, Donovan subsequently "learnt that the unfortunate baby had died: its death being due no doubt in a large measure to neglect" (202).

In his professional capacity as state representative of the law, it is clear that Donovan holds strict views on the nature of justice and the importance of adherence to legal procedure for the maintenance of social order. There is no sense of compassion or merciful delivery for criminals, whatever their motivation for committing crimes. In fulfilling his duty, Donovan is acting in accordance with a moral rule. Given his entrenched views on the importance of laws and the deterrence of crime for societal cohesion, rigid application of the law provides for him a sound justification for punishment. Evidence of his inflexibility is further illustrated in "All for Love's Sake" (1889). In the story, a young man is found to have pilfered goods from his employer to impress his sweetheart, and on being arrested by Donovan, is left in despair of any happiness and commits suicide. Stealing, in Donovan's view, is morally wrong and cannot be excused for any reason. In contrast to Holmes and Hewitt, Donovan is unyielding in his response to criminality. However, he disparages the official police force in similar fashion, commenting on blundering inefficiency. Official fictional police detectives were less successful than their amateur counterparts, and it was not until 1905 and the publication of Bertram Fletcher's *The Chronicles of Addington Peace* that a literary official police detective seriously resonated in the public imagination.

"A Railway Mystery" (1896)

In 1864, the brutal assault and murder of Thomas Briggs, a sixty-nine-year-old banker traveling first class from Fenchurch Street Station to Chalk Farm on the North London Line, marked the first murder on a moving train in Britain. (Brandon and Brooke, 43). It heightened anxiety over the perils of railway travel in public spaces where class barriers could be invalidated. Hans Muller, a German tailor, was arrested and hanged for the heinous crime, which served to highlight the dangers of railway travel in enclosed first class carriages where there was no possibility of escape in the event of assault and robbery. The theme of murder and mayhem on the railways was one that provided endless possibilities for a range of crime fiction writers, including Arthur Conan Doyle in the Sherlock Holmes's short story "The Bruce-Partington Plans" (1908) and in the adventures of Victor L. Whitechurch's detective, Thorpe Hazell, the vegetarian railway enthusiast who appears in a series of escapades in the *Strand*, later published in novel form in *Thrilling Stories of the Railway* in 1912 (Brandon and Brooke, 169). Baroness

2. Professional Detectives

Orczy, Freeman Wills Croft, Ernest Bramagh, Agatha Christie and Ronald Knox, amongst others, continued the trend into the twentieth century, and it remains a popular motif to this day, with Edward Marston's *The Railway Detective* series.

Sir Peter Ellsworthy, in Muddock's "A Railway Mystery," bears more than a passing resemblance to the unfortunate victim of the first railway murder, Thomas Briggs. Like him, he is wealthy and well respected by all who share his acquaintance. On his journey in a first-class compartment from Euston Station in London to Birmingham late one night, he shares a carriage from Rugby with a heavily veiled woman who deposits a bag on the rack and sits silently in the corner of the carriage. The train is held up for twenty minutes behind a luggage van, after which the guard, having decided to check on Sir Peter, finds him lying in a pool of blood from a wound in his forehead, occasioned by being struck with a life-preserver, and no sign of the veiled lady. As far as anyone can tell, nothing has been stolen from Sir Peter, for the box of documents he brought from London is still there, together with ten pounds in cash and a large gold watch, making robbery an unlikely motive. Sir Peter recovers consciousness but suffers amnesia and is eventually subjected to a process of trepanning, whereby much of his memory is erased and he is unable to recall any of the events. The family sends for Donovan to investigate in a private capacity, as he advises that his work is quite apart from the police, who "even at the end of a fortnight were utterly without the faintest shadow of a clue" (212). The official police believe it to be "an habitual criminal," a view which Donovan quickly scorns for "an habitual criminal would not have committed so desperate an assault for nothing" (221). Donovan assumes the veiled lady perpetrated the crime and he sets out to find out who she is. Fortunately for him, she has forgotten to remove her bag from the rack when she left the carriage, and he is able to examine its contents. Along with the general contents of a lady's bag, including a comb, hairbrush, toothbrush and scented bottles, he finds a chewed briar-root pipe and a tobacco pouch, an incongruous find. Since robbery is not the motive, and since the attack is so vicious and prolonged, he believes the motive to be revenge for some past wrong Sir Peter has committed. On application to the family for access to Sir Peter's papers and diaries to access a clue to his past and to his correspondence, we learn that class barriers can only be transgressed to a certain extent; although he is permitted to question the family and servants, a line is drawn at accessing personal papers, and he is denied access. On enquiring at Northampton about properties Sir Peter owned and rented out, he discovers a ramshackle property let to Joseph Marsden and his wife and three children. An honest workingman, he applied to his landlord, Sir Peter, for repairs to be done to the property, which he refused to do. Subsequently, Mr. Marsden's family contracted diphtheria and died. An examination revealed that "the cesspool had been defective and the ground round about had been saturated with sewerage," making Sir Peter "morally guilty" of their deaths, in Mr. Marsden's opinion.

In his search for evidence, Donovan considers that since Joe Marsden had recently been discharged from the lunatic asylum, there was every possibility that his mind was still deranged, and he had perpetrated the crime for revenge. Donovan deliberates on his options:

> Although at this stage there was a certain amount of presumptive evidence that Joe Marsden might have committed the crime, there was nothing, which, from a legal point of view, would have been accepted as a justification for placing him under arrest [224].

Finally it transpires that Joe Marsden's reprobate son, George Greenwood, falls under suspicion. His physiognomy points him out as singular:

> He was a remarkable looking man. He had a round head, a flat face, small eyes, a pug nose, a square chin, large mouth, and a peculiarly sullen expression of countenance. It needed no great amount of experience in facial and craniological study for one to determine that the man was of a sullen, fretful disposition, capable of dangerous outbursts of passion, and of a display of artful cunning [230].

From this socially Darwinian perspective, it is clear Donovan has found the culprit. He shadows him closely, tracking his movements in Gaboriau-like fashion as he meets up with his sister, Ellen, who, in contrast to her brother, is a hard-working, honest and upright individual. She has dropped her father's name because of his sojourn in the asylum and her brother's previous conviction, but unfortunately the bag her brother used in the crime belongs to her. Donovan is loath to do anything to sully her good name, for, in his estimation:

> The world takes precious good care that the sins of the father shall be visited upon the children, and a person, though he be as white as snow, and as blameless as a saint himself, will be pointed at with the finger of scorn, if it should be his misfortune to be connected by family ties with someone who has broken the law and suffered for it [233].

The expectation of clemency, then, to protect Joe Marsden's daughter from disgrace by shielding her involvement is foiled when Donovan declares that he is "compelled in the interests of justice and right" to ensure that for such a serious crime "the law had to be appeased" (233). Her reputation is sacrificed in his approach to justice.

For the fictional Joe Marsden whose family was destroyed due to the landlord's negligence, there was no redress. Demonstrating the power of those with wealth and influence over the less fortunate at the time of writing, and the limitations of the law with regard to the protection of tenants, according to *Every Man's Own Lawyer* in the section on "Houses and Lands," we are advised:

> A landlord is not liable to repair, except where he has agreed to do so. Nor, except in the case of a furnished house, is there any implied undertaking on the part of the landlord that the property is fit for habitation or occupation. An intending tenant must satisfy himself on these points before making his contract.... A landlord who lets an unfurnished house, even in a dangerous condition, is not liable to the tenant or to any other person using the premises, for personal injuries due to the defective state of the house [374].

Most people would agree that, although not legally responsible for the maintenance of the property at the time, the landlord is morally and socially responsible for the provision of safe housing for his tenants. Due to his disregard of the pleas of his tenant, Joe Marsden, Sir Peter Ellsworthy set in motion a veritable cascade of calamities including the destruction of his own well being and that of Joe Marsden and his family. Donovan refrains from comment on the moral or emotional elements of family tragedy in the narrative, accentuating instead the criminological aspect of the crime and those caught up in its entanglements.

Conclusion

Moretti suggests that the detective "sacrifices his individuality to his work" and is consumed by what an investigation entails. Abandoning the "individualistic ethic," he suggests, the detective retains the memory of it, and, steeped in the criminal world, he understands how the criminal operates and is potentially a criminal himself, furnished with the ability to commit crimes (142). The professional detectives, Hewitt and Donovan, are clearly in this mold, able to spot criminality where others might be deceived into believing in innocence. In their view, everyone has the capacity for wrongdoing as they look beyond surface appearances. In doing so they operate outside the legal framework and tackle crime that would otherwise go unheeded. The notion of good character is evident in Hewitt's response to the child stealer in "Mrs. Seton's Child." He empathizes with her sorrowful state and acts nobly through his generous gesture to ignore her criminality in stealing the child. By performing a magnanimous, altruistic act in the interests of someone else, Hewitt reaps the benefits of virtue, which as Aristotle points out, will become customary through practice. Here, his morality conflicts with legality, yet achieves a fairer justice than would be possible under the law. His actions are in line with a virtue ethical approach, for he disregards any disadvantage to himself if it were discovered that he colluded with a criminal. He is motivated by a spirit of generosity. Donovan displays no such kindness in his approach to criminality, considering it a form of guerrilla warfare, as he reveals in his story. Punishing those who transgress is paramount in a utilitarian approach to justice, where his values entail the belief that judgments should be made rationally rather than emotionally and should ensure the distribution of "just desserts" rather than mercy (Sarat and Hussain, 25). Acting as a deterrent to would-be criminals, he ensures offenders suffer the consequences of their actions.

3

The Female Gaze

Marsh, Hume and
Pirkis's Unsuitable Women

RICHARD MARSH (1857–1915): JUDITH LEE

In the first year of its publication in 1891, the *Strand Magazine* ran a series of articles entitled "The State of the Law Courts," delivering a stinging critique of the justice system in England. From the lack of talent at the Criminal Bar to the ineptitude of aged and infirm judges, whose decline in mental faculties presented "a source of danger to the public," remedies, it claimed, were long overdue (Vol. 1, 402). Public perceptions of a just society are invariably at odds with its practical administration in the Victorian era, as evidenced in many fictional representations of its workings. From Dickens's scathing critique of the Court of Chancery in *Bleak House* (1853), a novel, in Jan Melissa Schramm's words, "preoccupied with distributive and procedural justice" that resulted in energized legal reform of the laws of equity, to Mary Elizabeth Braddon's exposure of the impenetrable nature of upper class power and privilege in *Lady Audley's Secret* (1862), fictional representations of the law of the period reveal a range of distortions and corruptions at the core of the legal system (*Atonement*, 27).

Given the stark realities of how the judicial system works and the opportunities for miscarriages of justice it presents, it is unsurprising that the fictional law-breaking amateur and professional detectives who offered a personalized form of alternative justice grew in popularity toward the end of the nineteenth century and achieved recognition that continued into the Edwardian years and beyond. This chapter forms an appraisal of three female detectives who operate under the thrall of patriarchy, which in reality excludes them from active and professional participation in any aspect of the criminal justice system. The female detective's approach to justice and her quasi-legitimate use of power and authority create an anomalous fictional-ized account. In the context of the onset of modernity and the cult of the New Woman in fiction, the woman of independent means enjoyed oppor-tunities unavailable to her predecessors, yet she lacked any agency or repre-sentation in the judicial system, a situation remedied in the creation of fictive female detectives. Through close reading of the individual predicaments they encounter in the pursuit of justice in the narratives, we gain valuable insights into significant aspects of cultural and criminal history. In their inti-mate and personal interactions with official police, the victims of crime, the community in which they live and the criminals they confront, we develop a deeper understanding of how human relationships were forged, fractured and remolded in the era. Offering a contrast to male fictional detectives in "an unsuitable job for a woman," the female investigator combines her role as detective with that of respectable female and delivers her personal form of justice by extralegal means. I have chosen works by three authors: Richard Marsh (1857–1915), Fergus Hume (1859–1932) and Catherine Louisa Pirkis (1839-1910). Their fictional detectives Judith Lee, Hagar Stanley and Loveday Brooke emerged at a time of acute apprehension over gender identity shifts driven by the woman's movement, "race degeneracy" and industrial strife, as Kestner explains (*Sisters*, 181). The stories under review begin with Rich-ard Marsh's "Conscience" from *Judith Lee: Some Pages from Her Life* (1912). Fergus Hume's Hagar Stanley is explored in "The Seventh Customer and the Mandarin" and "The Eighth Customer and the Pair of Boots" from the col-lection *Hagar of the Pawn Shop* (1898), and Catherine Louisa Pirkis's heroine, Loveday Brooke, appears in "The Murder at Troyte's Hill" (1893).

Richard Marsh had a colorful past. Born Richard Bernard Heldmann, as a young author in 1880 he published fiction in boys' story papers, includ-ing *Quiver and Young England* and the *Union Jack,* where he encountered G.A. Henty and W.G.H. Kingston, favorite boys' writers of the time, as Minna Vuohelainen explains in her biography (3). By 1883 he had disappeared from the literary and social scene after his arrest in 1884 for writing forged checks. Sentenced to eighteen months hard labor, on release he changed his name to Marsh and began a prolific writing career. *The Beetle: A Mystery* (1897), a horror story, was sensationally popular and established his literary creden-tials under his new name. His fictional female detective, Judith Lee, exem-plifies a spirited depiction of the proto-feminist New Woman. Projected as a dedicated professional woman with a successful career as a teacher of the deaf and dumb, her particularized skill of lip-reading destabilizes the private realms of conversations and uniquely situates her within a locus of privileged communication and power. Her series of adventures was serialized in the

Strand Magazine from August 1911 until August 1912 before publication in novel form in *Judith Lee: Some Pages from Her Life* (1912) and *The Adventures of Judith Lee* (1916). According to Jean-Daniel Breque in his introduction to *The Complete Adventures of Judith Lee,* the second series was completed by Marsh's widow and published posthumously (Marsh, 12). Judith Lee's characterization builds gradually throughout the series as we discover that her lip-reading ability, inherited from her father, equates to "another sense" and is amplified by the ability to use her talent from great distances (Marsh, 17). As Kestner notes, her "epistemology is synaesthetic, that is combines two senses, those of sight and sound" (199). Judith Lee's Romany background adds an interesting dimension to the cultural and social nuances of the study. Her representation as a professional woman who originates from an ethnically marginalized community with a "reputation for misconduct" is doubly potent in its symbolic expression of sanction (Behlner, 235). Her stance on morality in decision-making reflects a compassionate response to potential victims of crime who are neglected by current legislation. It highlights the inability of the law to provide appropriate measures to deal with criminal encounters faced by ordinary people in the community by efficient and ethical means.

"Conscience" (1912)

"Conscience," the fourth story in the collection *Judith Lee: Some Pages from Her Life,* dramatizes the actions of a serial killer who perpetrates violent attacks on women traveling on the railway in first class carriages and reconfigures the Ripper murders and the failure of the official police force to catch the criminal. Contextualizing the narrative further, the success of the railways, which symbolized industrial progress and modern civilization, was offset by the host of new opportunities it provided for Britain's criminal elements. Pickpockets and perpetrators of assault and robbery found easy pickings on the railway network. Many crime fiction writers turned to newspaper reports for inspirational plots. Details of the sensational, unsolved railway murder of Mary Sophia Money on the Victoria to Brighton line in 1905 are echoed, to some extent, in the fictional reenactment of the story. The story "Conscience" begins in Brighton, where Judith Lee has gone to recover her health, for she "had nearly broken down in her work." This health crisis is an indication of the demands imposed upon Lee in her professional career, which involved attending overseas conferences, a measure of her success and achievement (Marsh, 47). Whilst seated on the pier, John Tung, a well-dressed, but odd-looking man with a Mongolian appearance, attracts her attention by surreptitiously murmuring the description of a woman, "Mauve dress, big black velvet hat, ostrich plume; four-thirty train," to two passing men, who avoid showing any recognition of him (Marsh, 46). The following day, she reads of the death of the very same woman on the Brighton line, found "lying on the ballast, as if she might have fallen out of a passing train" (Marsh, 47). Engaging in clandestine lip-reading of her fellow passengers, she discovers that the woman had been drinking, and was believed to have mistakenly opened the carriage door and stepped out on to the line. She fails to follow up on this peculiarity, putting it down to coincidence. However, following two further occurrences where wealthy women are targeted and murdered, she realizes that a serial killer and his accomplices are actively conducting a campaign of robbery and violence against vulnerable single women traveling on the railways. The coming of the railways promoted opportunities for women to escape from the monotony of imposed domesticity. As Sally Ledger observes, from the late nineteenth century onwards, "Far from being imprisoned by the private sphere of suburban domesticity, women of all classes … were pouring into the public spaces of the modern city in ever increasing numbers" (Ledger, 155). The replication of misogynistic hostility toward the itinerant flaneuse in the shape of the New Woman was rooted in media and fictional portrayals whose ideological discourses were shaped to "ridicule and control renegade women" as Ledger points out (Ledger, 9). Negative depictions linked them to sexually transgressive behavior, exemplified in earlier works such as Grant Allen's novel *The Woman Who Did* (1895) about a woman prepared to defy convention by raising a child as a single parent out of wedlock and refusing to marry her lover; it radically challenged conventional thinking about women's position and role in society (Ledger, 14). By shifting the boundaries of gender identity and imbuing their narratives with female empowerment, such writers exacerbated growing anxieties over the destabilization of the patriarchy, and there was a very real fear that the New Woman "may not be at all interested in men, and could manage quite well without them" (Ledger, 5). The story "Conscience" underscores the fact that the female victims were unaccompanied at the time of their murder, emphasizing the possible dangers of their predicament but for the actions of the female detective who outwits the villain in the final denouement. Unaccompanied travel is a risky venture for a young woman.

Re-emerging after a two-year absence, the criminal John Tung appears in the public gardens at Buxton, where he has earmarked his next victim: "Grey dress, lace scarf, Panama hat; five-five train" (50). His behavior is a catalyst for Judith Lee, who determines that since she "had seen sentence of death pronounced on an innocent, helpless fellow creature," she "did not propose to sit still … and allow those three uncanny beings, (his accomplices) undisturbed, to work their evil will" (51). Deliberating on her options, she reasons that without evidence there is little she can do, for the police will not respond to her accusations on the basis of her suspicions alone; her only course is to warn the woman concerned. However, due to a previous encounter with the woman, when she had tried to return a brooch that had fallen from her dress and met with a discourteous response, she was hesitant to place herself in the way of a second rebuff in engineering a meeting with her. Despite her apprehension, she approaches the woman. When she tries to avoid her, Judith Lee bars the way and exclaims:

> There is something I have to say to you, which is important—of the very first importance—which is essential that I should say and you should hear. I have not the least intention of forcing on you my acquaintance, but with your sanction [52].

To her amazement, she receives racial abuse rather than gratitude for her attempts to alert the woman to the danger she faces. The woman ignores her twice and then refuses to speak to her, finally announcing, "If you dare to speak to me again I shall claim the protection of the police" (52). Judith Lee's mixed-race appearance provokes racial antipathy from the woman and is confirmed later in the story. After Judith Lee's interventions on her behalf, the woman whispers to her companion, "I couldn't possibly remain in the same compartment with that half-breed gipsy-looking creature" (59). Despite Judith Lee's middle-class manners and dress, the wealthy woman, whose innate suspicion of the foreign precludes any form of association, marginalizes her. In response to the woman's racist remark, she replies, "I was the half-breed gipsy-looking creature. The experience she had had of me was when I saved her life at Buxton" (59). Prejudice and suspicion combine in the woman's dismissal of Judith Lee as an embodiment of unsavory appetites and exoticism; racial prejudice precedes the woman's subsequent exposure to mortal danger.

In the absence of any visible sign of apprehension or investigation by the official police into the deaths of so many unaccompanied young women, Judith Lee resorts to vigilantism, the legal definition of which is taking the law into one's own hands and effecting justice in one's own way. Assuming the mantle of intrepid defender of endangered women, she sends John Tung an ultimatum, warning him that she knows of his crimes and not to pursue his villainy further. Her missive states, "You may be sure that the day of reckoning is at hand, when you and your two accomplices will be called to a strict account. In that hour you will be shown no more mercy than you have shown" (53). Marsh imbues the tone of her threat with a retributive form of punishment for his continued villainy, contrary to the utilitarian principles of the time. Under the utilitarian system, if Tung were to be tried, the possibility of indeterminate sentencing would mean that mitigating circumstances left open the possibility of a lighter sentence (Tonry, 13). Because penalties were "adjusted to take account of the offenders'" sensibilities, a requirement impossible to quantify accurately, combined with the lack of tangible evidence, the result might be his being excused altogether (Tonry, 13). The prospect of his escaping justice would resonate with readers, reminded of the elusive Ripper and fearful of his reincarnation. Reflecting on the legality of her position, Judith Lee admits, "I was perfectly conscious that from the point of view of a court of law I had not the slightest right to pen a single one of the words which were on the sheet of paper inside that envelope" (54). Aware of the possibility of incriminating herself through her actions if she is mistaken, Lee considers the risks of her predicament, including the possibility of arrest, imprisonment and the end of her career. However, John Tung's reaction to the letter confirms her belief in his guilt, and she follows his victim to the station to ensure the woman's safety. Mr. Tung, having ignored Judith Lee's admonition, was waiting outside a train compartment for his quarry. Once more she scribbles a note inscribed, "You are watched. Your intentions are known," and she advises him that the police will be traveling in attendance on the lady with the grey dress, waiting to arrest him on sight, before adding, "Then heigh-ho for the gallows!" (Marsh, 54). This singular address panics the villain, who disappears from the station. Believing him to have learned his lesson, she is astonished to find him once more at Euston station and "inspired with a feeling of actual rage," as she considers him "well dressed, so well fed, so seemingly prosperous, with all the appearance about him of one with whom the world went well," she decides to write a final note (57). In it, the emotional rhetoric is heightened as she threatens, "You are about to be arrested. Justice is going to be done. Your time has come. Prepare for the end" (58). This final missive has its impact when he sees a constable and his assistant engaged on the company's business, advancing toward him. Mistakenly believing that they had come to arrest him, he blows his brains out—"killed by conscience" (58). Judith Lee's incitement to suicide seems vindicated when amongst his possessions the police find "feminine belongings of all sorts and kinds," indicative that he had been operating for years "with perfect impunity" (Marsh, 59). The lack of honest, law-abiding standards of behavior in some sections of society validated Sir Robert Anderson's opinion that "without statutory morality men had no incentive to virtue and nothing to hold them back from vice": a critique of the separation of law from morality (Rowbotham and Stevenson, 11).

3. The Female Gaze

Judging that the law has no positive response to control Tung's murderous behavior and realizing the futility of any attempt to incriminate him, Judith Lee administers a form of justice that most readers would applaud. Marsh's fictionalized articulation that it takes an amateur woman detective to unmask a serial killer and bring him to justice raises questions about the efficacy of the legal system in relation to threats to female bodily integrity and whether women are adequately protected in society. In situations like the one illustrated in the story, Judith Lee's incitement to suicide represents an individualized decision on the application of justice in answer to a gap in the law. Improvising in response to the circumstances, she exercises her discretion where there is no provision or remedy in the legal system. Lee's moral stance, like that of Holmes, is in line with a virtue ethicist approach where helping others to avoid harm, to the endangerment of one's own safety, is the charitable thing to do. Central to her belief system is the concept of virtuous character and behavior that encompasses generosity, courage and compassion in an Aristotelian mode. Although not judicially qualified as a judge, Judith Lee exercises an altruistic discretion based on her desire to prevent further harm to society and achieve a just solution, for without her intervention it is probable Tung would go on to murder other women. Also, it is worth considering Cook's proposition in support of Lee's actions as outline by Sandra Walkate in her article "Courting Compassion: Victims, Policy and the Question of Justice" (118). In it, Cook advises, "If a society cannot guarantee the equal worth of all its citizens, mutual and self respect and the meeting of basic needs, it cannot expect that all citizens will feel they have an equal stake in abiding by the law, and it cannot dispense justice fairly and enhance confidence in the law" (118). By this account, public lack of confidence and the marginalization of minority groups in society put the law's authority in jeopardy. In relation to the story, Judith Lee, by taking the law into her own hands, cannot guarantee a judgment that is certain, accurate and value-free; in foregoing any consultation with anyone, she undermines democracy. For as Rawls has pointed out, "Liberty requires the rule of law; otherwise the uncertainty of the boundaries of our liberty will make its exercise risky and less secure" (Kukathas and Pettit, 50). The exercise of discretion by the amateur detective raises ethical issues, especially when judgment is guided by personal rules that may not be consistently applied in all cases, potentially leading to disorderly and sporadic applications of justice.

Our fictional heroine Judith Lee waits for no invitation to the profession of teaching the deaf, as she asserts authoritative control over her own career and uses her talents for the good of society. Her sleuthing activities draw attention to the law's inability to protect women from predatory males in public spaces, once the preserve of masculine elites. By intervening to protect the lives of potential victims of crime in "Conscience," she draws attention to the deficiencies of the Railway Regulation Act of 1868, which was on the statute book at the time of writing and remains on the statute books in an amended form to this day. In its provisions for the safety of passengers, it outlines the railway company's liabilities:

> Every company shall provide, and maintain in good working order, in every train worked by it, which carries passengers and travels more than twenty miles without stopping, such efficient means of communication between the passengers and the Servants of the Company in charge of the train as the Board of Trade may approve.

These scant provisions for the personal safety of travelers fail to take into account a range of possible perilous situations that may face commuters, such as obstructions on the line, suicides, of which there were many, derailments and the sexual harassment of lone female passengers, making it less than adequate for passenger safety. In the section entitled "Carriage and Transportation of Goods" in *Every Man's Own Lawyer,* we learn that "carriers of passengers do not insure the safety of passengers, and are only responsible for injuries caused by negligence" (291). They are not liable for "unforeseen accidents," and in the event of a passenger falling from the train whilst it is in motion in the attempt to fasten a door that has not been secured, the proprietor would not be deemed guilty of negligence. An updated Regulation of Railways Act was passed in 1889, with further provisions for public safety including the improvement of the breaking and signaling systems.

FERGUS HUME (1859–1932): HAGAR OF THE PAWN-SHOP (1898)

> And the angel of the Lord found her by a fountain of water in the wilderness, by the fountain in the way to Shur. And he said, "Hagar, Sarai's maid, whence camest thou? And whither wilt thou go?"
> And she said, "I flee from the face of my mistress Sarai" [Genesis Ch. 16: 7–8].

In the preface to his 1879 book *The Gypsies and the Detectives*, Alan Pinkerton reveals how he left "the crowded populaces of great cities" and "travelled outside of the pale of civilisation" where he "entered into the camp of the gypsy" (Pinkerton, 9). His fascination with the "wild and romantic life" where "[t]he Gypsy Queen still practices the art of sorcery, and dives with shrewd prophecy into the regions of the future" links their "wild nobility to lawlessness," and to generating a sense of fear amongst the population of "sober law-abiding people" in England (Pinkerton, 9). The undertones of civic discord and rebelliousness associated with Gypsy culture is borne out in Fergus Hume's characterization of the fictional Gypsy Detective, Hagar Stanley, the second protagonist in this study of female detectives. With her links to disorderly behavior, Hagar embodies the Bohemian spirit of Conan Doyle's Sherlock Holmes combined with the pragmatism of Arthur Morrison's Martin Hewitt. By examining the fictionalized values, beliefs and anxieties she articulates in her conduct toward criminals and the victims of crime, I will establish where her empathy lies and the style of her ethical perspective. An interesting view of her complex relationship with the official police emerges in scrutiny of her interactions with them. In a gendered reading, I investigate how her status as a Gypsy and a woman detective differs from that of other fictional detectives of the era, such as Grant Allen's Lois Cayley and Hilda Wade, both of whom appeared in the *Strand Magazine* between 1898 and 1900. Cultural and legal issues surface repeatedly in the stories where Hagar's interventions address the discriminatory effects of an unjust legal system and biased laws. My focus on a second gypsy protagonist offers a counter narrative to that of Judith Lee. Like her, Romany traditions and customs may be read in the accounts, but unlike her, Hagar occupies the lower stratum of society and typifies the precarious predicament of survival as a marginalized single woman escaping from domestic violence. Fergus Hume's Hagar Stanley, the urban gypsy from Lambeth, has no amanuensis. Siting her in a pawn shop in the backstreets of Lambeth evokes Conrad's shop in *The Secret Agent* (1907), and her encounters with an assortment of customers places her in danger of assault from the criminal elements of society who pawn a range of intriguing articles. Unlike Judith Lee more than a decade later, she has no profession or means of support and must rely on her own initiative for survival in a lawless environment.

The stories under review are part of a collection of twelve episodes contained in *Hagar of the Pawn-Shop*, published in 1898 by the "already famous" Fergus Hume (Kestner, 107). Despite what Stephen Knight calls his "runaway success" with the crime fiction novel *The Mystery of a Hansom Cab*, first published in Melbourne in 1886 and declared "the first true best seller in the genre" with sales of over half a million copies within two years, Fergus Hume was unable to repeat this phenomenal success with any of his later work (*Secrets*, 76). This chapter examines two stories from the collection: "The Seventh Customer and the Mandarin" and "The Eighth Customer and the Pair of Boots." The first story is the eighth adventure, which dramatizes her run-ins with career criminals from London's organized crime rackets and emphasizes her ambivalent attitude toward criminal activity. It spotlights the proliferation of deviant characters and offers insight into contemporary views on criminality, with its roots firmly lodged in the emerging sciences of criminology, In the second story under review, "The Eighth Customer and the Pair of Boots," Hagar's actions highlight a recurring theme in Victorian crime fiction: the unreliability of circumstantial evidence for achieving justice. Hagar's class and gender-transcending role in this story reach their peak as the official police transfer power and authority in a murder inquiry to her, allowing her to lead the investigation and interrogate a prime suspect. Her behavior in this story confounds previous incidents of her dissociation from the legal forces of law and order.

Forming a chronological sequence that begins with her arrival at the pawnshop in Lambeth, the stories follow Hagar Stanley's exchanges with ten customers who deposit items for safekeeping at her pawnshop in exchange for money and an interest payment in case of redemption. In the introductory story of the collection entitled "The Coming of Hagar," the protagonist Hagar reprises the role of her biblical namesake, the concubine of Abraham. In the Bible story, Hagar is fleeing from the harshness of Abraham and his wife Sarah in Genesis and seeks shelter in the wilderness before being instructed by God to return to Abraham. Hume's Gypsy Hagar's flight is from her Romany tribe in the New Forest to the metaphorical wilderness of Lambeth and is undertaken to avoid a brutal marriage as the wife, or Rani, of Goliath, a formidable and evil member of the tribe. From the outset in the initial story, her arrival alone and late at night at the pawnshop iterates her rejection of social norms, behavior in consonance with that of Judith Lee, whose encounter with the German spy in "Two Words" occurs late at night. As a Gypsy, free from the repressive codes of Victorian respectability, Hagar repudiates the sexual connotations linked to her situation. Challenging her estranged uncle Dix to allow her entry to his shop and provide "Food and Shelter," she cautions him, "but you'd better shut the door; it might be bad for your reputation if any passer-by saw you speaking to a woman at this time of night" (Hume, 10). Like her, Dix is cast as a societal misfit, and, once assured that she was not the ghost of his long-dead wife also named Hagar Stanley, he assures her that it [his reputation] is "past spoiling" (Hume, 10). In breaching cultural taboos, she risks stigmatization as a woman of the streets and a criminal. As Rowbotham and Stevenson observe, since "Victorians saw much that was criminal in the strict legal sense as being also socially criminal," her socially offensive behavior was in reality a form of law breaking and would be viewed as "at least as important as the legal dimensions" (Rowbotham and

Stevenson, xxi). Her breach of social mores replicates that of Mrs. Pennefather in Donovan's "The Riddle of Beaver's Hill," where social convention is ignored despite awareness of the repercussions. Fergus Hume created another memorable women detective, the eponymous Madame Midas, who, along with Hagar Stanley, enriches the annals of empowered fictional female detectives operating toward the close of the nineteenth century and elevates them from relative obscurity.

"The Seventh Customer and the Mandarin" (1898)

The story of the "Seventh Customer and the Mandarin" opens with the arrival of Mr. William Smith, or Larky Bill, at the pawnshop requesting "two quid" for depositing a mandarin toy "gaily tinted to imitate the official dress of a great Chinese lord" and weighted within to allow it to roll around and "chime melodiously" (Hume, 153). In the ensuing conversation, Mr. Smith's use of language registers his criminal viewpoint, echoing Christiana Gregoriou's contention that criminal "language choices" reflect "how they [the criminals] metaphorically configure the world" (Gregoriou, 1). Hagar's immediate impression of Mr. William Smith is that she "did not like the man's looks at all" and that he was "[n]ot at all the sort of person likely to be in possession of so delicate a work of Chinese art and fancy," signaling her suspicion that he has stolen the mandarin (Hume, 154). Keen to discover whether this is so, Hagar asks him how he came by the mandarin, to which he replies that a sailor friend had given it to him. Voicing her concerns further she states, "I don't believe you came honestly by it, and I'm running a risk in taking it," before asking him why he has chosen a pawnshop so distant from his home (154). Refusing to answer, he agrees to take twenty shillings instead of his previous request for two pounds, likely proof that the mandarin is indeed stolen. Significantly, rather than contacting the police with her misgivings, Hagar enters into an altercation with Mr. Smith, who threatens to break her neck if the mandarin is missing when he returns in three months. Feminine propriety disintegrates as she leaps over the counter, seizes him by the ear, and practically ejects him from the shop, before finally agreeing the terms of credit and giving him the twenty shillings. The Pawnbroker's Act of 1872 required registration of all pawnshops and laid out a range of provisions, including the need for an annual license fee and strict adherence to a code of practice in an attempt to curtail criminality. By accepting the mandarin, she is complicit in the possible theft of the antique and lays herself open to accusations of aiding and abetting a felon, as well as placing herself in legal jeopardy. Hagar's gender-breaking behavior in physically tackling a violent individual could be viewed as foolhardy or courageous, but scarcely in keeping with the conduct of her counterpart fictional sisters in detection, whose ladylike demeanor is the antithesis of Hagar's. Even Judith Lee, a decade or more later and despite her entanglements with sundry evil villains, rarely took the initial offensive herself.

Once the mandarin has been pawned, Mr. Smith arranges to have himself arrested on petty theft and locked up for four months to escape the clutches of "a wizen-faced" accomplice villain called Monkey, who is keen to get hold of the mandarin (Hume, 155). Smith's manipulation of the legal system for his own purposes articulates the late Victorian and Edwardian debate about crime; its central concern was the problem of the professional or career criminal, which eventually led to the Prevention of Crime of 1908. Its terms provided for the incarceration of "those with incorrigible cravings for crime, on the principle that if they cannot be deterred they should be debarred the opportunity" (Turner, 620). During Mr. Smith's three-month sojourn in prison, Hagar's semi-villainous assistant Bolker discovers twenty-thousand pounds worth of diamonds hidden inside the mandarin, discreetly removes them and claims the reward on offer, before taking up a new position in an up-market bookshop in Leicester Square. Hagar's initial disregard of a minor infraction of the law prefaces an escalation in the seriousness of her offense.

When Mr. Smith returns to claim the mandarin and discovers that the diamonds are missing, Hagar calmly informs him that had she known diamonds were hidden inside the mandarin, she would have notified the police, placing her behavior more firmly in the realms of legality in relation to serious crime. Realizing the seriousness of the offense, she accuses Mr. Smith, "About the time you pawned this toy Lady Deacey's jewels were stolen. You stole them!" (159). Fully aware of the precarious position she finds herself in, facing an angry villain and the possibility of prosecution for aiding and abetting the theft of the diamonds, she lets slip her suspicions that Bolker, her assistant, is responsible for their removal. In a raging tirade, Mr. Smith threatens to "cut his bloomin throat" before turning his verbal and physical abuse on Hagar (159). As he prepares to assault her, she produces a "neat little revolver … lately purchased for defense" [sic]; living in Lambeth, where crime and violence are everyday occurrences, ownership of a weapon for protection seems a sensible precaution, borne out in Hagar's assertion, "I keep this always by me … to protect myself against rogues such as you" (160). In response, he hurriedly leaves the pawnshop in search of Bolker. Hagar's reliance on a weapon to protect herself against physical assault validates the notion that despite numerous social problems in Victorian England and the increase in crime, there was no control on guns and the importance of privately-owned firearms for self-defense was considered a basic right; unfortunately, this right applied to villains as well as law-abiding citizens (Malcolm, vii). Resorting to the use of a weapon highlights Hagar's willingness to use violence to counter violence and bears witness to the prevailing culture in Lambeth, where official forces of law and order are unable or unwilling to protect adequately all of the inhabitants. Her use of a revolver to defend herself prefigures the actions of Judith Lee, yet once again distinguishes her from her counterpart female detectives of the era, none of whom resort to the use of firearms.

Confronted with a situation in which Mr. Smith may return to murder her, and where he threatens the life of her one-time assistant Bolker, Hagar fails to contact the police to ensure his or her own safety. The enraged Bill seeks Bolker out, drags him to a ruined wharf and threatens to murder him by placing "the cold steel" of a knife against his throat (162). Well-versed in criminality, Bolker escapes by implicating the other villain, Monkey, in the removal of the diamonds and absconds as soon as Bill loosens his grip. By this time Hagar realizes that "on the whole … it would be just as well for society at large, and herself in particular, if Mr. Smith were restored to the prison from whence he had lately emerged" (160). Hagar's sidelining of the official police once more arises when she discounts their mediation or assistance in solving the dilemma of how to proceed, and instead consults a solicitor friend of her uncle Dix, named Vark, about what to do next. Described as a lawyer "who carried on a shady business, in a shady manner, for shady clients," Vark devises a plan to entrap Mr. Smith, reminiscent of the scene in Gay's *The Beggar's Opera* (1728), where Captain Macheath is captured by Peachum. Luring him to a meeting where Mr. Smith hopes to procure the diamonds, Vark betrays him to the police for a hefty reward for his capture. The single official police role in the story is the apprehension of the criminal in the final denouement. Hagar takes the law into her own hands to demonstrate that in communities where the law ceases to operate, she will respond to crime independent of the law.

Described by Kestner as "one of the most intriguing of all amateur female detectives" (*Sisters*, 107) in fiction, Hagar Stanley's characterization accommodates what Slung terms the "natural shrewdness and perspicacity of her race" (Slung, 361). Practicality supersedes legality in her daily life in the pawnshop, as we witness skilled financial haggling in interactions with the customers. The antithesis of Holmes's demure, self-effacing woman, Hume endows her, instead, with a streak of ruthless determination and the primitive desire for revenge, justified under the right circumstances. Notably, in "The Silver Teapot," the seventh story in the collection which forms a critique of the institution of marriage and friendship betrayal, Hagar urges the wronged woman, "Revenge yourself, Miss Snow! Tell John the truth [that his new wife had deceived him about his former fiancée, Miss Snow, who had not deserted him as she had claimed] and punish these vixens," before exhorting Miss Snow, "Ruin her! She ruined you": harsh words that reveal Hagar's belief in a form of retributive justice, evocative of the biblical "an eye for an eye" (144). Ably confronting lower-class criminals rather than the middle-class rogues that Judith Lee frequently encounters in her adventures, Hagar evokes a code of values and principles comprising a mixture of guile, common sense and survival instincts. Existing as she does on the margins of society, racial and gender status render her open to physical and verbal abuse from some of her customers, which she adroitly deflects with instinctive defense mechanisms. Like Judith Lee, she suffers racial jibes, which fail to penetrate a seasoned operator.

Hagar's attitudes and behavior in this story reveal a splintering of gender identity in keeping with Epstein Nord's contention that "writers who used Gypsy plots and figures also often chafed against patterns of gender conformity" (Epstein Nord, 12). Her deviation from conventional forms of female behavior is juxtaposed with her physical presentation as an exotic beauty. Hume characterizes grim determination to survive in the face of adversity in masculine tones, which presage the arrival of the silent movie heroines of the silver screen more than a decade later. Richard Abel's description of such heroines with "athletic exuberance and unyielding zeal for risky experiences" is emblematic of the actions of Hagar and Judith Lee, always ready to confront violent physical assault and face danger head-on (Abel, 173). Reviewing her attitude to legality in the story, it is clear at the beginning of the story that she suspects Mr. Smith of theft, yet agrees to lend him money on a stolen antique. Once it becomes evident that a more serious crime has taken place, she reverses her previous stance and distances herself from the thief, demonstrating that though petty crime may be ignored, the theft of twenty-thousand pounds in diamonds cannot be condoned. However, Hagar's fictional interactions with the characters in the story should be considered in the context of the narrative setting, one with which most readers would be familiar. In choosing Lambeth as the location for Hagar's pawnshop, Hume echoes the strains of Somerset Maugham's *Liza of Lambeth* (1897) and Arthur Morrison's *Tales of Mean Streets* (1894), whose images of slum conditions, brutality and the daily deprivation suffered by inhabitants in working class neighborhoods caused a stir on publication. The infamy of Thomas Neill Cream, the Lambeth Poisoner, hanged in 1892 for the willful murder of four women, still lingered in the Victorian popular imagination, adding to Lambeth's already tarnished reputation and alerting readers to the shady nature of Hagar's neighborhood. The criminal Mr. William Smith conforms to the stereotypical description of the time, described by criminal anthropologist Cesare Lombroso in his 1876 study *L'Uomo Delinquente*, in which he suggests that criminal man is identifiable by physical characteristics. In harmony with Lombroso, Hume directs the reader to his striking physiology: "a low forehead, a snub nose, a large ugly mouth, and two cunning grey eyes which never looked anyone straight in the face" (154). Clearly, Mr. Smith's intimate knowledge of the penal system is emblematic of the problem of recidivism, central to debate about crime toward the end of the nineteenth century, with its focus on the existence of a class of persons for whom crime was a way of life. Mr. Smith's criminal attributes are mirrored in J. Holt Schooling's article in an 1898 issue of *Harmsworth* magazine, "Nature's Danger Signals: A Study of the Faces of Murderers." In it, his advice to readers is to listen to their instincts when faced with someone for whom you feel a "certain instinctive aversion," since it is nature's way of alerting you to danger, a response articulated by Hagar on first meeting him. Notably, in Lombroso's construction of the criminal as a member of a different race, his physiological signs pronounce him guilty in advance of criminal action.

Apart from their detention of Mr. Smith once he has deposited the mandarin in Hagar's pawnshop, the official police remain in the background throughout the story. By consulting the shady solicitor Vark to capture the criminal Smith instead of the legal representatives of the law, Hagar endorses his superior ability to resolve criminal matters over that of the official police, perhaps in the belief that it takes a criminal to capture a criminal. Ethically, Hagar's failure to act in a situation which leads to disturbing consequences, as in the case of Bolker who is threatened with death, places her actions in a morally dubious light, for a negligent conscience falls short of readers' expectations of a mythical heroine. Despite being an urban Gypsy, whose work is based in financial transactions more akin to a busy city than a rural idyll, Hagar's sexual conduct is construed in line with Gypsy codes of conduct outlined by Rodney Smith. In his experiences of growing up with the Gypsies in Victorian England, he explains that "while his people may have been pilferers of fruit and potatoes, they observed a strict moral code in other respects … he could not recall knowing even one fallen woman in a Gypsy tent" (Behlmer, 235).

"The Eighth Customer and the Pair of Boots"

In her in-depth study into the growth of police investigators in Victorian and Edwardian England entitled *The Ascent of the Detectives* (2011), Haia Shpayer-Makov raises the issue of what a reading of literary detectives tells us about public attitudes to police detectives and to the system of law enforcement as a whole from their fragile beginnings with the formation of the Metropolitan Police in 1829 to a position of prominence and power later in the nineteenth century (Shpayer-Makov, 248). A wealth of cultural, legal and social history can be read in the fictionalized relationships of literary detectives and their official counterparts through the narrativised situations of their accounts. In the previous exploration of her relationship with the official police and legality in "The Seventh Customer and the Mandarin," Hagar's relationship with the forces of law and order can be read as one in which she marginalizes them in the story, except where their involvement is crucial to the final denouement, and they are called upon to arrest and detain the criminals. An air of insecurity and doubt about her personal safety and the level of protection she receives from the police can be inferred from Hagar's use of a revolver to protect herself in the violent neighborhood of Lambeth, where police patrols may be less visible than in other areas of the city. Her willingness to use violence to counter violence shows a complex relationship with legality and a readiness to disregard legal constraints when threatened. Contrary to Shpayer-Makov's assertion that amateur detectives were "mostly gentlemen" who were "financially independent" (248), Hagar Stanley belongs to an underclass of people whose mythical, shared Jewish-gypsy ancestry links them to Orientalism and anti-Semitism in the Victorian imagination, contributing to her unconventional charm (Epstein Nord, 6).

The ninth story in the collection of *Hagar of the Pawn-shop*, "The Eighth Customer and the Pair of Boots," is significant in its highlighting and remodeling of Hagar's previous relationship with the official police force by aligning her behavior and interactions with them in keeping with that of other fictional detectives of the era: as superior in every respect despite her othered status. No longer keeping them at arm's length, as she did in the previous story, her detachment is replaced by a willingness to collaborate, as she converts into the unofficial director of operations in a murder inquiry. Supplanting the official police detective in the legal process, she solves the mystery by noting the vital missing detail in a chain of evidence that would have sent an innocent man to the gallows. Hagar's function as a mediator of justice in this story remedies judicial errors by identifying critical gaps in the knowledge of official detectives and identifying flaws in the legal process. Picking up the thread of legality in her pattern of behavior in this story causes comparisons with her fellow Gypsy protagonist, Judith Lee, to emerge. A harsh code of conduct in keeping with her biblical connections materializes in her behavior as evidences by her willingness to bend the law.

Hagar's eighth customer at the pawnshop is a "ragged barefooted urchin" called Micky Dooley, a red-haired Irish child who has been sent by his mother to pawn a pair of strong, hob-nailed, laborer's boots for which he wants seven shillings (Hume, 173). Alert to the provisions of the Pawnbroker's Act that it is illegal to accept an article in pawn from anyone under the age of twelve years of age, she takes a risk and shows compassion for the child. Noting his "sharp, keen face, intelligent beyond his years with the precocity taught by poverty," she advances the money he requests in return for the boots without too much remonstrance. His ability to haggle was quite as sharp as Hagar's as he heaved them onto the counter with a mighty clatter, and demanded seven shillings thereon:

> "I'll give you five," said Hagar, after examination.
> "Ah, now, would ye?" piped the brat, with shrill impudence. "Is it takin the bread out 'ave me mouth ye w'uld be afther? Sure, me mother sid sivin bob, an' 'tis sivin I want…. Sure it's breakin' me hid she'd be afther, wid a quart pot" [Hume, 174].

A traveller herself, Hagar identifies with Mickey's difficult circumstances and is familiar with the poverty and hardship of travelers such as he in their nomadic wanderings. Noticing the letters G. K marked in nails on the soles of the boots, she asks how he came by them. Micky replies that they were a present, before adding, "If it wasn't for thim boots we got in Marlow, it's without a copper we'd be," a sign of the depth of his poverty (174). Suspecting they may have been stolen, Hagar nevertheless places the boots on a shelf in the pawnshop and thinks no more about them until two days later when she reads in the newspaper of a murder in which the boots are mentioned as forming part of "a chain of evidence likely to hang the assassin" (175). The newspaper report claims that Sir Leslie Crane of Marlow had been shot by his gamekeeper, George Kerris, who was engaged to marry a farmer's daughter, Laura Brenton. Sir Leslie, it claimed, had been paying her more attention than he ought, and when George Kerris complained of the inappropriateness of his behavior, the gamekeeper had been sacked. A week later Sir Leslie went for a stroll and was found by a pond, shot dead. Muddy footprints close to his body revealed that the boots worn were marked with the letters G and K, obviously belonging to George Kerris, who had acquired them through a Marlow bootmaker. Arrested and charged that in a fit of jealous rage he had killed Sir Leslie and disposed of the incriminating boots and the pistol he used to commit the murder, he oddly refuses to confirm or deny his guilt.

Taking the initiative to delve into the curious developments of the boots that had been presented for pawning by Micky, and which were central to a police investigation, Hagar's perusal of the newspaper article registers discrepancies in the reported timing of events leading to the murder. She reasons from the evidence presented that since the boots had been given to Micky seven days previously, and that since Kerris had been "under lock and key" in prison at that time, he could not have given Micky the boots on that day (176). From this, she further concludes that he could not have committed the murder, and that unless she was prepared to intervene, the convincing narrative of events would lead to the death of an innocent man. The evidence in the case is purely circumstantial, for no witnesses had been present when Sir Leslie was killed. However, since the evidence seemed incontrovertible, his guilt appears certain. Circumstantial evidence, as Carol Christ explains, derives from "a visible trace," and it shows the Victorian's fascination with the way the visible could reveal events of which we have no firsthand visual knowledge (Christ, xxv). The track of the boots presents a version of finger-prints, which is acceptable as evidence in court. Alexander Welsh confirms this preoccupation with circumstantial evidence in the era, noting that it "flourished nearly everywhere—not only in literature but also in criminal jurisprudence, natural science, natural religion and history itself" (Welsh, ix). In legal proceedings involving a criminal trial, the narration of events and the presentation of evidence had previously relied on witness statements or direct testimony, often considered biased or even totally fabricated. However, the introduction of an adversarial form of trial where lawyers represented the facts rather than statements from eyewitness accounts heralded the replace-ment of direct with indirect testimony, or circumstantial evidence, mooted as more reliable through its emphasis on "facts that speak for themselves," and, unlike witnesses, they could not lie (Welsh, 8). Notably, in the same year as the publication of the story, 1898, the Criminal Evidence Act confirmed that "from the moment a suspect is arrested by the police until the end of his or her trial he or she has the right to remain silent" when questioned by police. However, the difficulty still remained that refusal to speak "was often considered as an admission of guilt," as John Hostettler informs in his work *A History of Criminal Justice in England and Wales* (241).

Although George Kerris had refused to give testimony on his own be-half, his reliance on any alternative narrative would be unsupported by the facts, and his class status in relation to other suspects in the case also places him at a disadvantage. Hagar surmises that since "[n]o-one would let themselves be hanged for a murder which they did not commit," there must be an accomplice whom Kerris wishes to protect (176). Entering into the full spirit of the law, Hagar contacts the police. They send Julf, "a lean, tall, dark and solemn creature" who "had a conscience" and "would never forgive himself" for "hang[ing] the wrong criminal" (177). The figure of the official detective in the narrative is portrayed in sympathetic terms as he describes "how often circumstantial evidence helped to condemn the innocent" and how likely "even the most acute detective was to be deceived by outward appearances," showing his awareness of the fallibility of evidence (177). In his discussions with Hagar, we learn how impressed he is with her insight and how she enters fully into his confidence in terms of the details of the case. Her close liaison with the detective positions her firmly on the side of law and order, in contrast to the previous story in which the official police figured simply as symbols of narrative closure.

"I wish I had this case in my own hands," states Hagar during a lengthy debate with Julf in which she raises a number of salient points related to the evidence. Those points include the whereabouts of the missing pistol used in the murder and the question of finding Micky to prove Kerris's innocence, for upon his evidence the whole case turns (178). The detective Julf takes no exception to her promoting her own more skillful abilities to extrapolate details over his and declares his belief that the strength of the evidence is convincing enough to prove Kerris's guilt. Hagar's reflection that she would like prime authority to lead the case presents a critique of the legal approach to circumstantial evidence, whereby police fail to ensure all the links in a chain of evidence are secure before arresting a suspect. Critical of the administration of justice in a system heavily reliant on how facts are interpreted, she credits narratives other than the most obvious one followed by the police. In investigations they frequently mistake the wrongdoer and continue to cast around for evidence to support their convictions rather than trawling more widely to find all the possible suspects. In elevating Hagar to a position of dominance over the official detective, it is worth considering Kathleen Gregory Klein's assertion that, unlike the police who are "bound by bureaucracy, hierarchies and politics," the fictional female detective "has no client responsibility and no commitment to investigation as a profession" (Klein, 6). Her accepted lack of credentials means that readers have no standard against which to compare her. Following the guidelines of his profession from this perspective, Julf operates in a competent and acceptable way, but he is outmaneuvered by the narrative imposition of an alternative reading of the crime. The weak link in the chain of evidence produced by the police, and identified by Hagar, is that Kerris was in prison when Micky was given the boots. By finding Micky, they would discover who had given him the boots, and by locating the missing pistol, the case would be solved.

The story takes Hagar to Marlow in search of evidence to support her theory that Kerris is innocent, which means a journey into the country away from the stultifying atmosphere of Lambeth and the opportunity for "a breath of fresh air" (179). By this stage in the investigation, Julf, despite still being convinced of Kerris's guilt, meets Hagar at the train station, and offers her a "free hand in resolving the mystery" (180). Declaring, "You see I have agreed to let you assist me in finding out the truth in this case; though to my mind the truth is already plain enough," he places responsibility for the inquiry into her capable hands and could be accused of compromising his professional integrity (179). By giving Hagar the duty of resolving the mystery, the detective process enters the realm of an alternate reality, for it is inconceivable that her intervention would be sought in this way in real-life. Confident of her investigative ability, Julf delegates the role of unsupervised interrogation of the new baronet, Sir Lewis Crane, the brother of the murdered man, at his residence in Welby Park. In an allusion to Hagar's racial background, we learn that "at first, owing to her gipsy-like appearance, she was refused admittance; but on mentioning that her business had to do with the murder of the late baronet, Sir Lewis consented to see her" (180). Having astutely summed him up as a "miser" with a "mean, yellow face stamped with an expression of avarice," she tells Sir Lewis that she has "come on the part of Mr. Julf to see about this murder," to which he remarks, "I did not know that the Government employed lady detectives!" (180). Unabashed, Hagar clarifies her position as the representative of Julf rather than as an official employee, prompting Sir Lewis to agree to answer her questions about the murder without further demur. By inverting the power relations in this scene, whereby the marginalized female Gypsy has authority to question a member of the aristocracy on intimate family matters, Hume presents a radical view of gender and class status. The extent of Hume's innovative elevation of Hagar Stanley to a position of dominance over a member of the aristocracy is remarkable in the light of Victorian perceptions of the status of Gypsies.

After an incisive interrogation of Sir Lewis, Hagar asks to be shown the pond where she believes the missing pistol may be found. She discovers from the servants that Sir Lewis frequently argued with his brother Sir Leslie, who "hadn't a sixpence but what he got from Sir Lewis," thus providing her with his motive for the murder (182). She also discovers that he had quarreled about Laura Brenton with Sir Leslie, for he too was infatuated with her. Laura Brenton, for her part, accuses Sir Lewis of his brother's murder and is described as being in a highly emotional state. Having searched the scene of the crime for the missing pistol, Hagar locates it in a marble urn. Sir Lewis Crane's name is engraved on the silver plates, proving that he committed the murder. Establishing an alternative narrative solution to the circumstances, Hagar is still dissatisfied because of Kerris's refusal to deny the murder and pursues a further interpretation of events involving Laura Brenton. With the revelation that Sir Lewis is suspected of the murder, Hagar tricks Kerris into confirming his innocence. Julf arrives in time to disclose that Micky had been found and had identified Laura Brenton as the person who had given him the boots, pointing to her as the murderer. Sir Leslie "had promised to marry her, and because she could not force him to keep that promise she killed him," perhaps confirming that she had a compromised sexual relationship with him, whilst deceiving George Kerris into believing she loved him (189). In presenting a range of potential narrative solutions to the circumstances of the crime, Hagar signals the precarious nature of untested circumstantial evidence as the sole criterion for judging innocence or guilt in a court of law. The case validates Welsh's contention that "where testimony is built on inferences," proof requires that the chain of evidence should be constructed from "circumstances causally connected in a believable narrative … that connoted strong connections, links of iron, but also a story that fell apart if one of the links was broken" (Welsh, 4).

Pointing up discrepancies in the presentation of evidence forms a central theme in the story, which also posits Hagar's dogged commitment to the truth and her estimable ethical conduct in pursuing the mystery to its coherent conclusion. Allowing Hagar to impersonate a police assistant in a murder inquiry and sanctioning her interrogation of suspects constitutes a breach of professional conduct by Julf and amounts to a case of fraudulent deception on the part of Hagar. Tied to restrictive procedures and with accountability to higher authorities, Julf would be unable to use his sole discretion to resolve the case. By consigning it to Hagar, who continues to pursue the investigation thoroughly and omitting nothing in terms of evidence, Hagar prevents a travesty of justice, allowing the reader to commend her moral values and conduct. Kerris's ability to achieve justice as a member of the working class without Hagar's intervention would be questionable. As Sir Edward Abbott Parry, an honorable judge, noted in his work examining judicial bias in the application of the law, *The Law and the Poor* (1914), "In every age your judge will be tinged with the prejudices of his time and his class, and I cannot see how you can expect to grow middle-class judges in hot beds of middle-class prejudices without the natural formation of a certain amount of middle-class bias in the thickness of their middle-class wood" (Parry, 100). He goes on to explain how "wealth and position" are deciding factors in achieving favorable treatment in the criminal courts. Hagar, who is not an official public servant, assumes the mantle of savior of the innocent and, to some extent, rehabilitates the reputation of the detectives, whose credibility had suffered due to widespread corruption and negative press coverage in the 1870s and 1880s. In actively participating in the inquiry, she is instrumental in promoting what Shpayer-Makov refers to as a "certain shift" in public attitudes after the turn of the century toward greater appreciation for the performance of Scotland Yard detectives in literary works (253). Noting the arrival on the scene in 1904 of B. Fletcher Robinson's Inspector Peace of the CID in *The Chronicles of Addington Peace*, she points out that his literary depiction as a "highly intelligent, civil and somewhat mysterious bachelor with principles" recalibrates his skills in line with those of the amateur detective (253). Equally committed to promoting the image of Scotland Yard as a great machine designed by society to uphold law and order, Vivian Grey's *Stories of Scotland Yard*, published in 1906, dramatizes their skills as "masterful," leading to their elevation in the public consciousness (254). By conferring with the detectives, as Hagar does, the image of unreasonable tunnel vision in dealing with crime prevalent in Victorian and Edwardian detective fiction is reformed. Her actions give credence to Oliver Wendell Holmes's contention that "the community cannot be enforced by laws that go against the individual conscience," and literary characters will reject its mandates if they believe it is unrepresentative of their moral outlook.

CATHERINE LOUISA PIRKIS (1839–1910): LOVEDAY BROOKE (1893)

The pages of *Ludgate Monthly Magazine* hosted the career of the fictional female detective, Loveday Brooke, in six stories from February to July 1893, with a further story added to the collection, *The Experiences of Loveday Brooke, Lady Detective*, published in March 1894. The last work of fiction of its author, Catherine Louisa Pirkis, its importance lies in the creation of a female professional detective, penned by a woman, who challenges not only gendered stereotypes but also the newly crafted scientific definitions of criminality of the day, outlined in the works of Havelock Ellis and Francis Galton. With dubious morality, she roots out crime as an undercover operative in domestic spheres, placing her methods and actions in the category of spy.

3. The Female Gaze

Her liminality lies in her willingness to infiltrate private homes where no male detective could hope to trespass, and where she is privy to personal lives and family secrets not genuinely deserved. In her presentation as a female detective who works for a living, holds no aspirations for matrimony and who is completely dedicated to her profession, she personifies Gissing's odd woman. Electing to live an independent, mobile and self-sufficient lifestyle, she also typifies the New Woman. Pirkis was already an established novelist and journalist with an active interest in the anti-vivisection movement before submitting her final work to the *Ludgate Monthly* and taking up activism full-time as the chairman of the National Canine Defense League. The second of six stories from the collection, *The Experiences of Loveday Brooke, Lady Detective,* "The Murder at Troyte's Hill" is significant in its challenge to scientific theories of criminality that propose a method of identifying criminals through their physical characteristics. In suggesting that beautiful faces are rarely found among criminals, Havelock Ellis's work *The Criminal* (1890) lays the groundwork for eugenicist beliefs that later contributed to Nazi atrocities. "In it he asserts that, 'prejudice against the ugly and also against the deformed is not without foundation,'" equating outer ugliness and disability with inner immorality. In Pirkis's stories, the mad and bad do not conform to the stereotypical casting of ugly, poor or foreign, but are those whom society ranks as beyond suspicion: physically attractive, seemingly rational and well-educated, and giving every semblance of innocence. Loveday Brooke, Pirkis's female detective, is a woman of average appearance, defined as neither fair nor dark, handsome nor ugly, her common sense and pragmatism are well suited to her job as detective. In her ability to slide almost unnoticed into company across class divides, she prefigures Agatha Christie's Miss Marple when she adopts a range of functions in households that enable her to gain access to the details of crime, reminiscent of Magdalen in Wilkie Collins's *No Name* (1862).

Ebenezer Dyer, the head of a flourishing Fleet Street detective agency, informs Loveday Brooke of the murder of Mr. Sandy Henderson, the lodge-keeper at Troyte's Hill. Griffiths of the Newcastle Constabulary has requested her services as an agent to investigate the domestic sphere in which it occurred. Death was caused by a heavy blow from a blunt instrument, and the murderer then ransacked the cottage. The clock was turned over, and the bedclothes were rolled into a bundle and stuffed up the chimney in a baffling crime reminiscent of Edgar Allan Poe's "The Murders in the Rue Morgue" (1841). Robbery is not the motive, and the general consensus is that a passing tramp or lunatic is the perpetrator. The household comprises Mr. and Mrs. Craven and the young Miss and Master Craven, along with a body

109

of long-standing servants. Griffiths has determined that the young Master Craven is the culprit, for he declares him to be "a thoroughly bad sort and as much a gentleman blackleg as it is possible to be"; his appearance marks him out as criminal, confirmed in his wayward behavior and gambling debts (Slung, 32). Mr. Craven senior, on the other hand, is "a quiet old fellow, a scholar and learned philologist" who broke down when giving evidence at the inquest into Sandy's death and alluded to the "confidential relations" that existed between the murder victim and himself (32). Identifying the most likely suspect by appearances, Griffiths sets about finding the evidence to convict the young Craven while Loveday diverges into a different path of inquiry. Engaged as an amanuensis for Mr. Craven senior, her role places her on a par with a nursery governess: slightly below a lady's maid but above a housemaid. In assuming a disguise in a fictitious role in order to criminalize a member of the family, her moral conduct is questionable, for the use of deceit to weed out information in a private family setting marks her out as spying on the family. On the other hand, the sanctity of middle-class homes made it near impossible for the official police to investigate domestic crimes. This difficulty is made clear in the murder at Hill House in 1860, when Inspector Jonathan Whicher was tasked with finding the murderer of Francis-Saville Kent, a child of almost four years of age. Concentrating on a missing nightdress that belonged to Constance Kent, the sixteen-year-old daughter of Mr. Kent from his first marriage, Whicher was heavily criticized for invading the domestic affairs of the family and for accusing Constance of the murder. His accusation ruined his reputation, which never recovered. Constance later admitted the murder, and elements of the story were later used in several literary works, including Wilkie Collins's *The Moonstone* (1868), Mary Elizabeth Braddon's *Lady Audley's Secret* (1862) and Dickens's *The Mystery of Edwin Drood* (1870).

It transpires that Sandy was disliked by most of the servants for his high-handed ways and for his interference in household affairs beyond his station that Mr. Craven failed to rebuke. Aware of the suspicions surrounding young Master Craven, Mrs. Craven fabricates a plan to keep him out of harm's way, informing the household that he is in the grip of typhoid fever and cannot be disturbed. Miss Craven and the servants who are worried about infection are bundled off to friends and family, whilst Mrs. Craven undertakes to care for him and rejects all requests to visit him. Griffiths tells Loveday to investigate the invalid and find out where he was on the night of Sandy's murder. Loveday meets Mr. Craven senior the morning after her arrival and describes him as "a man of really handsome personal appearance, with a fine carriage of the head and shoulders, and eyes that had a forlorn appealing look in them" (35). He almost lives in his study, writing a treatise in seven or eight volumes on comparative philology. Having returned from Natal on the death of his brother to take up residency in Troyte's Hill, he has trouble making ends meet, yet increases the lodge-keeper's wages to the extent that the butler had to take a pay cut. A congenial gentleman, evidence of mental illness emerges when he discusses his work at breakfast and falls into a reverie. Loveday advises Griffiths, "As a matter of collateral interest find out if a person, calling himself Harold Cousins sailed two days ago from London Docks for Natal in the *Bonnie Dundee.*" Griffiths is puzzled by this advice and tells her he has found evidence incriminating the young Master Craven. He had stolen some valuable plate from the house and visited McQueen, a lowly innkeeper, asking him to lend him one hundred pounds on it. Griffiths turns up the next day with his constables to arrest young Master Craven in his sick room, only to discover that his sister has engaged in cross-dressing to give him time to escape to Natal on the *Bonnie Dundee,* as Loveday had deduced. On an evening walk around the grounds, Loveday discovers the dead retriever, Captain, bludgeoned in the same way as Sandy, confirming her belief that the killer is mentally unstable. She notifies Griffiths to come immediately and goes to work in the study with Mr. Craven. Awaking from one of his reveries, his character transformation surfaces gradually as Loveday persuades him to reveal the truth. Until 1912 the rules for extracting confessions from suspects by police had no guidance in law. By then complaints about the procedures used to elicit confessions had been the subject of comments, both judicial and otherwise, as T.E. St. Johnston advises (85). "Judges Rules" were set up to prevent breaches of citizen's rights and included "no inducements, threats or trickery" in extracting a confession. Loveday's method of extracting a confession from Mr. Craven would most likely in the twentieth century prevent its use as admissible evidence, given how she coaxes and leads him sympathetically to admit guilt for the crime. A further rule endorsed by "Judges Rules" relates how groups such as the mentally handicapped should only be interviewed in the presence of an appropriate adult. "He must have been a bad man, that Sandy," she suggests (50). To which he responds by springing from his chair and seizing her by the hand, declaring, "If ever man deserved his death, he did. For thirty years he held the rod over my head, and then—ah, where was I?" (50). She wheedles the truth out of him, discovering that an earlier indiscretion when Mr. Craven had married a disreputable barmaid in his youth gave Sandy power over him. Mr. Craven had killed Sandy and the dog in an attempt to crystallize his theory on elemental sounds emitted in agony. Seizing a large geological hammer, he locks the door and pockets the key, ready to test his theories on her and whispers with his lips close to her ear, "It has only this moment occurred to me that a woman in her death agony, would be much more likely to give utterance to an elemental sound than a man" (54). Fortunately, at this moment Griffiths and his constables seize her and drag her through the open window to safety.

Mr. Craven's madness remains buried throughout the investigation because his probity remains unchallenged—his outward respectability, charming manners and handsome appearance mask the serious nature of his mental condition, attributed to eccentricity. However, the fact that Mr. Craven successfully deceived the inquest about his relationship with Sandy raises questions as to whether he was genuinely insane. His actions in ridding himself of a tyrannical blackmailer imply premeditation, even though he justifies his actions as performed for the greater good of academia. Similarly, in locking Loveday into the study and pocketing the key with the intention of murdering her, he displays a certain amount of rational thinking, indicating mens rea. Establishing cases of insanity in criminal trials was notably contentious. The politics of mental health came under scrutiny following the publication of details about the wrongful confinement of Louisa Lowe in 1883, Georgina Weldon in 1879 and Lady Rosina Bulwer Lytton in 1880 (Bachmann, 6). New legislation in the form of "The Lunacy Act" of 1890 established legal control over asylums, requiring extra authorization from a Justice of the Peace to validate confinement and regular inspections to ensure legal practice. The changes in the law only applied to private institutions, which it was hoped would be phased out, and pauper asylums remained as they were. As Roger Smith explains, the psychiatry profession saw the legal interventions as an assault on their professionalism, and the battle between legal and medical definitions of insanity intensified (*Trial by Medicine*). The argument revolved around the medical belief, based on scientific knowledge of neurophysiology, that madness was a somatic condition, in contrast to the legal definition "where the intention was central to determining the presence or absence of mental states." With the use of medical experts in trials becoming more widespread in the late nineteenth and twentieth century, the medical expert, Mr. Henry Charlton Bastion, was engaged to testify at several trials in the 1890s. At the trial of Joseph Wood, charged with the murder of his daughter, Nelly Wood, on March 13, 1890, he offers his opinion:

> When I first saw the prisoner, I saw that he was a man of low type of head, nothing very noticeable, except a peculiarity about the pupil of the eye which is very commonly met with in epilepsy ... it was so marked that I drew Dr. Gilbert's attention to it ... his pulse was extremely irregular and intermittent rather unnaturally slow ... there does seem to have been insanity in three generations of the family [t18900519-457].

His conclusion was that he could find no evidence of insanity but that Joseph

Wood was an epileptic. His findings concur with Ellis's construction of criminality as a hereditary disease where he declares:

> The influence of heredity, even in the strict sense of the word, in the production of criminals does not always lie in the passing on of developed proclivities. Sometimes a generation of criminals is merely one stage in the progressive degeneration of a family [*The Criminal*, 92].

In debunking such wild theories, Pirkis played an important role in shedding light on the illusion that criminality, low intelligence and insanity were linked. Her female detective, one of twelve in the period between 1890 and 1910, according to Kathleen Klein (56), defied convention by subverting gender norms and fulfilling a vital role in the detection of crime, when in real life no women police officers existed until 1915.

Absent from courtrooms, either as jury members, barristers or judges, women could only achieve fictional redress in the usurpation of authority for dispensing judgments and gender transcendence in the way they deliver it. Since it was not until 1918 with the Representation of the People Act that women over thirty achieved a measure of suffrage in recognition of their work in the Great War, the female protagonists in this study outdo their male counterparts in subverting both gender and legal ideology. The year 1918 was also significant for the enactment of a bill to allow women to stand for Parliament and heralded the arrival of Lady Astor as the first woman to be elected to Parliament the following year. In her account of "British Women's Emancipation Since the Reformation," Helena Wojtczak advises that 1919 ushered in the Sex Disqualification (Removal) Act, which paved the way for women to enter the professions (www.historyofwomen.org).

Conclusion

Despite the profusion of fictional female detectives, and in particular Baroness Orczy's official female detective, Lady Molly of Scotland Yard, who was head of the Female Department of the Yard in 1910, it was not until 1919 that the Metropolitan Police appointed its first woman police officer, Sofia Stanley. They waited until 1921 before appointing the first female Inspector of the Criminal Investigations Department. Haia Shpayer-Makov notes that prior to this moment, women who were admitted to the force were involved in "conducting searches of female suspects"; "guarding female prisoners and taking statements: unlike their fictional counterparts, they were never part of the ordinary police force" (83). The female detectives in this study each have a different approach to questions of moral decision-making in response to crime. For Judith Lee, the ability to recognize the morally important aspects of a situation embolden her to disregard legality when adhering to it would cause further harm. Despite encountering racial intolerance, she does her utmost to ensure the safety and wellbeing of others in a spirit of generosity that endangers her own reputation if discovered. Her approach is in line with a virtue ethical direction in this instance. In contrast to Lee, Hagar's talionic approach to justice in seeking an eye for an eye iterates a form of justice practiced in both biblical and early Roman law. Defined by the *Encyclopedia Britannica*, Roger L. Lévesque explains that such an approach to justice is centered on retaliation for harm inflicted to be returned in equal measure. "Proportionality is inherently a retributive concept, and perfect proportionality is the talionic law," he advises (532). Hagar is in tune with the community she inhabits and responds to crime in a way that harmonizes with the way of life in Lambeth. Rather than adhering to a body of law rigidly imposed without due consideration of the life experiences of those living in her neighborhood, she operates outside legal processes and delivers fairer outcomes. As Emsley points out, the police were always troubled about "pawnbrokers acting as receivers," yet they "provided a vital financial service within these [urban working class] communities" by helping the poor survive until the next wages arrived (*Crime and Society,* 178). The legal standing of pawnshop owners in the Victorian era was often under scrutiny, evidenced in the number of trials brought to the Old Bailey with accusations leveled against them, implying their liminal status as sites for the redistribution of stolen goods. At the end of the Hagar series, in keeping with the Romantic vision of gypsies as exotic and mysterious, she finds true love and returns to the nomadic open-air lifestyle, unlike Judith Lee, who remains an unattached professional detective throughout. As for Loveday Brooke, her resemblance to the real-life detective Kate Warne, the first female detective in the United States, employed by the Pinkerton detective agency between 1856 and 1861, is striking. Describing her in his book *The Spy of the Rebellion* in 1883, Pinkerton remarks on her "handsome, honest and intellectual appearance" and her ability to root out criminals in private spaces, echoing the attributes of Loveday Brooke. With a professional eye to the beneficial consequences of her actions to the community rather than their impact on the rights of the individual, her behavior is consequentialist in nature.

4

From Detective to Spy

Justice for the Greater Good

"Good old Watson! You are the one fixed point in a changing age.
There's an east wind coming all the same, such a wind as never blew on England yet.
It will be cold and bitter, Watson, and a good many of us may wither before its blast"
["His Last Bow," 622].

In a solemn warning to the House of Lords on July 10, 1905, Earl Roberts of Kandahar, the hero of the Boer War, voiced his outrage at the lack of spending on military expansion. He declared, "History tells us in the plainest terms that an Empire which cannot defend its own possessions must inevitably perish" (Le Queux, *Invasion,* 4). His warning comes in the wake of expenditure cuts to the military budget and at a time when Edwardian society experienced a "crisis of confidence" that started in the 1880s and gathered momentum toward the end of the Victorian age, creating a growing sense of pessimism about Britain's fading global influence and vulnerable status. England was once "the superpower of the day," dominating the seas and holding sway over more than four hundred million people; now a sense of foreboding prevailed (Poplawski, 529, 532). General apprehension arose in response to the fashion for Invasion literature established in the 1870s with works like George Tomkyns Chesney's *Battle of Dorking* (1871) about the consequences of German attack and invasion of England, which heralded the advent of spy fiction at the beginning of the twentieth century.

Also contributing to national anxiety at the end of the century was concern over the nation's health, evidenced during recruitment campaigns for the Boer War when an overwhelming number of young men were rejected as unfit for service due to malnutrition and ill health. Public awareness in the period detected a "new sort of crime," linked to the existence of spies and the harm posed by foreign threats, not to individuals or property, but to the state, as Ernest Mandel explains in *Delightful Murder* (1984). He suggests that new structures of society engender new types of crime story reflecting the current values and principles (64). From 1880 until 1914, tales

115

of future warfare gained in popularity and spawned the emergence of spy fiction by writers like William Le Queux and E. Phillips Oppenheim, whose works reflected the rivalry of great powers and the dangers they posed to national security. Each international crisis, such as the alliance of France with Russia in 1894 or the Fashoda incident in 1898, was explored in fictionalized accounts where patriotism triumphed over a despicable enemy, initially France and Russia, and later Germany. Incidents of critical national concern called for the interventions of brave and indomitable spies in the public imagination to ensure the safety of the nation, protect vital security intelligence and ensure the safekeeping of pioneering plans for defense capability and weaponry (Clarke, 95). Conscious of the public appetite for narrative solutions to foreign incursions into national sovereignty, popular writers tapped into the world of international intrigue and fear of impending disaster. In its rooting out of enemy aliens and the protection of state secrets, the new genre of spy fiction readily accommodated the profile of detective and sleuth, prompting the transformation of well-known detectives into spies. For popular writers like Conan Doyle, Morrison, Muddock and most of the writers in this study, conscious of market trends, the recasting of familiar detective figures as detective-cum-spy is straightforward, yet requires a new code of conduct justifying moral realignments to accommodate the new role. Already adept in negotiating the vagaries of the law in circumstances where it proves to be more of a hindrance than a benefit, their decision-making is based on the unique context of the situation, taking into account a range of factors other than the purely legal and using means that would otherwise offend their sense of morality. Adopting a pragmatic stance to legality, in keeping with the principles of William James's philosophy of pragmatism that emerged in the 1890s, they consider the implication of their actions for the future wellbeing of the country rather than the strict limitations of legal boundaries. In its concern for concrete results rather than abstract notions of justice, James's pragmatism rejects static perceptions of morality and custom, advocating instead actions linked to the practical consequences of conduct for the community.

In this chapter, as the detective is recast as embryonic spy, I explore his infractions of the law, together with the methods he uses to achieve his purposes, and seek to identify the ways in which the boundaries of morality and legality alter his behavior in the face of threats to national security. In the stories under review, the theft of secret documents and England's complacent response to alien threats is countered through the mediation of Sherlock Holmes, Martin Hewitt, Dick Donovan and Judith Lee. Arthur Conan Doyle's Sherlock Holmes provides the initial platform for investigation in two stories from the canon. Beginning with "The Adventure of the Second Stain," first published in short story form in the December 1904 edition of the *Strand Magazine* and subsequently in the collection *The Return of Sherlock Holmes* in 1905, it provides an insight into the prevalence of foreign spies in the center of urban London and exposes the deviance of an upper-class client whose treasonous behavior escapes criminalization and the loss of reputation. The second Holmes story for review is "His Last Bow: The War Service of Sherlock Holmes," which locates Holmes as a full-fledged wartime spy in his final appearance in the *Strand Magazine* of September 1917, the same year as Conan Doyle's journalistic reports on "The British Campaign in France," where he charts the progress of the war. Arthur Morrison's Martin Hewitt assumes the role of sleuthing spy in the fourth story of the first collection *Martin Hewitt: Investigator*, published in 1894, in "The Case of the Dixon Torpedo." It mirrors elements of Conan Doyle's "The Adventure of the Naval Treaty" (1893) in dealing with the theft of plans for a top-secret weapon by Russian government spies who are threatening the future security of the nation. In "The Strange Story of Some State Papers," Muddock's Dick Donovan is approached by the Austrian Ambassador to the Court of St James's to uncover the traitor who has stolen a draft treaty likely to endanger international relations. Finally, Richard Marsh's female detective, Judith Lee, proves equally competent in her role as secret agent, embarking on a close encounter with German spies in the fifth story of the second collection, *The Adventures of Judith Lee*, "Two Words," published in 1916, where she nullifies the threat they present to England's air defenses in a show of gamesmanship and double-cross.

Sherlock Holmes, "The Adventure of the Second Stain" (1904)

Under the laws of the United Kingdom, high treason is the crime of disloyalty to the Crown, and until 1870 it was punishable by being hung, drawn and quartered if one were a man and burnt at the stake if one were a woman. The severity of the punishment was such that juries were often unwilling to convict defendants, which in turn led to changes in the law designed to ensure the conviction of traitors while protecting the security of the state. The last person to be sentenced to death in this way was Colonel Edward Despard in 1803 when he was found guilty, along with six accomplices, of organizing a conspiracy against the British government and of planning an assassination attempt on George III. As John Gardner points out, there were eight executions for High Treason in 1820. Five were in London, including

Arthur Thistlewood and his co-conspirators in the Cato Street Conspiracy; they were hanged and decapitated on a conviction of treason for trying to assassinate the cabinet. The Cathkin Rebellion in Glasgow resulted in one execution, with a further two executions taking place in Bonnymuir, Stirling, during the Radical War of Scottish Insurrection (Gardner, John, "Preventing Revolution: Cato Street, Bonnymuir, and Cathkin"). The Treason Felony Act of 1848, some of which is still in force today, created a new offense known as treason felony with a maximum sentence of life imprisonment. *The Old Bailey Proceedings Online* relates how on April 20, 1885, James George Gilbert and Harry Burton were indicted under this act and charged with "feloniously conspiring with other persons whose names are unknown to depose the Queen from her Royal name and style of Queen of Great Britain and Ireland" in commissioning an explosion in Victoria Station in London; they were sentenced to penal servitude for life (*OBO,* t18850420-532). This could have been the fate of Lady Hilda Trelawney Hope and Sherlock Holmes who colluded with her to conceal her crime of treason in "The Adventure of the Second Stain," one of thirteen stories in the collection *The Return of Sherlock Holmes.* Released for publication in 1904 and set in the late 1880s, this adventure is credited by Watson as "the most important international case" that Holmes has ever been called upon to handle (Conan Doyle, 536). Holmes makes his entry into the newly evolving spy fiction genre, pioneered by Rudyard Kipling in his novel *Kim* (1901) and Erskine Childers in his critically acclaimed novel *The Riddle of the Sands* (1903), by rising to the challenge of espionage and proving to be a worthy combatant. An earlier encounter with international diplomacy occurred in 1893 in "The Adventure of the Naval Treaty" when Holmes was called upon to recover an important naval treaty, stolen from the offices of Mr. Percy Phelps, an old schoolmate of Watson's. Tailoring his disregard for the legal processes to the exigencies of state security in "The Adventure of the Second Stain," he proves himself an able and effective government agent whose deductive abilities enable him to prevent both war and scandal. International tensions existed at the time in terms of military alliances and provide a framework for the events, which mirror Britain holding a tenuous balance of power in Europe. Prior to the publication of the story, Britain signed the Entente Cordiale, joining France and Russia against Germany and Austro-Hungary, a treaty referenced in one of the stories (Poplawski, 520). Despite his unofficial status as spy in the narrative, Holmes's undoubted success and renown as a skilled detective, coupled with his brother Mycroft's connections, place him in a unique position of trust and authority. It becomes clear from investigation of Holmes's response to complex matters of state that he is ready to abandon the dictates of due legal process in cases of national significance and is willing for morality to take a back seat to pragmatism as the order of the day.

In "The Adventure of the Second Stain," Lord Bellinger, the British Prime Minister, and the Right Honorable Trelawney Hope, Secretary for European Affairs, entreat Holmes to recover a document stolen from Hope's dispatch box, which he kept for safekeeping in his bedroom at home. The only people in residence that evening were his wife and loyal servants, whom he trusts implicitly. After an initial show of reticence about sharing the details of state secrets included in the documents, the ministers are forced to accept Holmes's terms of full disclosure. It transpires that the missing document is a letter written by a foreign potentate, possibly Kaiser Wilhelm II, according to Baring-Gould, in which he uses indiscreet and inflammatory language to express his outrage at Britain's behavior regarding recent colonial developments (304). If the letter were to be published, it would lead to serious breaches of trust, heightened tension and the likelihood of hostility in the region expressed by the Premier: "There would be such a ferment, sir, that within a week of the publication of that letter this country would be involved in a great war" (537). The idea of a provocative letter providing the catalyst for war evokes the circumstances surrounding the Franco-Prussian War of 1870–71, when Prussia goaded France into a war by means of an incendiary letter: Bismarck's "Ems Dispatch" (Wawro, 34). It also echoes Britain's later interception of the Zimmerman Telegram in 1916 using "SIGINT" [signals intelligence], sent to the German Ambassador in Mexico proposing that Germany would be willing to assist Mexico to acquire Texas, Arizona and New Mexico in the event that the United States joined the Allies against Germany in WW1. The telegram was communicated to the U.S. government "as an inducement for it to join the war on the side of the embattled Europeans" (Hitz, 163).

Having established the significance of the stolen letter, Holmes questions to whom a thief would take such a missive and concludes that the likely recipients would be one of three top international spies and secret agents whose names were "tolerably familiar to me" and about whose whereabouts he seems very well informed (Conan Doyle, 538). Holmes proves his capability to act as spy through his knowledge of all the foreign intelligence agents operating in London, naming Oberstein, La Rothière and Eduardo Lucas as those "capable of playing so bold a game" (538). The government approach to Holmes begs the question why the special section of CID, forerunner to Special Branch, was not consulted along with Holmes. As an organization set up in 1883, its specific role was to counteract the terrorist threat of the Irish Republican Brotherhood and later to dedicate itself entirely to intelligence gathering and running operations designed to frustrate the subversive activities of continental anarchists (Andrew, 5). The lack of suitable intelligence personnel may relate to Stephen Wade's observation that from the 1880s onwards, it was impossible for Britain to successfully manage "espionage and the military intelligence" of such a vast empire (Wade, 145). And, as Christopher Andrew explains: "The myth of a far-flung intelligence network," encouraged by a range of Edwardian writers, such as Kipling and William Le Queux, had "the incidental advantage of avoiding public revelation of British intelligence weakness" (Andrew, 4). He recounts that rather than an efficient intelligence agency, the British operation was small and underfunded, spending much of its time and resources on Irish Republican terrorism (Andrew, 3). For the purposes of the story, we must assume that Holmes's connection with his brother, Mycroft, who is well known in government circles, coupled with his superior knowledge, deductive ability and gentlemanly status precluded the need for the involvement of anyone else. Further, it may reflect the minister's belief that a discreet individual agent like Holmes would be more successful in preventing an international incident, and, importantly, his amateur status allows him to function outside the law if need be.

Lady Hilda Trelawney Hope, wife of the European Secretary, arrives at Baker Street in a state of flux immediately following her husband's departure. On her visit to Holmes, Watson, ever appreciative of feminine allure, describes her in glowing terms, largely with respect to her physical attributes. She is imbued with "subtle delicate charm" and "queenly presence," which frame feminine innocence and virtue afflicted by tragedy, echoing similar portrayals of women in crises, such as Helen Stoner in "The Speckled Band" and Mary Sutherland in "A Case of Identity" (Conan Doyle, 539). Declaring her only desire in visiting Holmes to be the search for information to protect her husband's interests, she questions whether his political career would likely suffer as a result of the theft of the documents, to which Holmes naturally replies affirmatively. Characterized as a woman deeply immersed in her role in the private sphere, dedicated to her husband and his career yet unaware of the importance of her husband's role in government, she explains to Holmes:

> There is complete confidence between my husband and me on all matters save one. That one is politics. On this his lips are sealed. He tells me nothing. Now, I am aware that there was a most deplorable occurrence in our house last night. I know that a paper has disappeared. But because the matter is political my husband refuses to take me into his complete confidence. Now it is essential—essential, I say—that I should thoroughly understand it [539].

Holmes refuses to divulge any of the particulars of her husband's meeting with him, and after her departure, he speculates on her motives for visiting him, concluding, finally, that her actions are propelled by conjugal devotion rather than otherwise. Initially perplexed in his search for the missing letter, we are left in no doubt of its importance to national and international security when Holmes declares, "If it's on the market I'll buy it if it means another penny on the income tax" (538). In a plot reminiscent of Edgar Allan Poe's "The Purloined Letter" (1844), he uncovers Lady Hilda's culpability and the way in which she procured the letter for the spy, Eduardo Lucas of Godolphin Street, who was subsequently found, murdered at home, by his estranged wife. Holmes receives hourly reports from the government on whether any trouble has yet arisen in response to the theft of the letter and is finally conducted to the murder scene, where he observes "an ugly irregular stain upon the carpet" (541). The clue to the puzzle emerges when he discovers the stain on the carpet does not match the one on the floor underneath, proving it has been moved. Beneath the carpet is a hinged cavity, now empty, but once clearly used to conceal the letter. Lady Hilda, who is the thief, is confronted by Holmes over her crime and admits that Lucas was blackmailing her with an indiscreet letter she had written before her marriage: "a foolish letter, a letter of an impulsive, loving girl" she declares, affirming, "I meant no harm, and yet he [her husband] would have thought it criminal" (544). Only when threatened with exposure does she finally confess to Holmes how she came to steal the document from her husband using a duplicate key and, through a series of events, managed to regain possession of it by returning to Lucas's house and retrieving it after the murder. The final difficulty she faces is how to replace the letter without alerting her husband to her treachery, an obstacle which Holmes removes. The prevalence of foreign spies in Britain at that time, initially, "most prominently from Imperial Russia," was linked to the arrival of a large population of foreigners, including anarchists and revolutionaries who sought refuge and asylum in the country, as Shpayer-Makov explains (58). In response to Lady Hilda's initial denials that she has the letter in her possession, Holmes is patient yet persistent, declaring that only if she gives up the letter will he be able to avoid a scandal. He insists, "Give up the letter, and all will be set right. If you will work with me, I can arrange everything. If you work against me, I must expose you." In his desire to protect Lady Hilda, Holmes's chivalric spirit springs to the defense of a conscience-stricken aristocratic woman and entails conspiracy to conceal a criminal act (Conan Doyle, 544). In the final denouement, Holmes colludes with her in replacing the letter in the dispatch box before her husband's return a short time later.

Holmes's assertion to Lady Hilda that he will allow her to escape punishment reflects his potential for using power and influence to subvert the legal process in a way unique to his position. His ability to manipulate the situation toward a resolution that could be construed as illegal, yet appropriate to the circumstances, appears in line with William James's pragmatic approach to problem solving, tied to the importance of context and justifiability for social wellbeing. Balancing a tough mental stance—if she persists in lying—with that of a more "tender-minded" response if she accepts culpability, he implements a response that takes into account the practical consequences of his actions (*Pragmatism*, 29). In his 1907 work *Pragmatism: A New Name for Some Old Ways of Thinking*, James proposed a pragmatic approach to solving problems that integrated scientific empiricists' preoccupation with adhering to facts along with rationalist religious idealism in a way that combines science and religion in a system "rooted in experience" (White, "Joseph Butler" www.iep.utm.edu). Holmes's willingness to shield Lady Hilda from exposure has utilitarian undertones, reflecting the belief that inflicting pain on an offender is only justified if more pain (stemming from more crime) is thereby avoided, as Hudson advises (Hudson, 18). Undoubtedly, Lady Hilda's treasonable act in stealing the letter and delivering it into the hands of a foreign agent, Eduardo Lucas, may be considered treasonous, yet Holmes refrains from further rebuke in recognition of her strong attachment to her role in the private sphere. A utilitarian approach to her behavior may consider her criminality and the seriousness of the offense, which threatened to lead the country into war, as one that merits punishment commensurate with the crime of treason. Her behavior, stemming from an initial imprudence in penning an indiscreet "criminal" letter to forging a duplicate key to her husband's highly confidential dispatch box, compounded by an unaccompanied evening assignation with a foreign spy, casts doubt on her judgment and integrity. From a contemporary perspective, we might consider that Lady Hilda's duplicitous nature in lying convincingly to cover up her crimes signals the possibility that this may not be an isolated incident, and that she may re-offend if given the opportunity. Tammy M. Proctor, in her study of women in espionage in the First World War, notes that historically women who were spies were "characterised either as self-sacrificing patriots bent on saving their countries or as whores with an inherent character weakness driving them to treason and betrayal for the sake of money and fame"; however, this is a far cry from Lady Hilda's characterization (7). Holmes clearly considers it unlikely that she is a spy or that she had criminal intent when she stole the letter. In his view, it is unlikely that she would ever again engage in criminality because her main motivation was the avoidance of scandal and its consequences, a significant mitigating factor. Additionally, she was, by her own account, unaware of the severity of the offense and, therefore, punishing her would do more harm than good. Holmes may have believed that in regaining the letter, Lady Hilda had redeemed herself and that punishing her would serve no purpose; the consequences would deliver no positive good to anyone and, on the contrary, scandal linked to government ministers would destabilize the country. Holmes digresses from the utilitarian stance where deterrence is an important aspect, for in this case he ignores the contention that an unpunished crime leaves the path of crime open since, as Hudson points out, "Punishment inflicted on the individual becomes a source of security to all" (Hudson, 18). In allowing Lady Hilda to escape punishment, the deterrent aspect has been ignored; there is no reassurance that she will not commit the offense again, particularly as there is no mention of her surrendering the duplicate key. In the words "I am going far to screen you, Lady Hilda," Holmes defines his own criminality and awareness of their combined guilt (544).

The morality of state punishment, according to Hart, views it as a "paradigmatically legal practice, a reaction to an offense against legal rules," which does not necessarily fit the individual circumstances of each case, but rather is designed to offer general punishments within a certain range (Hart, xxv). Given the return of the letter with no apparent external adverse effects and to avoid a national scandal, Holmes acts beyond the boundaries of the law in the belief that his superior logic and intelligence will bring about a just and practical resolution. A sense of honor, duty and chivalry predominantly characterize Holmes, whose attitude to life is shaped by willingness to compromise on legal principles on occasions where he feels it to be for the general welfare of chosen individuals in a spirit of pragmatism. He reflects an idealistic belief in innate female honesty, avoiding the depiction of women as criminal, unlike Baroness Orczy, whose professional detective Lady Molly of Scotland Yard unmasks a range of deviant female criminals including women who kill. Fergus Hume's Hagar also unmasks the killer, Laura Brenton, in the story "The Eighth Customer and the Pair of Boots," and highlights the offenses of several women criminals in *Hagar of the Pawn Shop*. In his study of Conan Doyle as a writer, Douglas Kerr writes that "[m]ale writers were commonly assessed not only in terms of writing but also in terms of manliness" and maintains that Conan Doyle's writing exhibits the "manly" model of masculinity in contrast to that of Oscar Wilde, whose work he admired (24). The heroic model of masculinity depicted in Sherlock Holmes offers a more complex mixture than the muscular form of masculinity of his counterparts, for his sometime decadent behavior aligns him more readily with the aesthetic appeal of Wilde and with the disruptive tendencies of rogue heroes.

"His Last Bow: The War Service of Sherlock Holmes" (1917)

The image of the spy both in literature and in real life conjured up for Victorians all that was dishonorable, deceitful and disagreeable in the fight against criminals in society. Linked to "despotic states on the Continent," as Shpayer-Makov explains in her study *The Ascent of the Detectives,* "negative connotations of the word spy" were used to oppose the introduction of the detective branch of the police force in England in 1842 by a public wary of the stealthy and underhand methods they employed (28). The clandestine nature of their work where they dressed in plainclothes, making them indistinguishable from the ordinary man in the street, raised fears over the possibility that such "secrecy provided temptations … to exceed their legal authority and resort to all kinds of insidious practices" (28). Rehabilitated and romanticized by the likes of Dickens in his laudatory articles in *Household Words*, the image of the detective improved in the 1850s until its despoliation in the Turf Fraud Scandal of 1877, which evoked memories of the spies and thief-takers of the early years of the century. The scandal created by the subsequent trial of the detectives involving four senior police officers accused of fraud, forgery and bribery destroyed public confidence and trust once more in the incorruptibility of the detective police and led to the formation of the Criminal Investigation Department in 1878.

The image of the detective was later enhanced on the publication of police memoirs and positive media depictions of them. Despite the perception of an affinity with spies and close intimacy with thieves remaining into the twentieth century, Shpayer-Makov believes most police officers were viewed with respect and approval, a view that is contradicted by their continued depiction as less astute than their fictional counterparts (302). Robert Baden-Powell's advice to readers in his 1915 work *My Adventure as a Spy* addresses adverse public opinion of spies in his rejoinder to "disabuse one's mind of the idea that every spy is necessarily the base and despicable fellow he is generally held to be" (10). It is clear, however, that more than thirty years after the trial of the detectives, considerable suspicion and hostility toward all manner of spies still existed in the public imagination. Secrecy, fraud and deceit, the *sine qua non* of a successful spy, were dubious practices that could never be reconciled with the moral high ground of a fictional hero like Sherlock Holmes (415). Yet, Conan Doyle successfully harmonizes the fictional attributes of a legendary detective with those of an accomplished unofficial spy for his readers in his wartime spying escapade entitled "His Last Bow: The War Service of Sherlock Holmes." The role of spy replicates that of the detective in many ways, such as the hunt for and discarding of clues, identification of the criminals, the use of disguise and specialized knowledge in unraveling the mystery in the pursuit of justice, but it differs in relation to the shifting moral and legal parameters of its functions. Secrecy and unaccountability provide possibilities for transgression, as do zealous patriotism and unfettered power, so by examining Holmes's behavior as a spy in this story, the focus is upon his altered perspectives on legality and morality. Like the detective who often works in secret, as Cole points out, he may be inclined to get the job done "regardless of the means." By shedding light on the methods, activities and motivations of Holmes in resolving issues of national security, we gain clarity on the entrenched Edwardian cultural, legal and moral values encoded in the narratives about war, explored in Cole's ethical study of espionage in *Just War and the Ethics of Espionage* (21).

By the time Conan Doyle had composed the Sherlock Holmes adventure "His Last Bow: The War Service of Sherlock Holmes," the Great War itself was in full swing, and the effects of its military campaigns echoed throughout the pages of the *Strand Magazine* of 1917. It appeared in the September issue of the magazine, along with titles such as "The Tanks" by Colonel E.D. Swinton, "War Workers" by May Edginton in the October edition; "Life on a Battleship" by E. Ashmead Bartlett in the November edition and fictional tales of wartime derring-do from the likes of H.C. McNeile (Sapper) (Vol. 54, 270, 386, 471, 563). Like the protagonists of the stories, readers were urged to feelings of optimism, appreciation for the bravery and endurance of those involved in the war effort and an understanding of the hardships they faced. In the story, Sherlock Holmes has been requested by the most powerful people in the land, the Foreign Minister and Prime Minister, to come out of retirement where he is tending bees on his farm on the Sussex Downs and apply his considerable skills in the service of his country. Assuming the role of secret agent, he is tasked with tracking down and capturing a German agent described as one "who was in a class by himself" and "a bit too good for our people" (Conan Doyle, 620). At the time of writing, images of war and national threats to security were mirrored in cinema productions, including the 1914 films *The German Spy Peril; Guarding Britain's Secrets* and *The Kaiser's Spies* and in the 1915 adventure *The Crimson Triangle* (Proctor, 25). Along with John Buchan's popular novel, *The Thirty-Nine Steps,* questions of national loyalty predominated in the popular imagination, and such images constructed ideological paradigms of heroic behavior.

The story opens just prior to Britain's declaration of war on Germany on August 4, 1914, as two famous German spies discuss the upcoming invasion of England and put together the final touches to their evacuation plans. Von Bork, "a man who could hardly be matched among all the devoted agents of the Kaiser," had assumed the identity of an English squire some four years earlier, and, through his skill and love of upper-class sporting activities such as hunting, shooting, yachting and polo, had succeeded in installing himself in society's influential circles where he was privy to confidential discussions on matters of state during the course of general conversations (Conan Doyle, 616). Baron von Herling, his counterpart, is Chief Secretary of the German Legation and has come to discuss von Bork's acquisition of British secret military intelligence relating to "Harbor defenses, Aeroplanes, Ireland, the Channel," amongst other things, and to retrieve the final "gem of the collection": British Naval Signals, encoded "Sparking Plugs." These are to be delivered that evening by the traitor, Altamont, who is selling them to the Germans for five hundred pounds (617). The ensuing dialog between the Germans focuses on the gullibility and myopia of England, who, despite Germany's introduction of a war tax, which von Herling points out "one would think made our purpose as clear as if we had advertised it on the front page of the *Times,*" somehow fails to galvanize the British government into action and make ready for war (617). Pressed for time, the Baron remarks that the old lady housekeeper, Martha, who is the only other occupant of the house "with her complete self-absorption and general air of somnolence" as she bends over her knitting and strokes the cat, personifies "Britannia," blissfully unaware of the perils ahead (618). On the Baron's departure, Altamont arrives with the information on Naval Signals tucked inside a package under his arm. Characterized as a "real-bitter Irish American," he speaks in a heavy Irish brogue interlaced with American colloquialisms and is barely intelligible. Noting the safe in von Bork's study, Altamont deceives him into revealing its codes before commenting on the recent imprisonment of five German secret agents and accusing von Bork of treachery by selling them out to the British. Von Bork, incensed, replies, "How dare you speak in such a way!" to which Altamont replies, "If I didn't dare things, mister, I wouldn't be in your service…. I've heard that with you German politicians when an agent has done his work you are not sorry to see him put away" (619). Having resolved their dispute, Altamont insists on having his reward of five hundred pounds before delivering the codes and adding, while procuring them from his navy contact, "The gunner turned nasty at the last and I had to square with him an extra one hundred dollars, or it would have been nitsky for you and me" (619). Gunners held an important role as guardians of naval secrets, and their integrity needed to be above reproach.

Altamont is Holmes in disguise and, having received his fee of five hundred pounds, he passes the parcel to von Bork who, on opening it, discovers that instead of naval signals it contains a copy of *Practical Handbook of Bee Culture*, a humorous touch from Holmes. He then grips von Bork on the back of the neck in "a grasp of iron" and uses chloroform to knock him unconscious (619). This first physical act of violence from Holmes is a departure from his usual code of conduct where he would refrain from force unless attacked. His strike first approach signals the beginning of his retreat from gentlemanly conventions to a more aggressive means of achieving his ends. We learn from Watson, who arrives in the guise of the chauffeur, that Holmes's assumption of a new identity as the traitorous Irish American took him two years to fully embrace. His deception involved a complete immersion in a semi-criminal artificial persona, starting in Chicago, then on to Buffalo where he enrolled in an Irish secret society before building his camouflage by giving trouble to the constabulary at Skibbereen in Ireland. Having created a history of subversion, he was finally approached by a German subordinate of von Bork who recruited him as a spy. The transformation of Holmes into a convincing spy by immersing himself in a criminal identity illustrates the potential moral damage inflicted on spies when carrying out clandestine operations. As Cavallaro points out, there is the risk of "loss of moral agency" when the new identity absorbs that of the former and releases the spy from the moral constraints of the law (678). Despite his fictional status, Holmes's character must adapt to the changing circumstances in which he operates. Since character is bound up with experience by spending a lengthy period of time as a rogue, the harmful effects of constant exposure to criminality on Holmes may influence his judgment and decision-making, perhaps explaining his ready recourse to violence as the best method for resolving problems. This view of harm is confirmed in Cole's work when he suggests that "the tactics used by spies may be more potentially damaging to character than the tactics used by soldiers" with whom they are often equated (Cole, 21). Although soldiers may be brutalized by hand-to-hand combat, because "spies are often called upon to lie, deceive, play false roles for long periods of time and act treacherously," their character may be corrupted (Cole, 21). The use of humor throughout the narrative, for example, with Holmes's use of the manual on bees instead of naval signals and his reference to "sparking plugs" as the code name for naval signals, introduces a lighter note to a very serious topic; Holmes's jocund and flippant manner gives the impression that he relishes the opportunity to outclass his rivals in a show of bravado, a metaphor for Britain's superior wit and ability.

Having bound von Bork hand and foot, Holmes next raids his safe, removing all the documents, burning some and retaining anything useful. In response to von Bork's threat that he will get even with him "if it takes me all my life," Holmes cheekily repudiates the threat, declaring, "The old sweet song…. It was a favourite ditty of the late lamented Professor Moriarty. Colonel Sebastian Moran has also been known to warble it. And yet I live and keep bees upon the South Downs" (621). In a friendlier tone, Holmes informs von Bork that he, the expert detective, was responsible for solving several cases in Germany, including that of the King of Bohemia and Irene Adler and that he should feel less aggrieved since "it is better than to fall before some ignoble foe," a comment that further ruffles von Bork's feathers (Conan Doyle, 621). Countering his initial pugnacious approach to von Bork with a more conciliatory attitude, Holmes then treats him as a man of honor vouching, "But you have one quality which is very rare in a German, Mr. von Bork: you are a sportsman and you will bear me no ill-will when you realise that you, who have outwitted so many people, have at last been outwitted yourself. After all you have done your best for your country, and I have done my best for mine" (621). Explaining the lack of antagonism toward German spies, as sympathy and understanding replace hostility and resentment, Hitchner contends that spying "connects rather than divides Britain and its rival" (418). This same cultural sympathy and appreciation of values can be read in Erskine Childers's *The Riddle of the Sands*. Antipathy toward spies was not confined to Britain, as Proctor reminds us, for stories of spy mania were emerging in most combatant countries too (26). Holmes and Watson finally manhandle the struggling von Bork into their car and ignore him as he remonstrates against the illicit restraint and kidnap imposed upon him in a time of peace by unofficial undercover agents, as he protests bitterly, "I suppose you realise Mr. Sherlock Holmes that if your government bears you out in this treatment, it becomes an act of war," a last attempt at protest, for he knows war is already imminent (Conan Doyle, 622). Von Bork raises a legal challenge to Holmes's authority and charges that as a private individual, without professional state recognition or an arrest warrant, Holmes has no lawful right to detain him. He declares the "whole proceeding is absolutely illegal and outrageous" (622). Holmes, however, disregards his invective before moving to the terrace which overlooks Harwich and utters his famous words to Watson, "There's an east wind coming," in reference to the approaching war (Conan Doyle, 622).

Holmes, in his characterization of spy, is willing to apply his own particularized code of conduct where his actions border on the morally dubious and illicit and in which he embraces a pragmatic approach to the situation. Viewed through the lens of pragmatic justice, where the law may be seen to operate in an instrumental variation to the traditional method, and given that the story is set before the outbreak of war, he is justified in using violence and abduction to nullify the major threat to the nation's safety. Since pragmatism is "rooted in the specific context" of the situation at hand, the consequences of his actions for future wellbeing entitle his response to the threats posed by von Bork. However, in seizing von Bork's property and subjecting him to violent rendition into the custody of the Metropolitan Police and thence to his German superiors, no doubt facing trial and possible execution, his actions may violate von Bork's human rights. As an unofficial spy, endorsed by political leaders who have invested in him unlimited freedom to act as he sees fit, he lacks professional training in the role. The lack of oversight and official status places him beyond the law, and allows him to act with impunity. In mitigation of Holmes's behavior, however, it is worth considering Allan Hepburn's observations on the duties of citizenship in relation to the law. In his work *Intrigue, Espionage and Culture* (2014), he points out that "certain unjust acts, if undertaken rationally to combat other unjust acts, are not judged by universal laws but according to the context in which they transpire": a pragmatic view of legality (5). In this light, the preemptive use of force by Holmes on von Bork could be condoned as a means of preventing his [von Bork's] unjust appropriation of state and military secrets for an enemy state to the detriment of national security. Holmes's good intention is to safeguard Britain's welfare using whatever means are necessary under the circumstances. Edwardian fears over the infiltration of German spies into British society created "xenophobic paranoia," according to Hepburn, much of which was found to be misplaced as Christopher Andrew has explained (11). Far from inundating Britain with spies, "German military intelligence concentrated exclusively on Russia and France … which helped to alert the Prussian General Staff to Russian mobilisation at the end of July 1914," Andrew points out (52). Holmes's pragmatism in balancing his illegality with that of the German spies accommodates a form of dual morality in keeping with his altered role as spy. His conduct reflects his altered status, for unlike his role as detective, where he addresses the grievances and complaints of individual members of society, his duty as an undercover agent is bound up with the wellbeing and safety of society as a whole. Despite Holmes's dubious methods of engagement, his behavior reflects cultural attitudes toward the treatment of aliens. Evidence of public disquiet over the failed prosecution of supposed spies due to the inadequacy of the 1889 Official Secrets Act is exposed in the rapid pursuit of a new Official Secrets Act, which came into force in 1911. Under its provisions, it was illegal "to obtain or communicate any information useful to an enemy as well as to approach or enter a prohibited place for any purpose prejudicial to safety or interests of the state" (Andrew, 39). Alongside the setting up of a secret Register of Aliens, its terms strengthened Britain's ability to prosecute enemy agents. In the shady world of espionage where the boundaries of ethics and morality are fluid, the fictional Holmes soothed the angst of his Edwardian readers.

Arthur Morrison: Martin Hewitt, "The Case of the Dixon Torpedo" (1894)

The jewel in the crown of the British Empire was India, and securing its borders from Russia's incursions was a priority for military intelligence toward the end of the nineteenth century. The Great Game of espionage between Britain and Russia gathered pace after the Crimean War, and the focus of Afghanistan as the gateway to India featured heavily in military circles, with Sir Francis Younghusband, a lone officer, embarking on a journey across Asia as a surveyor of the landscape. In reality, his journey was undertaken with a view to gauging Russia's intentions toward India (Wade, 50). Fear of Russian interest in British naval capability and its growing imperialist tendencies can be read in Martin Hewitt's adventure "The Case of the Dixon Torpedo," the fourth story in the first series *Martin Hewitt: Investigator.* As he enters the world of espionage, Hewitt's detective profile is readily adapted to the necessary legal and moral adjustments to be made when dealing with an undercover Russian agent. The need for ruthless methods and decisive action in his dealings with a serious threat to national security is indisputable as he raids the home of the culprit, Mirsky, a Russian immigrant living freely and openly in London. Operating as a spy for the Russians, Mirsky's behavior in the narrative gives expression to the general unease over the influx of Russian immigrants into Britain from the 1880s onwards. As Sarah Young points out, approximately 30,000, mostly Jewish, working class immigrants, arrived from the Pale of Settlement between 1881 and 1891 following the assassination of Tsar Alexander II, adding to existing anxiety over Eastern European anarchist activity in London (sarahjyoung.com). Like Joseph Conrad's 1907 novel, *The Secret Agent: A Simple Tale,* set in the 1880s, the story identifies the Russian Embassy as the hub of espionage activity that poses a threat to national security in contravention of its agreed status as a diplomatic mission in keeping with the Vienna Convention, as Michael Herman points out (257). Fueling stories of Russian criminality linked to treachery, the spy in the story operates an illegal coining operation in addition to his spying activities, differentiating him from those engaged in covert operations for Britain.

Lunch is fast approaching when Martin Hewitt is called upon by Mr. Graham Dixon, the mastermind of a "new locomotive torpedo," whose speed, accuracy and ability to travel farther than any yet designed, is under Admiralty contract and remains a closely guarded secret (17). Despite the fact that no one has left or visited his office in Chancery Lane, a set of drawings has been stolen, and Dixon's fear is that they will be offered for sale to some foreign government. He has two employees who work alongside him: Worsfold, a draftsman, "a very excellent and intelligent man ... quite beyond suspicion," and Ritter, a tracer, "quite a decent young fellow, but not very smart, both of whom seem beyond suspicion" (18). In the course of Hewitt's search of the office, Dixon assures him of the impossibility of copying the plans, due to the complexity of "hydrostatics, chemistry, electricity and pneumatics" involved in the design, a paean to the wonders of science and technology of the era. During their discussion, a visitor arrives purporting to be a Mr. Hunter, yet betraying a foreign accent and prompting Hewitt's curiosity. He had called earlier looking to interest Mr. Dixon in a railway project of steam-packing. On being told of Mr. Dixon's unavailability, he seizes his walking stick from the hat stand and leaves in high dudgeon. After his departure, Hewitt discovers the missing plans hidden inside the hollow of a walking stick in the hat stand identical to that of Hunter, and concludes that the return of the plans means the culprit, Hunter, has photographed the plans and returned them in the hope that no one will have noticed their disappearance. Since time is crucial to the recovery of the negatives, Hewitt observes:

> I must act at once, and I fear, between ourselves, it may be necessary for me to step very distinctly over the line of the law in the matter. You see, to get at those negatives may require something very close to housebreaking. There must be no delay—no waiting for legal procedure—or the mischief is done. Indeed, I very much question whether you have any legal remedy, strictly speaking [21].

His contention that there is no legal remedy justifies illegality, though he further complains that "the consequences to me, if I were charged with housebreaking might be something that no amount of guarantee could mitigate," adding, "However, I will do what I can if only from patriotic motives" (22). Patriotism provides sound rationale for his actions in the public interest, regardless of the cost to himself and his professional reputation—a great deal is at stake.

Confronting Ritter, whom he has discovered is implicated in the plot, Hewitt insists that he inform Hunter the plans have been changed and that he should return to the office for the adjustments. Having ferreted out Hunter's address from Ritter, Hewitt hurries to Carton Street in Westminster where he lives, and learns that the real identity of Hunter is Mirsky, a Russian émigré. Popular literature and media representations of the influx of migrants to Britain, particularly from Eastern Europe and Russia in the late nineteenth century, heightened feelings of anxiety and resentment over the effects of cheap labor and exacerbated fears of alien invasions on a grand scale. Russian pogroms in the 1880s that witnessed the persecution of the Jewish population and caused them to flee the country saw their arrival in large numbers in the East End of London and the subsequent rise of anti-Semitic sentiment. On Hewitt's arrival at Mirsky's apartment, the thief opens the door to Hewitt, rapidly excuses himself and rushes downstairs carrying a bundle wrapped in brown paper under his arm, leaving Hewitt free to enter the apartment. Taking advantage of the opportunity, Hewitt enters and locks the door behind him to prevent Mirsky's re-entry. Rooting around he finds and destroys the negatives of the plans and discovers that Mirsky is running an illegal coining operation forging Russian twenty-rouble notes: a sideline in criminality. On returning to his apartment and finding it locked against him, Mirsky, who had been divesting himself of the criminal evidence of coining materials, rattles the door violently and shouts, "Who are you there inside? Why for you go in my room like that? Open this door at once or I call the police."

Smashing the photographic plates of the torpedo plans and destroying all that he can find, Hewitt remarks, "I suppose nobody ever did so much devastation in a photographic studio in ten minutes as I managed" (24). Having completed the ruination of the negatives and the plates, Hewitt now sees it his duty to communicate with the police from Scotland Yard from whom he learns of the circulation of a large number of forged Russian notes on the continent. A letter arrives for Mirsky bearing the Russian Imperial Arms, indicating its source as the Russian Embassy and expressing an interest in the important information he has to offer. Hewitt concludes that Mirsky, when caught, "will probably get something handsome at St. Petersburg in the way of imprisonment, or Siberia" (27). After the assassination of Tsar Alexander in 1881, the formidable Russian secret police organization, the Okhrana, built a wide network of international spies targeted at rooting out revolutionaries and anarchists who threatened the autonomy of Tsarist Russia; their reputation for efficiency and brutality in equal measure made them an organization to be feared.

Tensions and rivalry between Britain and Russia were played out in the Great Game of espionage in Central Asia toward the end of the nineteenth century, ending in 1907 with the signing of the Anglo-Russian Entente relating to Persia, Afghanistan and Tibet, the areas of greatest anxiety. Nevertheless, literary dramatizations of the threat posed to Britain by Russia continued apace until public realization of the colonial aspirations of Kaiser Wilhelm II of Germany, with his expansionist military and naval plans, ratcheted up global concerns. Popular literature of the period is rich in examples of alien criminality, including Oriental mystics and the Sino-Japanese threat entitled the Yellow Peril, encapsulated in the hero of Sax Rohmer's 1913 novel, *The Mystery of Fu Manchu,* whose adventures continued for decades. The narrative subtext of Martin Hewitt's "The Case of the Dixon Torpedo" reflects fears over the lack of immigration control and supervision of immigrants that leave them free to exploit their hosts with actions likely to disrupt the security of the state. In the story, Mirsky, in bringing important information to the attention of the Russian Ambassador, is characterized as criminal rather than patriotic; his criminality is twofold because not only is he a thief in British eyes, but he undermines his own homeland by engaging in coining activities, a treasonous offense in Russia. Hewitt's departure from legality appears proportional in relation to the harm he prevents from the theft of the plans. His lack of concern over Ritter's fate is demonstrated when he is asked how to deal with the treasonous Ritter and responds, "Here's his stick—knock him downstairs with it, if you like" (29). By allowing him to go free, like Holmes, he assumes the royal prerogative of mercy, based on the traitor's assistance in locating Mirsky and his genuine contrition for his actions. However, in reality, the conditions for such a pardon entail a high threshold before implementation. Despite the difficulties with extradition in the Victorian era, we learn that Mirsky was finally caught and extradited to Russia for his crimes. Although they have been absent from the scene throughout the narrative, Hewitt's successful counter-intelligence operation concludes by informing the police of events.

J.E.P. Muddock: Dick Donovan, "The Strange Story of Some State Papers" (1898)

A year before embarking on Dick Donovan's adventure "The Strange Story of Some State Papers," J.E.P. Muddock penned a novel entitled *The Chronicles of Michael Danevitch of the Russian Secret Service* in which he recounts the exploits of Michael Danevitch, "one of the foremost detectives in the world," whom he met in the course of Danevitch's quest to find the would-be assassin of Tsar Alexander II (6). His admiration for and friendship with Danevitch led him to act as scribe for him, detailing his work in the Russian embassies of Europe along with his fraternizations in the upper echelons of diplomatic society. In a similar vein, Dick Donovan's adventure "The Strange Story of Some State Papers" relates to international relations with Russia and the perilous predicament of upsetting the balance of power between nations when papers go astray. Betraying his partiality for aphorisms, morality fables, French writers and detectives, Donovan begins his tale of espionage by advising his readers to "cherchez la femme" as the source of misfortune. Coined by Alexandre Dumas, *père*, the phrase was first used in *Les Mohicans de Paris* (1864) by the Sherlockian detective, Mr. Jackal, in a classic crime drama that hints at the moral imbuing Donovan's account.

"The Strange Story of Some State Papers" begins at the Court of St. James's where he has been summoned in answer to an urgent call from the Austrian ambassador, an unnamed count, for his assistance. Awaiting his invitation to the Count's presence, Donovan meets his son, Ferdinand, a handsome twenty-four-year-old who acts as attaché for his father. The young man's gracious manners fail to impress Donovan, who describes him as vain and affected. In conversation with him, Ferdinand reflects on "the number of crimes that have gone unpunished" where "the inventors must be cleverer than the solvers," raising Donovan's suspicions about his honesty and integrity (50). During the subsequent interview with the Count, he is asked to retrieve a highly controversial draft treaty that had been securely locked in the dispatch box but had gone missing in the night. Containing politically sensitive information of a proposed treaty between Britain and Austria, its contents will be incendiary if revealed. When asked the object of such a theft, he replied, "But one object. The treaty is framed against Russia, and someone in the pay of Russia has carried it off" (51). The realization that there is a traitor in their midst who may cause serious disruption to the relationship between Austria and Russia, possibly war, is of great concern to the Count: constant international rivalries amongst the great powers of Europe and Russia in which the balance of power was precarious meant that slight shifts in relationships could alter the dynamics of empire. The dispatch box was stored in the Count's bedroom, and he describes how the use of an ill-fitting duplicate key has damaged the lid, which has been forced open. Donovan concludes that the person who carried off the state papers must be "directly or indirectly interested in Russia," or is someone who "has been corrupted by Russian agents" (53). Outlining his plan for clandestinity in finding the traitor, Donovan instructs the Count to put aside his "models of chivalry, of honor, of all that is noble" and allow him to root out the black sheep by spying on his household, to which the Count reluctantly agrees. On examining the Count's bedroom, Donovan discovers a smaller chamber at the end of the room which is Ferdinand's bedroom. Requesting half an hour's private inspection of the Count's bedroom, he subsequently pens a note requesting that the Count receive as his dinner guest that evening a French priest, Paul Vernay, a non-English speaker who must not be hampered in any way.

The denouement occurs next day when Donovan restores the stolen documents to the Count and reveals how he discovered a piece of wax in

Ferdinand's room indicating his attempt at duplicating the key, together with love letters written in Russian and a photograph of his paramour. Inquiries led to "the daughter of a Russian lady, well-known in London society, where she was regarded as a spy and an intriguer of exceptional cleverness" (66). In his disguise as the French priest, he had followed Ferdinand after dinner to Grosvenor Mansions, the home of the Russian lady. On the following day, he returned and spoke to the daughter, whom he discovered was "as unprincipled as she was clever," and threatened to ruin her with a public scandal if she failed to return the papers. (67). Ferdinand was so infatuated that she was able to manipulate him into the betrayal of secrets to the Russian government. Donovan informs us:

> At that time it was pretty well known that, owing to certain menacing movements on the part of Russia, directed principally against Hungary, the Austrian ambassador had managed to enter into a treaty with England bearing on the point [67].

Ferdinand was banished from his father's sight in disgrace and was sent to India, never again to return and ended his days in a second-rate consular post in France.

Once again Russia takes center stage in this story of intrigue and romance, where the detective, Donovan, expands his investigation of domestic crime into the realms of diplomacy and espionage as a counter-intelligence agent. Highlighting the incidence of Russian spies operating with impunity in high society, the story offers a critique of the lack of supervision of the immigrant population. As a feature of popular media accounts of the day, it later led to the creation of the Royal Commission on alien immigration in 1903, described in J.C. Bird's account *Control of Enemy Alien Civilians in Great Britain, 1914–1918*. In his emulation of the state's reliance on individual men of character and capability to weed out spies rather than professional operatives with reputations for dishonesty and treachery, Muddock offers a palliative to the public distrust of spies, still prevalent in the era. The sexualized portrait of the female Russian spy in the story, posited as older and more worldly-wise, evokes that of a Mata Hari ready to use her sexuality to gain political information and mirrors that of contemporary honey-trap strategies. Betraying his sense of distaste for the proposed group surveillance at dinner reflects the Count's ambivalent attitude toward the methods used by Donovan to identify the culprit. By subjecting his own family and friends to deceptive practices and the intrusive gaze of an outsider with the purpose of criminalizing one of them, the Count reveals his natural antipathy for spies. Status of spy leads to the uncovering of conclusive evidence of guilt as Ferdinand betrays his interest in the Russian lady and her daughter.

Although the use of covert methods to unmask the traitor proves worth the effort in this instance and justifies the reduction of ethical standards for a higher purpose, his actions normalize the decline of trust and morality in society, in a literary context, where things are not as they seem. Instructing his host to put aside his scruples, Donovan imitates the code of practice implemented by Eugene Francois Vidocq, the criminal turned founder of the Sûreté Nationale, whose work inspired the French writers Honoré de Balzac and Victor Hugo, and whose own criminality provided the basis for catching villains.

Richard Marsh: Judith Lee, "Two Words" (1916)

A year or so ago, when the first crude aeroplanes were flying yards instead of miles, and when no flight of any kind was possible unless there was practically a dead calm, there were clever men who smiled when aircraft were spoken of as a possible weapon in time of war. Now, in 1911, a man whirls through the air at sixty-three miles an hour, lunching in London and having tea in Paris, and amazing the whole world by bridging the distance between the two capitals in a monoplane in three hours less time than the fastest train and the quickest turbine steamer ["The Aerial Menace: Why there is Danger in England's Apathy," *Strand Magazine*. Vol. 42, Jul-Dec, 1911, 3].

In his July 1911 article in the *Strand Magazine*, Claude Grahame White complains bitterly of the short sightedness of England's War Office for failing to strengthen Britain's air defenses in line with the growth of militarization occurring in Europe. A common object of discourse in the years leading up to World War I, it was a theme still eagerly pursued in popular literature five years later in 1916 at the height of the war. As a popular writer alive to current trends and anxieties, Richard Marsh capitalizes on England's complacent response to alien threats through the remolding of his fictional detective, Judith Lee, into a patriotic female spy, an already popular trope in early cinema productions. The power of images of heroic female characters in espionage was shown in the success of such films as *Girl Spy*, a series running from 1909 to 1910 that featured a Civil War heroine fighting on behalf of the Confederacy. Later film characterizations include the tale of *Joan of Plattsburg* by Wesley Alan Briton, a 1915 melodrama depicting the transformation of a young heroine into a contemporary Joan of Arc who foils a German plot (4). Alongside fantasy exemplars, the courageous actions of real-life nurse Edith Cavell proved that gender is no obstacle to heroism. Her death received worldwide condemnation when she was shot on October 13, 1915, for harboring fugitive British and French soldiers from the Germans. Reports of her "merciless execution" appeared in *The Manchester Guardian* of October 22, 1915, fueling anti-German sentiment in propaganda reportage and saw her memorialization in an Australian silent movie *The Martyrdom of Nurse Cavell,* 1916. In the story "Two Words," the fifth story of the second collection of her adventures *The Adventures of Judith Lee,* published in 1916, Judith Lee is characterized as courageous and resourceful. Her ingenuity and swift actions avert a significant threat to England's air defenses in a fictional encounter with German spies. Her portrayal as spy challenges the stereotypical view of the seductress female spy, epitomized by Mata Hari. Sliding effortlessly into duplicity, her progressive characterization is coupled with a distinctly pragmatic reaction to circumstances where the law has its limitations and requires broader interpretation in a situation critical to maintaining national dominance in air defense technology.

Blindley Heath is a "remote Surrey common" in the story "Two Words" which, along with echoing White's fears of threat to empire, disparages German manliness embodied in the shape of a German agent by subjecting him to Judith Lee's verbal asperity and superior acuity (Marsh, 317). In a similar vein to Holmes, Hewitt and Donovan, the story records her mutation into spy working in the interests of national security whilst simultaneously securing the release of an innocent man. Since the art of spying alters the moral and legal parameters of behavior in response to threats to state security, Richard Marsh effects a corresponding shift in Judith Lee's characterization. No longer simply a detective who engages in the accepted craft of her trade in the course of uncovering the truth—deception, disguise and eavesdropping—her campaign methods now extend to more dubious practices like lying, cheating and coercive interrogation, reminiscent of Vidocq and the thief-takers of a bygone era. In his description of the spy's role in society, Darrell Cole presents some validation for the altered parameters of societal norms in times of war. In his reasoning for the just war hypothesis, he points out that since "One of the necessary functions of any government is to protect its people from harm" by employing spies to preserve order, justice and peace, then the professional "may act at the very limits of what morality may allow and will certainly act in ways that may contravene accepted laws and conventions" (Cole, 12). Taking into account his justification for the shifting moral boundaries expected of real-life spies in carrying out their duties, we gain a better understanding of the extent to which the norms of social and legal behavior were revised in the era when issues of national security arose.

The story opens with a dinner party, arranged to provide an opportunity for Mr. Philip Collier, the lawyer for Mr. Charles Sinclair who was arrested for the murder of Gerald Tansley at Blindley Heath, to entreat Judith Lee's help in clearing his innocent client of the charges. Rudely rejecting his appeal for her sympathy, she resists gendered expectation, instead placing professional integrity above benevolence and compassion. Defending her role as a professional teacher, she rebukes him, saying, "What do you take me for Mr. Collier? A professional detective or what? I am a teacher of the deaf and dumb; I take the profoundest interest in my profession" (Marsh, 314). Her outright rejection of his entreaty, she argues, is due to the excessive demands for her services as a detective, for she receives numerous similar emotional requests on a weekly basis. Complaining that, at times, she has to shut her eyes and ears in "self-defense" when subjected to so many entreaties, the story emphasizes her now much enhanced reputation, both as a detective and as a teacher of the deaf and dumb (314). A further poignant entreaty for assistance to help clear Sinclair comes from his fiancée, Gertrude Alloway, who explains how Sinclair and his partner, Tansley, had invented a new aircraft "which could move in any direction, regardless of wind, or storm, or anything, just as easily as if it were on land," clearly a valuable weapon in time of war (316). Affirming Sinclair's innocence, she discredits the purely circumstantial evidence that will shortly lead to his execution unless something is done. Once again Judith Lee summarily dismisses her request in sharply contrasting characterization to that of previous stories, assuming a dispassionate attitude verging on the ruthless. Her harsh tone chimes with that of the credible spy, infusing it with authoritative self-possession and grim determination in readiness for imminent conversations with the bullish agents of foreign powers. Called to attend a conference in Berlin, Lee's lip-reading skills flicker into life on overhearing two Germans utter the words "Blindley Heath" (317).

A German speaker herself, she eavesdrops on the conversation between the Germans and witnesses the delivery of documents (stolen aircraft plans) from one Gustav von Hertzheim of the aviation department to Major Schrattenholtz of the German Secret Service. As she monitors the ensuing conversation, it becomes clear that they are involved in the death of Tansley and are aware that an innocent man, Charles Sinclair, is accused of his murder. The Major's opinion with respect to Tansley's death, "You cannot make omelets without breaking eggs," demonstrates his complicity in the crime offset against the potential benefits to be gained for German home security from his actions. With regard to the impending death threat to Charles Sinclair, he theorizes that "if this other one also dies, as from the latest advice seems likely, then the secret will be ours only"; he rationalizes that the sole possession of the newly invented aircraft plans justifies the deaths of two foreigners (318). Evaluating the morality of their actions by Darrel Cole's reasoning that all nations are "potential adversaries" and that governments may need to rely on treachery and perfidious acts as the only way to protect their citizens from harm, his logic seems defensible; the Major is acting within the ethical boundaries of his profession (Cole, 13). Since spying is a justifiable profession for the common wellbeing, and since nations expect to be spied on by friend and foe alike, the Germans in seeking to procure plans that would impinge on the security of their own state, were acting "for the protection of the common good" and therefore morally justified in their actions (Cole, 13). On the other hand, as the story is set prior to the outbreak of war, evidenced in Judith Lee's invitation to Berlin, their involvement in what appears to be an assassination of a citizen from a friendly state could be construed as reprehensible. Critiques of German culture and integrity appear in several articles in the *Strand Magazine* of the period. One such is Sir Ray Lankester's article "Culture and German Culture" in the January 1915 edition of the magazine. In it, he excoriates Kaiser Wilhelm II, stating: "It is truly marvelous that this man who suffers from a morbid condition of both body and brain, whom most Englishmen have regarded as a megalomaniac, should have been able to infect the whole German people with his insane audacity and his infamous lack of honor and morality" (Vol. 49, 3). His implication is that the Kaiser is innately evil and that his moral necrosis represents a contagion whose symptoms induce a blatant disregard for justice and human life, vices portrayed in Marsh's fictionalized German spies.

In pursuit of the truth, Judith Lee is soundly rational and now fully convinced of Charles Sinclair's innocence, she connects the chain of events and travels to Blindley Heath in search of proof. By visiting the crime scene and interviewing local witnesses, an omission on the part of the official police force which further indicts reliance on purely circumstantial evidence, she uncovers a crucial page of the stolen aircraft plans and evidence that von Hertzheim had flown to Blindley Heath from Germany on the night of the murder. Paradoxically, her own case supporting Charles Sinclair's innocence is also based on circumstantial evidence linked to inference, and requires direct evidence to generate proof. Engaging the assistance of the Crown solicitor in the Sinclair case, she invites von Hertzheim to a rendezvous in which she plans to blackmail him into a confession in return for the missing page. Noting that his arrival at eleven o'clock at night was "an uncanonical hour for a single woman to receive a visit from a solitary man," she remarks that despite his fine figure, his appearance was "coarse-featured," foreshadowing his characterization as superficially masculine and uncultured (324). During his visit, she accuses him of having flown to Blindley Heath, murdered Gerald Tansley and stolen the plans for the new aircraft he [Tansley] had invented along with Charles Sinclair. Warning von Hertzheim of his precarious legal position, she threatens, "In England killing is murder, even when a distinguished officer kills an insignificant civilian" (326). In reply, he reproaches Lee for her deceit and denounces her unexpected mendacity with, "Then what is contained in this letter is false?" (326). Having successfully lured him to England with the promise of repatriation and the missing page from the stolen plans in exchange for his testimony on behalf of Charles Sinclair, Lee's deception could be viewed as morally justified and the right thing to do in the circumstances; procuring the release of an innocent man balances the scales of justice. As Jan Goldman observes in her handbook for those working in the field of intelligence *Ethics of Spying: A Reader for the Intelligence Professional* (2010), "As in life, the intelligence profession is sometimes filled with moral and ethical dilemmas for which no law, policy or regulation can assist in developing the proper response in doing the right thing" (Goldman, xi). Given von Hertzheim's subsequent resistance to verbal pressure to admit his guilt, Judith Lee resorts to blackmail to achieve her ends, threatening to inform his superior, the major, of his failure to complete his mission successfully. "You have lied to Major Schrattenholtz ... you did not dare tell him that you had not brought to Berlin what you knew to be the most essential part of the drawings of that aeroplane"; he had forged the missing page to hide his ineptitude (328). Under the heavy verbal onslaught, von Hertzheim finally concedes defeat and relates how Gerald Tansley, who had previously agreed to sell the plans to Germany, had fallen in a rage and "struck his head against the edge of the table" and died, a fact later confirmed by the medical examiner (329). Agreeing to testify, he later discovers Judith Lee's further duplicity for the stolen plans is now obsolete; the threat of foreign ascendancy in aerial combat is crushed and German hubris subdued.

In the final analysis of the judgments made by Judith Lee in her discretionary response to crime, which could arguably be consistent with Sarat's description as "unmoored from an anchoring system of justice," mitigating factors in support of her actions are plentiful. Firstly, the stories are set in a pre-war England, where the still-credible threat of invasion by Germany dominated media, and popular magazines would strike a chord of sympathy with readers anxious for fictional redress for past German transgressions. Living through the horrors of World War I, in the midst of which the collection of stories was published, galvanizes popular approval for the narrative discrediting a detested enemy. Secondly, acting primarily as a detective whose primary intention is the release of an innocent man tempers any disapproval of the morally dubious methods she uses to achieve her goal. Deception, coercion, blackmail and the promise of immunity from prosecution outweigh the negative consequences of flawed justice that condones the death of an innocent man. Finally, although once perceived as "dirty and unacceptable," the image of the spy "defined and mythologized" by Kipling's 1901 novel *Kim* is validated in recognition of the need for agencies and spies tasked with ensuring the safety of the nation (Wade, 57). The remodeling of the spy followed the success of the "male adventure genre in popular fiction, which showcased 'the spy as a type' engaged in warfare 'that asked questions about morality as well as politics'" (Wade, 49). Its popularity was accelerated by the notoriety of the Dreyfus Affair in France, where a Jewish army officer was controversially found guilty of selling secrets to the Germans in 1899. In this new world of spies, a revised framework of ethical values arises. It is one where the criteria may be altered in line with national security interests in opposition to a Kantian, or deontological, disposition where moral rules, such as "Do unto others as you would be done by," no longer apply. As Raymond Wacks points out, the Kantian view where "certain moral virtues exist independently of our minds or of convention" condemns a state that engages its own subjects as spies "even in self-defense" as morally unacceptable. Those who perform such activities, Kant claims are "unfit to be citizens" (qtd. in Goldman, 132).

In his incarnation of the female detective Judith Lee, Richard Marsh equips her with the necessary capacity to compete on par with male spies who are adept in the skills of subterfuge. With interrogative cunning and the moral flexibility to adjust her ethical practice to suit the hostile actions of clandestine foreign agents, Judith Lee generates fictional reassurance of the elimination of threats to life and liberty. Her response is balanced against "competing claims of other values" in a time of emergency, as Dyzenhaus explains in his work *The Constitution of Law: Legality in a Time of Emergency* (306). In doing so, Richard Marsh confounds critics of the female detective who accuse her of passivity and relegate her to a reductive role in the annals of detective fiction. Contrary to Michele Slung's contention that the female detective is often either "abandon[ed] mid-career" or "finish[ed] off at the matrimonial alter," she remains firmly unattached throughout the series and thoroughly dedicated to her profession (Slung, 17). It is worth considering Raymond Wacks's thoughts on the evaluation of judgment and morality in his observation that "judgments may simply reflect emotion" for "there exist no self-evident first principles of morality from which all else may be derived"; ethical statements express only an individual's subjective state of mind and conventionalism (*Jurisprudence*, 34). In the light of Wacks's statement, contemporary readers are bound to connect with Judith Lee's code of morality, which reflects considered and balanced appraisal of the ethical arguments in conjunction with practical reasoning.

5

Spying and Lying
Childers and Buchan's Accidental Spies

> The subject of espionage is itself endlessly fascinating because it deals with the rawest, most elemental side of human behavior. People have been intrigued by the essence of spying since Judas betrayed Jesus with a kiss for thirty pieces of silver in the Garden of Gethsemane [Hitz, 7].

ERSKINE CHILDERS (1870–1922)

The Riddle of the Sands: A Record of Secret Service (1903)

The global world of espionage today presents a dynamic contradiction to that of the early days of Rudyard Kipling's *Kim* (1901), in which the celebration of the Great Game of intrigue and intelligence gathering between Russia and Britain occurred. From the kidnapping of dissident journalists to the electronic surveillance of embassies, Article 22 of the 1961 Vienna Convention on Diplomatic Relations invoking the inviolability of mission premises is constantly breached. The pattern of slippage in ethical and moral choices used by spies for the preservation of national security can be read in the shifting boundaries of lawful practice implemented in the early ventures of the fictional amateur spies examined in this chapter. Mysterious incidents linked to the operations of state protection, coupled with covert missions into enemy territory for the purposes of intelligence gathering, provokes profound curiosity in the reader and an appetite for narrative replication of the spy's exploits in the form of spy fiction. Earmarking the bridge between detective and spy, the final chapter explores the lawbreaking behavior of Erskine

142

5. *Spying and Lying*

Childers's accidental spies, Davies and Carruthers, in *The Riddle of the Sands*, alongside John Buchan's Hannay in *The Thirty-Nine Steps*. Charting the rise of militarism in the lead-up to the First World War, this chapter adds to our understanding of the way in which detectives morphed into spies, creating their own version of legality in the process.

The life of Erskine Childers, like that of the protagonists in his early modern spy story *The Riddle of the Sands: A Record of Secret Service,* reads like an imaginary tale of intrigue and adventure. Leonard Piper's biographical account of Childers's life relates how, after an honorable career and wartime record for which he was awarded the Distinguished Service Order, his life ended in execution by firing squad, shot as a spy by the Irish Free State in 1922 (230). His novel *The Riddle of the Sands* (1903) appeared in an atmosphere of invasion scares in England, and its message of a major, planned attack by the German Kaiser on the undefended coast of East Anglia echoed public anxieties of the time. The novel's verisimilitude also aligned with British press reports of the construction of German warships and a naval dockyard at Emden. Ignatius F. Clarke refers to a typical article in *Black and White* magazine in 1901, "The German Navy," which warns of the Kaiser's naval ambition and Britain's inertia:

> Then suddenly one day the world awoke to the fact that Germany was a great maritime power, and from that day to this, through the tireless exertions of the energetic and far-sighted Kaiser, she had gone steadily forward toward the fulfillment of her dream as the premier naval Power of the world [Clarke, 118].

The rapid expansion of the German fleet was viewed as a challenge to Britain's naval supremacy and led British authorities to agree with the press that the Kaiser intended to "live up to his new title: Admiral of the Atlantic" (Clarke, 119). According to Frederick Hitz's account in *The Great Game: The Myths and Realities of Espionage* (2005), in response to public concerns, the British government established a North Sea squadron and naval base on the east coast of Britain to protect its coastline from possible attack (77). Adding to the climate of paranoia, tales prophesying warfare by writers such as William Le Queux and E. Phillips Oppenheim enjoyed great success. Le Queux's alarmist account of a joint French and Russian attack on Britain, *The Great War in England in 1897* (1894), was published in several European languages, including German, and his work *England's Peril* (1899) presages the theme of German invasion, preparing the way for *The Riddle of the Sands* (Clarke, 63).

Generally considered a pioneering modern spy story, *The Riddle of the Sands* blends elements of detection, mystery and adventure successfully into a full-length detective novel, in contrast to the earlier short story form of detective fiction, and earned Childers critical acclaim and financial success for his efforts. As Panek explains, his work created a successful platform for future spy writers like Buchan and fused the emergent spy with the detective genre, a significant contribution to popular literature (*Special Branch,* 38). Childers's work is in perfect harmony with contemporary fears over Britain's unpreparedness for war in the face of threats to her empire and status as a world power. His protagonists in the novel, Davies and Carruthers, operate in the dual role of detective and spy, revealing how principles and personal values they once held sacred in a gentlemanly code of conduct are sacrificed on the altar of expediency and espionage, "tradecraft" appropriate to international politics. Life as an accidental spy presents a challenge to them when the welfare of the entire nation is at stake, and ruthless tactics are called for. Resorting to illegal methods to achieve intelligence information on a country not yet at war and with whom Britain continued to share diplomacy raises questions about the justification for such actions. Interweaving features of the budding espionage genre with those of detective fiction, the narrative of the story embraces altered legal and moral parameters commensurate with the fluidity of ethics in relation to patriotism and reflects contemporary historical and political issues. Cultural corroboration of the values of imperialism pervades the text alongside the theme of exposure of foreign threats to Britain's naval supremacy. Working in an unofficial capacity as detectives and spies, Davies and Carruthers constantly evoke moral apprehension over their departure from accepted codes of conduct and behavior. Testing the elasticity of moral and legal boundaries that constantly give way under the pressure of patriotic hyperbole, the image of hero is recast to overwhelm any lingering scruples and construct a popular modern identity for him. My analysis of the story *The Riddle of the Sands* explores the nature and extent of the use of illicit means in the uncovering of the German invasion plot. It charts evidence of cultural, readerly expectations and how these are satisfied by the abandonment of legal and moral principles on the part of the protagonists in response to alien threats to national security and illuminates the relationship of law with morality and justice in issues of national security and defense.

The story begins by establishing its credentials as a "true" account of events experienced by two young men, Arthur Davies and Charles Carruthers, on a yachting and duck-shooting adventure to the Baltic and the Frisian Islands off the north coast of Germany. Based on the diary and personal accounts of Carruthers, it charts their voyages with the help of detailed maps in and around German waters and the incidental discovery of a German plot to invade England's east coast. Carruthers is characterized as "a young man

144

who 'knows the right people, belongs to the right clubs [and] has a safe, possibly, a brilliant future in the Foreign Office,'" although he later admits to being a mere office administrator whose work is neither interesting nor important (Childers, 1). His position echoes that of William Le Queux's protagonist, Geoffrey Engleheart in *The Great War in England in 1897,* whose status as "the younger son of a very distinguished officer" guarantees him work as a clerk for two hours a day at the Foreign Office (Le Queux, 21). At the outset, Carruthers is characterized as a fashionable young man who is snobbishly effete and consumed with superficial concerns over sartorial etiquette and stylish manners. Since he has nothing better to do, he agrees to join an Oxford friend, Davies, on his yacht, the *Dulcibella,* for a yachting trip and some duck hunting in the Baltic. His initial encounter with Davies immediately illustrates their polarized attitudes on appearance, for Davies fails to live up to Carruthers's class-inflected ideas of how a yachtsman should appear; "No cool white ducks or neat blue serge ... [or] snowy crowned yachting cap ... that so easily converts a landsman into a dashing mariner" is how Carruthers appraises Davies (14). Davies's lack of concern for outward appearances is manifest in his dress, which comprises "an old Norfolk jacket, muddy brown shoes, grey flannel trousers ... and an ordinary tweed jacket" (14). The sight of the *Dulcibella,* a flat-bottomed, starkly furnished former lifeboat, housing basic accommodation and sparse comforts, further dismays Carruthers and erodes any expectation of luxury he has envisaged. Gradually, however, Davies's geniality, robust personality and nautical wizardry infect Carruthers in the course of the story, and he casts off the shallow accoutrements of his former life and embraces Davies's ethos of manly valor and daring in the unraveling of the ensuing mystery. According to Hitchner, the Edwardian novel, unlike future works of espionage such as Saki's 1914 work *When William Came,* advocates the benefits of a rugged lifestyle evocative of the public school ethos of good sportsmanship and healthy outdoor living (422). Offsetting the moral ambiguity of spying as a necessary evil, the sanitized lifestyle pursued by Davies and Carruthers acts as a palliative to the more questionable aspects of the behavior that follows. It implies that the inculcation of strong physical attributes builds strength of character and manliness that counter the negative psychological and moral damage linked to the dubious practice of espionage.

Davies explains to Carruthers that before his [Carruthers'] arrival and during his sailing trips around the Frisian Islands, he witnessed unusual shipping activity, including the existence of large sailing barges in the narrow channels that run in between the islands. His suspicions raised, he meets an Englishman, Dollmann, who claims to be German and whom he suspects of spying for the Germans. Explaining the reasons for his misgivings, he relates how Dollmann and his daughter, Clara (for whom Davies subsequently forms an attachment), entertain him on board their yacht, the *Medusa*, during which Dollmann interrogates him about his motives for being in the vicinity of the islands and rejects the possibility of duck-shooting at that time of year. Then, in an attempt to get rid of Davies, Dollmann offers to lead him safely through a short cut to the Elbe in his yacht but, instead, leads him into treacherous waters before abandoning him to inevitable shipwreck. However, with Davies's superior nautical skill and with the aid of Bartels, the German skipper of a nearby galliot, or barge, he escapes disaster. The detective and mystery element of the story is grounded in discovering Dollmann's true identity, his motives in wishing to dispose of Davies and in exposing the truth behind the flurry of naval activity in the waters around the Frisian Islands. In setting out his moral justification for spying on German shipping activities, Davies reasons:

> About this coast.... In the event of war, it seems to me that every inch of it would be important, *sand and all.* Take the big estuaries first, which, of course, might be attacked or blockaded by an enemy. At first sight you would say that their main channels were the only thing that mattered.... But now look at the sands they run through, intersected as I showed you, by threads of channels. It strikes me that in a war a lot might depend on these both in defense and attack ... the strip of Frisian coast adjoins the estuaries and would also form a splendid base for raiding midgets [Childers, 84].

Davies's argument for the legitimacy of his behavior in spying on German shipping is grounded in the exceptional circumstances of their position as they become aware of a possible threat to England from a surprise German naval attack. If an act of aggression is planned, their actions are justified as a means of defense and preventing the worse evils of war; its "object is to retain some semblance of a moral hold upon an activity that constantly threatens moral dissolution," as Anthony Coates explains in his study *The Ethics of War* (Coates, 3). Coates's view is in keeping with Anthony Taylor's description of the tradition of Just War theory where actions are initiated "not for revenge or personal gain but for the common good," making them morally sound (Taylor, 6). Davies proposes to Carruthers that they adopt undercover identities as young men on an innocent shooting holiday and engage in surreptitious logging of German shipping movements in the Kiel Canal, charting the depths of the sands around the Frisian Islands and spying on Dollmann's yachting activities. Carruthers initially expresses concern over the propriety of tracking Dollmann, observing:

146

5. Spying and Lying

"It's a delicate matter … if your theory's correct. Spying on a spy," to which Davies indignantly objects and insists "It's not like that…. Anyone who likes can sail about there and explore those waters. I say, you don't really think it's like that, do you?" [89].

His tone conveys feelings of guilt and apprehension over the probity of the proposed actions, based as they are on conjecture rather than solid evidence of a possible German attack, for, after all, the Germans are entitled to establish defenses of their own coastline, without question or intrusion from foreign visitors. Given that Germany and England are at peace with one another, the host country would regard the behavior of Davies and Carruthers as criminal since the German view of espionage mirrored that of Britain in many respects. Military and naval attaches were instructed to avoid espionage, confirmed in "Imperial directives of 1878, 1890 and 1900 [which] cautioned against illegal acts of intelligence gathering in host countries," as Richelson explains (Richelson, 14). The protagonists' plan to explore the waters around the coast for information on German naval strategy contravenes both the concept of innocent passage and the sovereignty of territorial waters, the subject of laws agreed to by Britain. Innocent passage of shipping on the high seas emerged during the first half of the nineteenth century, according to O'Connell, and was premised on a vessel's neutrality in transit (22). Clandestine gathering of information and surveillance of the shipping activities of a friendly state violate the sovereignty of that state, and arguably equate to the use of force, he argues (22). Since much of the action of the novel takes place within the territorial and inland waters of Germany, and since Britain agreed to abide by an international law in operation at the time which granted a range of three nautical miles to coastal states over which they have judicial sovereignty, Davies and Carruthers's actions are clearly in violation of the law. By engaging in clandestine spying, their actions must be kept secret because they transgress conventional moral or legal boundaries, as Cawelti and Rosenberg point out (*Spy Story*, 13). Under the cloak of disguise, the spy frees himself from responsibility, which allows him to do things he could not ordinarily do without serious consequences.

The heroes' suppositions of German intrigue are confirmed late one night by the arrival of an intruder on board their yacht, convincing them that the Germans suspect them of spying and raising the possibility that they may be arrested. Since they have no official standing or diplomatic immunity, the risk of arrest looms large when Commander von Bruning, a high-ranking officer in the German Imperial Navy, questions them on their intentions. Subtly alluding to his position as custodian of shipping, he recounts his suspicions about "a Dutchman trawling inside our limits" and warns, "That's my work you know—police duty" (Childers, 163). Carruthers had impressed on Davies the need to "lie like a trooper" (152) when the need arose, and he skillfully negotiates Davies's obvious embarrassment as von Bruning cross-examined them with "the most charming urbanity and skill" (Childers, 158). Von Bruning then offers a convincing counter-narrative for the animated naval activity around the Frisian Islands and Dollmann's involvement in it. Justifying Dollmann's presence in such a remote location, von Bruning claims he is part of a small local company involved in the reclamation of a French treasure ship, the frigate *Corinne,* that had been wrecked off the coast of Juist, the most westerly of the German Frisian Islands, carrying a million and a half in gold bars. Von Bruning lies as skillfully as Carruthers to preserve Dollmann's identity as a spy, but he fails to convince them; trust and truthfulness are casualties in the language of spying. Vitriol is reserved for the traitor, situated as the antithesis of the heroic image of the protagonists who determine to "scotch Dollmann," described by Davies as the "vilest creature on God's earth" (Childers, 169). No real account is given for Dollman's treason in the novel, yet the extent of his villainy is exposed when Davies and Carruthers discover his true identity from a small guidebook for yachtsman on the bookshelf of the *Dulcibella,* written whilst he was a high-ranking officer in Her Majesty's Navy. A moral and legal dilemma is presented and Carruthers, because Davies is torn between patriotism and love for Dollmann's daughter Clara, suggests that, despite having evidence of Dollmann's treachery, they should:

> [S]ail straight away and forget the whole affair. He's only some poor devil with a past, whose secret you stumbled on, and half mad with fear, he tried to silence you. But you don't want revenge, so it's no business of ours. We can ruin him if we like; but is it worth it? [Childers, 198].

Rejecting the suggestion of allowing a traitor to escape justice, Davies insists he will secure an outcome that accommodates saving Clara, yet reconciles his actions as honorable and dutiful as a citizen and patriot.

In the denouement of the story, Carruthers in his totally remodeled identity as a German seaman, dressed in oilskin jacket, trousers and muddy boots, stows away on board a tug, which is towing a barge in a trial run for the invasion of England. During the voyage, full realization of the significance of so many barges and the shipping activity in the sandy channels in between the Frisian Islands and off the north coast of Germany dawns on Carruthers; the Germans were using the cover of the Frisian Island to build barges to be used to ferry German troops to invade the coast of England. Managing to sabotage the tug, with the Kaiser onboard, by causing it to run aground on the shallow sands, he takes the opportunity to return to the *Dulcibella.* He and Davies then persuade Dollmann to sail with them, along with Clara, to

5. Spying and Lying

Holland and in a *volte-face* in relation to their previous attitude to treachery, offer, "We promise you immunity—on certain conditions, which can wait" (Childers, 309). Their offer of immunity from prosecution to a traitor configures their actions in line with the omnipotence of fictional detectives like Holmes, who bend the law to suit their actions in applying a just resolution.

Apart from the infringement of Germany's territorial sovereignty for the collection of information, a measure that is harmful to its political ambition yet essential to Britain's coastal security, a review of the behavior of Davies and Carruthers relates more palpably to questions of morality than legality. Their actions—eavesdropping, lying and deceiving their way to the truth— appear to be unreasonably unjust treatment of a friendly state in peacetime, yet mutate in the context in which they occur. By regarding them as the "duties of citizenship," they are not judged by universal laws and thus escape moral and legal boundaries, iterating a narrative pattern evidenced in the previous story of Holmes in "His Last Bow" (Hepburn, 5). Britain's position as an island nation and global trading empire that relies on the sea for what Lambert calls its "insular and imperial security" impels the protagonists to adopt an attitude of pragmatic realism in response to the German threat to national security. The foreboding of conflict can be read in Davies's assertion, "We're a maritime nation—we've grown up by the sea and live by it; if we lose command of it we starve" (101), a point of view inclined to apply what Raphael Bitton terms "the rules of necessity" (Bitton, 1025). In his insightful study of the legality of spying among nations, Bitton points out the dangers of a realist approach, such as the one adopted by Davies, which prioritizes national interests over moral duties, for it is based on the belief that the state operates in an anarchical sphere (Bitton, 1014). In this view, he argues, everyone seeks to protect their own interests. In the event of an emergency, such as the threat of war, a state will do whatever is necessary regardless of ethical considerations. Such an approach has serious implications, since difficult dilemmas of security and justice do not justify a suspension of ethics, and, considering the extent of moral harm allayed to spying, the lack of solid and legal underpinnings is worrying (Bitton, 1016). The decision by Davies and Carruthers to offer Dollmann immunity from prosecution may be interpreted either as an act of compassion in recognition of the damage inflicted on his daughter Clara by their unofficial actions or unauthorized sanction of the criminal act of treason. However, in the end, divine providence intervenes as Dollmann falls or throws himself overboard en route to Holland. Assuming judicial powers in resolving problems, Davies and Carruthers emulate the fantastic exploits of the detective and, in their role of spy hero, operate, in Cawelti and Rosenberg's words, to repair "the orderly fabric of society" (*The Spy Story*, 3).

An interesting perspective on the role of spy is offered by Rosanna Cavallaro in espionage fiction when she argues how it illustrates the demise of the law and suggests that the illicit behavior of official spies in fiction contributes to law's failure. Her reasons are based on the important function of the law as embodying "the moral norms of the culture for which it speaks." By divorcing his actions from morality and ignoring legal constraints, the spy undermines the law's legitimacy, for his actions are no longer in accord with the society in which he operates (660). Despite the rhetoric of invasion, Poplawski notes that the British Empire continued to expand from the 1870s through the end of the First World War, and for most of this period Britain remained, in effect, the superpower of the day (Poplawski, 529). An anonymous article in *The North American Review* entitled "The German Navy and England" by a German Naval Expert in August 1909 concluded by pointing out that England, by building Dreadnoughts, had itself compelled other nations to build larger battleships and that the aim of the German Naval Act in 1900 was "to prevent wars rather than win them" ("The German Navy and England," 253). Pre-emptive action, such as that undertaken by Carruthers and Davies, intensifies the likelihood of war as nations strive to match their competitors in the build up of arms. On the other hand, a surprise attack such as the fictionalized account of a German invasion arguably warrants defensive measures outside the normal parameters of legitimacy and resonates well with the public imagination.

JOHN BUCHAN (1875–1940): RICHARD HANNAY

The Thirty-Nine Steps (1915)

"Spy-hunting in Britain" is how John Buchan describes the actions of his South African fictional adventure hero, Richard Hannay, in *The Thirty-Nine Steps* (1915), written whilst Buchan was "pinned to [his] bed during the first months of war," according to his autobiography *Memory Hold-the-Door* (Buchan, 195). Buchan's views on creating memorable fiction and enduring heroes are clearly shown in an essay he wrote in 1931, entitled "The Novel and the Fairy Tale." In it, he rejects prevailing modernist criticism of Victorian novels as sentimentalizing and extols the virtues of Dickens, Hardy and Eliot as storytellers in the tradition of folk tales. Folk tales, he argues, "do not exalt passive virtue" but "daring, boldness, originality and brains … [because] the people who made them realised that the hope of humanity lay not in passivity but in action" (Buchan, 7). In his novel *The Thirty-Nine Steps,* Buchan's words resonate fully in the characterization of his energetic spy-cum-detective hero, Richard Hannay, the protagonist he created for what he called his shilling shocker. Presented as criminal and pursued by both police and enemy agents as he unravels the mystery of the thirty-nine steps, Hannay's rejection of the formal procedures of law and order for resolving his outlaw status offers an instructive insight into the construction of a popular transgressive hero of the time. Relying on his own initiative and active involvement in securing exoneration from false incrimination, he indulges in clandestinity and deceit to save himself and civilization from disaster. Analysis of the motivations and rationale underpinning the hero's behavior in responding to crime provides a contrasting picture to that of Holmes, Carruthers and Davies in the previous chapter. It charts the burgeoning use of force by the detectives for achieving successful outcomes and exposes their willingness to forego morality and legality in the interests of the state. By means of interdisciplinary analysis, this chapter explores how early spy fiction, exemplified in John Buchan's *The Thirty-Nine Steps,* builds on Victorian and Edwardian detective fiction's prototypical use of illegality for securing justice through unauthorized channels and in unlawful ways from the late nineteen hundreds to the end of the First World War. Focusing on the close affinity that exists between spy and detective fiction, it highlights the influence of genres such as adventure, romance and sensation narratives within the stories, factors that helped shape the visual image of heroic detective and spy in the upcoming silent movies. An early espionage thriller, the widespread appeal and success of *The Thirty-Nine Steps* is testimony to the ongoing ascent of spy fiction at the time and secures John Buchan's central contribution to the genre. John Cawelti and Bruce Rosenberg believe Buchan created the formula for the modern secret agent story and commend the quality of his work, in which his "moral earnestness, his sense of humor and his concern for literary values make the Hannay stories the very model of the early twentieth century spy story," a fitting tribute to Buchan's achievement in laying the foundations for a popular genre that still resonates today and that recognizes his erudition (*Spy Story,* 80). LeRoy Panek, in his assessment of key figures in the evolution of spy fiction, suggests in his work *The Special Branch: The British Spy Novel, 1890–1980* that "the modern spy story simply would not have developed along the same lines without him…. One simply cannot understand the development of the spy novel, or the detective novel for that matter, without a grounding in Buchan" (39).

Following in the tradition established by E. Phillips Oppenheim and William Tufnell Le Queux, who were instrumental in advancing the popularity of spy fiction in the wake of the war prophecy novels of the 1870s and 1880s, Buchan's *The Thirty-Nine Steps* is a novel of empire warning of threats to imperial power and styled to foster confidence in Britain's ability to neutralize them through the actions of an upstanding hero, as Panek explains (*Special Branch*, 7). Its narrative, replete with historical, social and political currency, was first published in serial form in *Blackwood's Magazine* under the pseudonym H de V from July to September 1915 before publication in novel form in November of the same year. Combining adventure and detection with political intrigue and drama, it emerged more than a decade after Erskine Childers's heroes, Davies and Carruthers in *The Riddle of the Sands* (1903). Its colonial hero, Richard Hannay, vividly encapsulates the attributes Buchan admires most in folk tale heroes: a champion striving for justice against heavy odds in the manner embraced by Sir Walter Scott, whose biography he completed in 1932. Like Davies and Carruthers, Hannay is an amateur gentleman spy who accidently becomes enmeshed in an international conspiracy. He grapples with an evasive ring of foreign agents named the "Black Stone" who are bent on destroying the British navy by stealing Admiralty plans and using them in a surprise attack. Hannay personifies the archetypal clubland hero of early spy fiction, aptly described by Richard Usborne in *Clubland Heroes*:

> In the 1920s the man of sufficient private income and absolute leisure did not excite comment. Naturally he had a West End club. The beefy type of hero was a man's man. So his club meant a lot to him. It offered him a fortress, with many of the amenities of home, but without the distractions of, or the obligations to, his womenfolk [Usborne, 3].

Usborne's description of the clubland hero of the 1920s equally applies to the many bachelor heroes who graced the pages of late Victorian and Edwardian detective fiction, including Sherlock Holmes's brother Mycroft, who notably transacted much of his business from an armchair in the Diogenes Club in London. Buchan's novel, *The Thirty-Nine Steps,* is the first of five Richard Hannay adventures whose narrative is framed, in Kestner's words, to "imprint[ing] codes of masculinity" (*Masculinities*, 1). It was written on the outbreak of war, when patriotic fervor and national interest took precedence over domestic problems, resulting in the relegation of the violent suffragette's campaign, industrial unrest in the shape of strikes and demonstrations and the issue of Home Rule for Ireland to future times. The accidental spy, Hannay, in this novel is depicted as a lonely hero who must survive in the wild conditions of a rugged Scottish landscape, an ideal location to apply his previous colonial experience acquired in the African veldt to help him stay alive and complete his mission of unraveling a political conspiracy and subverting the law in the course of his endeavors.

Boredom with London, "where he had been three months in the Old Country and was fed up with it," initiates Richard Hannay's entry into spydom. Evocative of Buchan's own opinions of London in 1903 on his return from South Africa where he was working as assistant private secretary to Lord Alfred Milner, the High Commissioner for South Africa, he writes in his autobiography:

> Those years were not the pleasantest in my life. South Africa had completely unsettled me.... I was distressed by British politics, for it seemed to me that both the great parties were blind to the true meaning of empire. London had ceased to have its old glamour [*Memory,* 127].

The hero Hannay, too, has recently arrived in London from a colonial career as a mining engineer in Bulawayo and, having accumulated a small "pile," complains that "the amusements of London seemed as flat as soda-water that has been standing in the sun" (Buchan, 5) A solitary figure in this novel "with no pal to go about with," his daily routine is framed by visits to the club, restaurants and music halls before retiring every evening to his flat in Portland Place (5). One evening, having "made a vow" to "[g]ive the Old Country another day" before taking the next boat for the Cape (6), the sudden appearance outside his flat of a "slim man, with a short brown beard and gimlety blue eyes" interrupts his ennui and draws him unwittingly into spying. Scudder is the man's name, an American journalist from Kentucky, with an interest in politics and characterized as a "sharp, restless fellow" who "always wanted to get down to the root of things" (8). Scudder confides that through his sleuthing activities, he has accidentally discovered an international conspiracy of what he claims to be Jewish agitators and anarchists, backed by financiers and designed "to get Russia and Germany at loggerheads" by assassinating Constantine Karolides, a Balkan politician who threatens to derail their plans (8). G.R. Searle points out that the entry of "rich Jews" into society at that time, particularly bankers and financiers who were welcomed into the entourage of Edward VII, created dismay amongst radical right politicians who feared their influence on British values (92). Claiming that he is aware the assassination attempt is due to take place during a diplomatic visit to England on June 15, Scudder's dangerous knowledge places him in jeopardy from enemy agents who have tracked him down. To elude his pursuers and secure his safety, he fakes his own death by acquiring the corpse of an alcoholic whose jaw he blows away with a revolver. Scudder's phlegmatic retelling of events in relation to the violence he perpetrates on an unknown corpse raises no moral apprehension in Hannay, who replies, "Hand me your key ... and I'll take a look at the corpse. Excuse my caution, but I'm bound to verify a bit if I can"; his concern lies with Scudder's veracity rather than the moral probity or legality of his actions (12). Hannay's response to Scudder reveals his indifference to the identity and subsequent fate of the alcoholic's body in keeping with his colonial heritage as a soldier in the Matabele War, where brutal encounters were a daily occurrence and death unavoidable in a wartime context. However, when Scudder is later discovered "sprawled on his back [with] a long knife through his heart which skewered him to the floor," Hannay's moral sensitivity is plain when he remarks:

> I sat down in an armchair and felt very sick. That lasted for maybe five minutes, and was succeeded by a fit of the horrors.... I had seen men die violently before; indeed I had killed a few myself in the Matabele War; but this cold-blooded indoor business was different [16].

For Hannay, there is clearly a marked difference between bloodshed in times of war, aggressive assault on an unknown corpse and the brutal slaying of a neighborhood journalist for whom he has provided sanctuary in his apartment for four days as part of a gentlemanly code of conduct. Consistent with the tradition of fictional amateur detectives who sidestep official channels of redress, Scudder fails to seek police protection or assistance in his predicament and relies solely on his own intuition and the use of whatever means are necessary to ensure survival. After Scudder's death, Hannay, too, discounts the law's ability to untangle the intricacies of an elaborate deceit framing him for Scudder's murder or to prevent national catastrophe—on the contrary, in fictional posturing of the futility of procedural justice, official police obstruct his attempts at uncovering the conspiracy by pursuing him as a criminal and undermining the nation's security in the process (15).

"Flight and pursuit" are essential elements in the spy story, according to Cawelti and Rosenberg, subsequently dramatized in Hannay's escape from the forces of law and order and the clutches of foreign agents (*Spy Story*, 83). Surmising, as he surveys Scudder's body, that "his number was up ... [t]he odds were a thousand to one that I would be charged with murder," and that circumstantial evidence was "strong enough to hang me," Hannay follows Scudder's lead and bypasses official legal channels in his attempt to find a fairer form of justice (17). His desire to retain control over his own fate empowers him rather than the official police force and calls for pragmatic judgments. Being recast as criminal forms a radical departure from the privileged middle-class status he once enjoyed and provides occasion for him, as Wark explains, to "endure flux" and "physical regeneration" like other characters in popular fiction, before achieving his ultimate goal (Wark, 32). As the victim of foul play heading for the gallows, his plight engages the reader's compassionate response and signals the need for resistance to standard means of legality which follow set norms and rules at odds with justice and ill-suited to his complex circumstances. Like the judge who "must find the answer that best fits the situation ... [he] may need to look beyond the strict letter of the law" in an interpretive framework, as Ronald Dworkin's approach to legality outlines in *Philosophy of Law* (43). Feeling like "a trapped rat in the city," Hannay's ingenuity comes to the fore when he devises a plan to vanish for three weeks to "some wild district, where my veldcraft would be of some use to me" and give him time to evade the enemy until the June deadline when he could "get in touch with the Government people," explain Scudder's findings and clear his name in the process (17).

Like Carruthers in *The Riddle of the Sands* in 1903, Hannay is unwittingly co-opted into espionage; however, despite a similar start to his spying career more than a decade earlier as he ventured into a life of disguise and deception, the conflicted ambivalence shown by Carruthers is absent from Hannay's personality. Indicative of time-hardened attitudes, Hannay expresses no qualms about lying and, entering into the spirit of "The Game," begins his adventure by bribing the milkman using a false cover story and adopting his identity. His tactics in securing the compliance of the milkman for his planned escape echo those of Sherlock Holmes in "The Adventure of The Blue Carbuncle" when he invokes the appeal of gambling for the working man. Influenced by his imminent arrest and the lack of other options, Hannay manipulates the milkman into aiding and abetting his escape by proposing, "I reckon you're a bit of a sportsman ... and I want you to do me a service.... Lend me your cap and overall for ten minutes, and here's a sovereign for you" (20). He then explains how he has made a bet in which he must be a milkman for ten minutes and offers the milkman "a quid for yourself" before making off with his "flat blue hat, white overall and milk cans" (20). Hannay's inventive solution for escape, despite its deceit, resonates with the reader's vicarious enjoyment, for after all, little harm has been done, and the unusual circumstances of his situation allow him to use minor deceptions for a graver purpose. However, it later transpires that the milkman has been held for Scudder's murder and has lost the tools of his trade; he could also be charged with aiding and abetting a felon. From an ethical point of view, Hannay applies a utilitarian view where "the end justifies the means" to achieve a greater good: his escape and the subsequent rescue of Britain's future. However, it runs contrary to Henry Sidgwick's contention in his 1874 work *The Methods of Ethics* that "common sense holds that we must not do a bad action from a good motive: to say that the end justifies the means is thought a pernicious paradox," and by this account, Hannay's sacrificing of the individual, who suffers the unintended consequences of his actions, throws doubt not only on Hannay's legality but also on his morality (Sidgwick, 179). His attitude reflects an individualist and class-inflected mindset where he believes his middle-class status and rights trump those of the milkman, who is less important in the scheme of things.

Heading for the remote hills of Galloway, Hannay begins his journey by boarding a train at St Pancras bound for Newton-Stewart in the borders of Scotland, exhilarating at the prospect of outdoor adventure and escape from arrest. However, on arrival at his destination, his excitement changes to a sense of isolation and dread as he reflects on his position as a fugitive from justice. Buchan's use of pathetic fallacy in the landscape to denote Hannay's trepidation creates a powerful mood of suspense and foreboding and exposes the vulnerability of an individual hunted down by a far-reaching enemy:

> There was not a sign or sound of a human being, only the plashing water and the interminable crying of curlews.... For the first time I felt the terror of the hunted on me. It was not the police that I thought of, but the other folk, who knew that I knew Scudder's secret and dared not let me live. I was certain that they would pursue me with a keenness and vigilance unknown to the British law, and that once their grip closed on me I should find no mercy. Crouching low in the runnels of the bog, I ran till the sweat blinded my eyes [27].

Enemy agents are construed as other: barbaric, uncivilized and without compassion, escalating the level of hazard to which he is exposed and creating justification for Hannay's operating outside the borders of legality as the only recourse for staying alive. Adding to Hannay's feelings of victimization, the appearance of a monoplane, circling relentlessly on the horizon in surveillance, adds to his fear of capture in a panoramic landscape devoid of any human shelter, reminiscent of Bentham's panopticon and entrenching a fear of the omniscient observer. Recovering from his panic, Hannay makes his way through remote moorland and encounters a young innkeeper with literary aspirations. Seeing mutual benefit in taking advantage of the young man's thirst for adventure by concocting a fictitious account of himself as a mining magnate from Kimberley who had a lot of trouble with a diamond association, Hannay exchanges creative tales of derring-do for the young man's complicity in helping him evade arrest (29). By this time, Hannay, immersed in his disguise and practiced in fabrication, enjoys the assumption of new identities and the clandestine nature of his role. As part of our popular fantasies, fictional images of clandestinity and duplicity appeal to readers, as Cawelti and Rosenberg explain, allowing them to uncouple the real from the imaginary world and ignore the realistic, moral ramifications of subversive actions (*Spy Story*, 3). In reality, as George Simmel asserts in an article evaluating the effects of deception and concealment of information entitled "The Sociology of Secrecy and Secret Societies," written for *The American Journal of Sociology* in 1906, the impact of secrecy on relationships and society in general has serious implications:

> [T]he person deceived is held in misconception about the true intention of the person who tells the lie. Veracity and mendacity are thus of the most far reaching significance for the relations of persons with each other. The lie that succeeds—that is which is not seen through—is without doubt a means to bring mental superiority to expression and subordinate less crafty minds [Simmel, 447].

By using his perceived mental acuity and true knowledge of the facts, Hannay gains furtive satisfaction in exercising power over the innkeeper whom he is able to manipulate for his own ends by lying. David Vincent in his study of secrecy *The Culture of Secrecy: Britain, 1832–1998* (1998), suggests in a wider context that due to the value placed on knowledge in a democratic system, "withholding information became at once a claim to probity and a demand for deference" (15). He goes on to explain how "it [secrecy] implied a sense of responsibility which arose from and defined a position of moral authority" (15). Adapting his argument to individual relationships, Hannay considers himself to be responsible for a secret that cannot be entrusted to the innkeeper, and that renders him more powerful as its possessor. However, in mitigation of Hannay's use of deceit, as Simmel points out, the lie is less harmful where relationships are relaxed and informal, as characterized in Hannay's relationship with the innkeeper. The comedy value of Hannay's trickery adds to its fictional appeal, for the more outrageous his tale appears, the more enthused is the innkeeper who willingly believes all he hears. By Hannay's account, a gang of diamond mining policeman had "pursued" him across the ocean, "had killed his best friend" and were now on his "tracks," a tale, partially true, that incites the young man's interest and secures his assistance (29). Hannay escapes by stealing the car belonging to enemy agents who have tracked him down, then assaults a policeman who is trying to stop him and who only desists "when he got my left in his eye" (35). Hannay's actions, like those of Watson in "The Adventure of Charles Augustus Milverton" when he assaults the man trying to impede his escape over Milverton's wall, incriminate him in resisting arrest by the official police. By now Hannay has decoded Scudder's notebook and discovered the significance of the date in June as the time when the Black Stone intends to steal documents relating to the disposition of the British Home Fleet, a key issue to be discussed between France and Britain at a secret meeting.

Having crashed the stolen car, Hannay then meets the radical Liberal candidate, Sir Harry, who requests his help by presenting a talk on Free Trade at the Masonic Hall and replacing the billed Colonial ex–Premier who has gone down with influenza. The novel's political message reflecting Buchan's conservative views is articulated through Hannay's rejection of the pacifist Liberal approach of Sir Harry's speech as "appalling rot," as he claims that "the German menace" was all a Tory invention (40). In contrast, Hannay's speech is full of rousing rhetoric about "the kind of glorious business [he] thought could be made of the Empire if we really put our backs into it." The thesis that resolute action rather than the spineless inertia of the Liberal approach of appeasement toward Germany will allow us to triumph in the end forms the substance of his discourse (40). Having confided the true state of affairs to Harry, he is assured of assistance from powerful friends. With the entitlement that comes from a government position and influential connections, Harry's godfather, Sir Walter Bullivant, the Permanent Secretary at the Foreign Office, has access to a higher level of authority that operates a modified version of state-sponsored legality. Harry instructs Hannay to head for Artinswell where Sir Walter lives, suggesting, "You can put in a week among the shepherds, and be as safe as if you were in New Guinea" (42). In the same way that the rigors of the sea sanitized and regenerated Carruthers in *The Riddle of the Sands,* the privations of the harsh outdoor trek over wild countryside reanimate Hannay.

During his pilgrimage Hannay encounters a range of individuals, including a spectacled roadman, whose identity he briefly usurps, before finally coming face to face with the villainous foreign agent, the Black Stone, in the guise of a bald archeologist. Commenting on Buchan's characterization, Cawelti suggests that each of the characters Hannay meets has a "Bunyanesque flavor in the allegorical style of *The Pilgrim's Progress* and represents some moral or social characteristic," an observation confirmed by Buchan in *Memory Hold-the-Door* (*Spy Story,* 87). He writes:

> Even today I think that, if the text were lost, I could restore most of it from memory … its spell was largely due to its plain narrative, its picture of life as a pilgrimage over hill and dale, where surprising adventures lurked by the wayside, a hard road with now and then long views to cheer the traveller [*Memories,* 18].

In imitation of Buchan's hero Christian in *Pilgrim's Progress* when he tumbles into the "Slough of Despond," Hannay reflects despairingly on his moral and legal decline from gentlemanly standards:

5. Spying and Lying

> As I sat on the hillside, watching the tail-light dwindle, I reflected on the various kinds of crime I had now sampled. Contrary to the general belief, I was not a murderer, but I had become an unholy liar, a shameless imposter, and a highwayman with a marked taste for expensive motor-cars [51].

A night spent sleeping "on the shelf of the hillside" acts as palliative to Hannay's troubled conscience and appeases his sense of guilt over the extent of his lawbreaking (52). In absolving himself he considers that since he is not guilty of the crime of murder, for which he is charged, the subsequent crimes of deception, car theft and assault on a policeman dwindle in significance and warrant exculpation on the grounds of exigency; the personal risk to his reputation is worth venturing for the benefit of humanity.

Finally, still on the run, Hannay encounters the face of evil in the "bald archaeologist," otherwise known as the Black Stone, leader of the foreign conspiracy, by inadvertently stumbling into his lair. He is construed as outwardly benign in the image of Mr. Pickwick yet inwardly malevolent, and Hannay fails initially to identify the threat the "old gentleman" poses as he commiserates with Hannay: "A fugitive from justice, eh? Well, we'll go into the matter at our leisure. Meantime I object to my privacy being broken in upon by the clumsy rural policeman" (56). The fictional representation of policemen as dull-witted is grounded in class and public perceptions, expressed in the media and explained more fully in the chapter on professional detectives. Its cultural roots lie in the nature of recruitment procedures for detectives outlined in Haia Shpayer-Makov's *The Ascent of the Detective: Police Sleuths in Victorian and Edwardian England* (2011). In it, she clarifies the role of policemen and detectives, pointing out that since they were not expected to handle "complicated investigations," "pursue long searches for clues" or engage in "lengthy readings of crime," it was assumed that "little ingenuity," "extraordinary genius" or "formal knowledge" was needed to satisfy the requirements of the job (74). Contrary to her assertion of their rehabilitation in twentieth century fiction, the novel provides confirmation of their continued undermining. Shpayer-Makov offers mitigation for the reductive view, opining that since there was a heavy focus on the physical demands placed on detectives, such as being prepared for those resisting arrest and withstanding long hours trailing suspects, an emphasis on physique rather than intelligence fostered their representation as large and clumsy. Due to their recruitment mainly from the working and lower middle classes, she suggests the powerful position they occupied in society did not correspond with the constraints of their class origins and generated "anxiety" amongst the middle-classes (258).

In his exchange with the bald archeologist, deception rebounds on Hannay, for he is initially outwitted by the expert artifice of a foreign spy in the guise of an English gentleman, equally skilled in fraudulent camouflage and duplicity. The synthesis of detective with spy is defined in the hero's superior instinct and perception, which allow him to identify the significant clue that incriminates the foreign agent. Realization dawns on Hannay:

> As he spoke his eyelids seemed to tremble and to fall a little over his keen grey eyes. In a flash the phrase of Scudder's came back to me when he described the man he most dreaded in the world. He had said that he could 'hood his eyes like a hawk [56].

In locating the visible trace of singularity in the villain's make-up, Hannay is able to isolate the criminal in our midst and expose the disguise of Englishman as fraudulent. The road to freedom materializes for Hannay when, escaping from the Black Stone, providence intervenes and he meets Sir Walter Bullivant, disguised as a dry-fly fisherman. Relieving him of his anxieties over his status as an outlaw, Sir Walter reassures him, "You may dismiss the police from your mind.... You're in no danger from the law of this land" (73). It transpires that having received Scudder's letter, Sir Walter had gone to Scotland Yard, made inquiries about Hannay, and, finding him "respectable," confirmed by Sir Harry's communiqué, he determined that Hannay should be absolved of all culpability for his actions (74). The ease with which Sir Walter expunges all traces of criminality from Hannay's record corroborates the existence of a higher authority than conventional legal channels, which raises questions over who is and who isn't subject to the dictates of the criminal law. Whilst we applaud Sir Walter's intervention on behalf of an innocent man, his mediation highlights Edward Parry's contention that "once in the dock all men are said to be equal, or very nearly so, but one may harbor a suspicion whether all men have equal opportunities of getting there;" prospects are enhanced through influential alliances (Parry, 201). Hannay's final act of disruptive lawlessness acts as the catalyst for the unraveling of the mystery of the thirty-nine steps when he engages in a violent fracas with a policeman and a group of young men of his acquaintance. Confronted by Marmeduke Jopley, whose car he had previously hijacked, he declares:

> I wasn't looking for any trouble, but my ill-temper made me play the fool. A policeman came up, and I should have told him the truth, and, if he didn't believe it, demanded to be taken to Scotland Yard, or for that matter to the nearest police station. But a delay at that moment seemed unendurable, and the sight of Marmie's imbecile face was more than I could bear. I let out with my left, and had the satisfaction of seeing him measure his length in the gutter [80].

In his frank admission that bad temper rather than the threat of personal danger prompted him to use force, he violates the Offenses Against the

Person's Act of 1861 and may be liable for prosecution for assault. We learn from Edward Jenks that "common assaults are summarily punishable by proceedings before magistrates, and are usually visited with a fine or short imprisonment, or both, according to the circumstances of the case" (208). Pursued by the policeman, whom he had "wrenched" off his feet, and the group of men with whom he had the altercation, Buchan heads for Sir Walter's house at Queen Anne's Gate where he recognizes too late the imposter, the Black Stone, masquerading as the First Sea Lord at a meeting of military leaders. The meeting concerns the details of naval dispositions that the Black Stone has absorbed using his photographic memory before exiting the house unchallenged. Unscrambling a series of clues leads Hannay to the final showdown at Trafalgar Lodge, a house with thirty-nine steps leading down to the sea and decked out in a style "as orthodox as an Anglican church" (97).

Conclusion

Set between May and June 1914, Buchan's novel presents a range of instructive historical insights into a period of intense international rivalries and events leading to the outbreak of World War I. Its political and cultural message, mirrored in the actions and interactions of the fictional detective-cum-spy Hannay, reveals a shifting narrative on traditional middle-class Christian values and attitudes that seeks to entertain more secular views in relation to truthfulness, courtesy and restraint in the use of force, fundamental features of the virtue ethicist model of detective, characterized by Sherlock Holmes. By representing the profession of spying and its concomitant ethics, which were once viewed with suspicion and disdain as worthy traits for the hero, a new construction of heroic detective and spy emerges in the public imagination, construed as one who is prepared to bend both legality and morality for the public good. The hero's willingness to indulge in physical skirmishes with the police as well as former acquaintances, if the need arises, conveys the image of a man of pluck and resolve who will stand up for what is right against all odds. Hannay's relationship with the official police and the type of justice he might expect if captured stands in sharp contrast to what he encounters with the higher legal authority invested in Sir Walter, who is party to an alternative approach to legality. Linked to hierarchical notions of justice and accountability and germane to the corridors of power, its approach replicates the tradition of casuistry, in which as Shapiro explains, "particular circumstances might alter judgment" and where "judgments of conscience" apply more readily (Shapiro, 234). Casuistry was discredited for its fraudulent use in exempting those with power and influence from prosecution for their crimes. Sir Walter is seen to operate a system where what is normally viewed as illegal may be condoned under certain circumstances. Twice in the narrative, Hannay assaults policemen by resisting arrest, yet his behavior is excused. Unlike Buchan's fictional representation, there are no instances of complete reprieve for offenders found guilty of this crime by the Old Bailey. The implementation of a parallel system of legality undermines democracy by invalidating the legal system as it stands. The likelihood of physical assaults on officers by criminals underscores the emphasis placed on stamina and stature when recruiting officers. Unlike the amateur sleuth detectives, their main function in carrying out their duties, as Shpayer-Makov explains, was "to become acquainted with the world of crime and its chief actors, with the devices used by veteran policemen to detect and curb violations of the law, and with criminal law" (74). More than a decade after Childers's novel *The Riddle of the Sands* and seven years after Conrad's anti-hero, Verloc, appeared in the 1907 spy novel *The Secret Agent,* the story chronicles a middle-class hero's struggle with conflicting loyalties, identities and codes of ethics. In the story, the boundaries of lawful enterprise employed by the protagonist shift dramatically, yet engage the reader's sympathetic acknowledgment of his rational discretion in negating the law's legitimacy. Underpinning the narrative, stark legal and moral challenges place the protagonist in a paradoxical framework where he is forced to use illicit means to procure legitimate ends. The motives and cultural messages implicit in the behavior of the protagonist may be difficult to define with contemporary hindsight, yet it is clear that there are tensions in juggling the need for loyalty to king and country with a gentlemanly code of ethics. The tone of censure of official forces of law and order in keeping with that of detective fiction accentuates the exceptional skills and heroism of the protagonist. At the same time, it locates inadequacies in a judicial process that has neither the time nor the skills to investigate crime thoroughly, preferring to rely solely on circumstantial evidence to incriminate. Faced with the dual challenge of dealing with inept and obstructive official police and subverting the threat to civilization from foreign conspirators, Buchan's portrayal of Hannay illustrates a vivid chronological progression of the increased use of illegality to achieve narrative closure in detective and spy fiction.

Epilogue:
The Vigilantes

McNeile, Wallace
and Retributive Justice

He who fights with monsters should be careful lest he thereby become a Monster. And if thou gaze long into an abyss, the abyss will also gaze into thee [Nietzsche: *Good and Evil*, 47].

In his essay "Raffles and Miss Blandish" (1944), George Orwell strongly condemns crime stories that focus their attention on glamorized criminals rather than on the successes of conscientious agents of law and order. He questions the reasons for their popularity, suggesting they offer a reflection of the morality of the times. The consequences of shifting boundaries of morality and legality in the behavior of fictional detectives and spies between 1890 and 1920 resulted in the ongoing normalization of increasingly graphic pictures of violence and corruption, once considered tasteless and beyond the pale in literature. For war-embittered readers, the law of just desserts meted out on the evil-doer by powerful fictional heroes replaced the popularity of chivalrous empathy of former investigators, keen on restorative justice, and served as a cathartic release for their sufferings and hardships. In his essay, Orwell compares E.W. Hornung's *Raffles, A Thief in the Night,* published in 1900 with James Hadley Chase's *No Orchids for Miss Blandish,* written forty years later, and demonstrates the decline of moral values and lack of principles implicit in the narratives. His conclusion that the crime story "greatly increased in bloodthirstiness' after 1918" is borne out to this day with more recent developments in crime fiction, including the rise in popularity of Domestic, Nordic, and American Noir, amongst others, sub-genres of the crime novel, assuming congruity with hard-boiled fiction (www.gutenberg.net.au).

Epilogue: The Vigilantes

Where Raffles, whom Arthur Conan Doyle referred to as an inversion of Sherlock Holmes, follows a distinct code of conduct that avoids violence, sex and murder, in Chase's novel murder, "dismemberment and exhumation" accompany unfettered cruelty and sexual perversion that premises corruption as the behavioral norm. Raffles finally redeems himself through honorable patriotic duty in the Boer War, exposing a spy and facing death with courage unlike the protagonists of Chase's novel, who die in unpleasant and seedy circumstances.

Orwell's comments on morality are apropos, to some extent, in the characterization of Herman Cyril McNeile's brawny protagonist, Bulldog Drummond, whose popularity rivaled that of John Buchan's Hannay. Drummond emerges after the war in 1920, a hero of the trenches cast in a distinctly less genteel mode from Hannay and his predecessors, embarking on a mission to prevent a coup d'état by Carl Peterson, an arch-villain, determined to bring about a Communist take-over of Britain. Drummond's actions mirror the changes wrought on fictional detective and spy heroes from pre to post First World War, part of a spiraling timeline of anti-authoritarian means for achieving justice in crime fiction. Operating in the space between detective, spy and adventurer, his code of conduct retains traces of chivalry in his attitude toward women whilst celebrating the victory of physical strength over brains in battles with the enemy, replete with anti-intellectual asides. His whimsical approach to danger and legality alternates between gentlemanly modes of heroism entailing codes of conduct where right and wrong are sharply defined, to one that prefigures the cynicism and ruthlessness of the hard-boiled school of detective fiction, characteristic of Dashiell Hammett and Raymond Chandler. Sapper, the pseudonym of Herman Cyril McNeile, a writer for the *Strand Magazine,* first introduced the popular hero in *Bull-Dog Drummond* in 1920, and took advantage of his success in ten collections of Drummond adventures until 1937, when his friend Gerald Fairlie, a "fellow novelist" and partial model for the hero, replaced him (269). In Sapper's fictional portrayal of a wartime hero caught up once more in the threat of foreign aggression on home soil, Drummond encapsulates a hero of the times whose response to crime relates to wider cultural, historical and political influences. By contemporary standards, his racist language and xenophobic attitudes appear inflated and outlandish. However, in the context of post-war Britain, their articulation and public endorsement, evidenced in the success he enjoyed as a writer, represents the deep resentment felt by many for the mass destruction caused by Germany's combative, imperial drive for world supremacy. As a spy-cum-detective acting in defense of the national interest rather than the pursuit of justice for one individual, the protagonist's patriotic duty presents a new and urgent form of necessity. In this remodeled arena of conflict, where events are dictated by military and political affairs, the normal rule of law is subject to ever more flexible boundaries, creating tensions between privately held views on morality and the need for pragmatic judgments. Testimony to the durability and continuing influence of public school mores and their acceptability as defining traits for mythical heroes in popular fiction, Drummond's code of conduct eschews mercy and compassion for vengeance and retribution. As Anthony Coates explains, "Realism resists the application of morality to war"; by implication, showing compassion reveals a form of weakness rather than strength that may spark a string of undesirable consequences (Coates, 17). The rejection of legal means of procuring justice introduces vigilantism, a pervasive theme throughout the narrative as he enlists the help of his former army friends in collective action that validates the efforts of the many over that of the individual, analogous of war. The mass-mechanized nature of war illustrated that an individual is powerless against many, but in using a vigilante force to defeat the enemy, the odds are greatly enhanced. As Stephen Banks suggests, "Groups who penalized others with their own particular view of the legal environment were not usually conscious of being part of an oppositional counter-culture" (viii). They claimed the right to "moral probity" with their imposition of informal sanctions on offenders, evocative of bygone eras where community punishments were often accompanied by collective bullying (2).

Transposing the belligerent events and actions of the war to the domestic sphere of a country house establishes the "commodification of violence," to use Robert Morrison's expression, in the introduction to *Thomas De Quincy*. Resorting to violence in response to lawless behavior, his retaliation echoes the actions of the criminal; once used in exceptional circumstances, it quickly becomes the norm (vii). The standards Drummond adopts in relation to legality in the stories emulate, to some extent, those of the villain. By excluding the forces of law and order and using physical force to repress their attempts to disrupt society, he not only usurps their function but remodels justice in a heavily retributive form of an eye for an eye. His form of justice occurs on the spur of the moment, usually without discussion and in response to unforeseen circumstances. Arguably, by ignoring legality and disrespecting authority, he undermines democracy and the rule of law, but since there is no viable alternative for destroying the enemy within, which appears outwardly to be deeply ensconced in English tranquility, he is vindicated. Sydney Horler's Tiger Standish, a character cloned in Drummond's image, achieved similar success after the appearance in the *News of the World* of Horler's crime novel *The Mystery of No. 1* in 1925.

Epilogue: The Vigilantes

In the same year as publication of *Bull-Dog Drummond*, Edgar Wallace, whose influence on the development of the detective genre Julian Symons reckons significant, published a story of vigilantism entitled *Jack O' Judgment:* a vigilante ex-policeman, bent on the elimination of a ruthless gang of blackmailers and murderers whose power and influence enable them to escape justice. Dressed from head to foot in a long coat of black silk and with his head and face camouflaged under a slouch hat and white handkerchief, he deals out his own brand of justice to compensate for the law's inability to protect society in anticipation of the masked heroes of comic fiction. Jack's token of impending punishment is a playing card that warns the evil members of the gang that their time is up. Famous for his creation of the iconic monster, King Kong, in 1931 and the J.G. Reeder detective series, Wallace's affinity with vigilante heroes whose resistance to using authorized legal channels as a means of achieving justice first emerged in his 1905 work *The Four Just Men*. It chronicles the illegitimate actions of a group of wealthy men who have devoted their lives and fortunes to setting to rights injustices that have gone unpunished. In five sequels to the book that gained Wallace an audience of enthusiastic devotees, they engage in wholly unlawful acts of vengeance and retribution ending with criminals' pardon on condition they operate within the law. Frank L. Packard's *The Adventures of Jimmie Dale,* (1917) whose American hero, similarly, operates in vigilante mode, is a society figure in the daytime and by night a Robin Hood character engaged in illicit operations.

Running parallel to the thread of steely fictional detectives and spies like Drummond who were fighting for what they believed to be right was an alternate vision of spying which emerged in 1907 with Joseph Conrad's amoral anti-hero Verloc, out for his own ends, in *The Secret* Agent (1907). Anti-heroic stances were further pursued in the complex and conflicted characterization of Somerset Maugham's *Ashenden: or The British Agent* (1928), lauded as the first realistic spy story with what Cawelti calls its "anti-heroic vision" of the intelligence agent. Ashenden reveals the reality of life as a spy, where operations go wrong, instructions are misinterpreted, people do not always respond to threats of violence in the way expected of them and fate often plays a hand in the outcomes of missions. Later, John Le Carré's depictions of spies, notably *The Spy Who Came In from the Cold,* feature a weary anti-hero following the rules of espionage in which both sides exploit their operatives for political gain, and spies are portrayed as the antithesis of refined upper middle-class clubmen of the early years of the Great Game (*Spy Story,* 45). More than a decade later in 1938, Eric Ambler, credited as the creator of the modern spy story, again dispels the myth of the suave, sophisticated model of espionage operative, epitomized by the likes of Bulldog

166

Drummond, and offers an alternative vision in his portrayal of the anti-hero Joseph Vadassy in *Epitaph for a Spy* (1938). In the story, Vadassy, a Hungarian language teacher whose passport is out of date, is mistaken for a spy and arrested by the French police. A murder has been committed at his hotel, and he is charged with finding out the real spy and murderer before he will be allowed to return to Paris to take up his teaching duties. Unlike earlier patriotic heroes, his characters are victims of circumstances beyond their control who courageously confront enemy agents in a battle of survival that entails frustrated intentions, false hopes and mistaken assumptions. Ambler's characterizations resisted the proliferation of heavy-handed, brawny protagonists like Drummond whose success clearly illustrated cultural acceptance of changing patterns of legality and morality. Such revisioning of societal values, inherent in the characterization of Drummond that is compliant with legal infractions and diminishing standards of propriety and virtue in fictional heroes, subsequently led to the arrival of Ian Fleming's James Bond. Representative of the total transformation from morally conflicted protagonists like Hannay, whose conscience generally precludes unprovoked violence or vengeful retaliation, Bond is ruthless and has a license to kill on state authorization when the national interest is imperiled by enemy threats. Post-war fears of German invasion were supplanted by the fear of Bolshevik subversion and its anarchic influence on the working man, themes fully exploited in the political narratives of popular detective and spy fiction.

The model of the hero who is prepared to sacrifice some of his own values, such as respect for the rights of others for the sake of patriotic duty, chimes with the utilitarian doctrine of seeking to maximize the welfare of many at the expense of humanitarian concerns. It also demonstrates the value placed on nationalism by the hero. Michael Cavanagh in *War and Morality: Citizen's Rights and Duties* (2012) suggests that in terms of the "othering" of the enemy, nationalism entails the view that "the nation is the center of the moral universe and the rights of individuals are secondary or have little or no importance in the overall process of governing" (6). Constructing the foe as atavistic, a strategy used in propaganda campaigns during the war, demonstrates the influence of eugenicist views of humanity that endorses a diminishing of the moral code. With the arrival of film adaptations, the visual appeal and comedic interpolations of Captain Hugh Drummond, DSO, MC, late of His Majesty's Royal Loamshires, and similar heroes, added to the appeal of handsome, witty and swashbuckling men of courage and ensured their success for decades to come.

Conclusion

In Search of Alternative Justice

In their pursuit of justice, the fictional detectives and spies in the stories examined in this work embody the shifting boundaries of ethics and morality endorsed as the norm in the societies in which they operate. Ranged over historical periods that experienced social and political flux, these stories form an archive of cultural attitudes and issues that demonstrate patterns of kinship with the present. The waning influence of morality in decision-making by the fictional detectives and spies occurs at a time of transition from strict religious enforcement of moral values to a society more attuned to secular morality in which the modern criminal justice system "rested on utilitarian foundations," as Michael Tonry explains (4). Where once judgments were based on the idea of justice and morality derived from the law of God and enshrined in the sanctity of Natural Law, Jeremy Bentham's ridiculing of Natural Rights in 1832 as "nonsense upon stilts" culminated in its demise (*Anarchical Fallacies,* Article II). Impinging on the relationship between morality and legality, utilitarian thought assumes a more cynical view "denying the existence of any deontological, mind-independent moral values" and claims instead that morality is a "matter of personal preference and subjective taste," as Wacks explains (*Jurisprudence*, 33*).* The separation of law from morality in a judicial system based on the utilitarian philosophy, a form of consequentialism, of "achieving the greatest good for the greatest number" went "hand in hand with indeterminate sentencing" and allowed judges wider discretion in determining sentences, according to Philip Smith and Kristin Natalier (4). Opportunities for abuse and miscarriages of justice increased in a judicial system heavily reliant on deterrence rather than individual justice and provided sustenance for authors and popular media writers. Demonstrating reconfigurations of justice in response to the flaws and vagaries of the law, their legal interventions reflect the changing sociological and historical conditions existing between 1880 and 1920 that gave rise to public concern. Betraying sensationalist roots, their use of illegal methods to solve crime in fictional narratives sets the stage for the anti-authoritarian behavior in crime fiction that continued to resonate throughout the century. The relationship between fictional and real detectives in the era of the study was a contentious one. Amateurs like Sherlock Holmes were posited as "specialist," as opposed to the more mundane plodding policeman, creating problems for Scotland Yard detectives who were "easy to blame for failing to prevent or solve crime" (Glazzard, 29). The depiction of official detectives as ineffectual thwarts their likelihood as fictional heroes and raises the appeal of subversive champions of justice like the lawbreaking detectives in fiction. However, in flouting the law and operating outside its constraints, the fictional detective negates its validity whilst professing to uphold its tenets. It was not until the appearance of the likes of B.F. Robinson's *The Chronicles of Addington Peace* in 1905 and Freeman Wills Croft's Inspector French stories in 1924 that official police detectives truly assumed the role of champions of justice. In modern times, the fictional lawbreaking state detective is more common than the amateur and is epitomized in the characterization of *Luther,* the television hero whose approach to crime is to disregard due process in most situations where it would hamper the realization of equitable justice. Despite his status as a professional with ethical standards, Luther uses a pragmatic form of constructive illegality to by-pass legal authority in the interests of a more individual resolution.

Improvements in the legal system in the early years of the twentieth century are reflected in Edward Parry's assessment of its impact on the poor when he applauds the "three recent acts of Criminal reform that have done much to safeguard the interests of innocent men, especially if they are poor: the Criminal Evidence Act, 1898; the Poor Prisoners Defense Act, 1903 and the establishment of the Court of Criminal Appeal" (Parry, 195). However, writing in 1915, he goes on to complain about how long it has taken to bring about change, and admonishes, "If we had such an outburst of criminal reform every ten years we should be doing well" (195). Not everyone approves of the commingling of genres in detective and spy narratives. Offering a critique of the immorality and dark view of humanity espoused in the later spy fiction of John Le Carré, Jacques Barzun laments the adulteration of detective fiction with spying narratives and remarks, "Nothing in this world can be accomplished without trust," for deception creates conditions of insecurity for all since credibility disintegrates and leads to chaos (Barzun, 167–178). Further he complains, "Under a surface likeness the purposes of spying and criminal detection are opposite: the spy aims at destroying a polity by sowing confusion and civil strife: the detective aims at saving a polity by suppressing crime" ("Findings" 167–178). Despite his protestations, the appeal of spy literature and spies, both then and now, attests to its allure and to the magnetic

Conclusion

charms of its champions; it provides a fantasy indulgence of surreptitious power, adventure and subversion, an escape from the humdrum or a thrilling encounter.

Simon Joyce in *Capital Offenses: Geographies of Class and Crime in Victorian London,* 2003, reminds us that cultural texts rarely function simply as ideological repositories of progressive or reactionary attitudes to be subsumed by readers, and points out the difficulties in ascribing motivating factors to readers from a bygone era. Nevertheless, mindful of the pitfalls of subjective interpretation, there is no doubt that popular fiction in its ubiquity and range of readership presents fertile ground for interdisciplinary analysis in any age. Influential in forming and representing the prevailing tastes, opinions and anxieties confronting the reading public, it provides a fascinating insight into a bygone era. In the context of each story, we encounter a legal framework that highlights the mismatch between legal provision and materiality boosting its fictional appeal. Detailing the dramatic infringements of the law and the rationale underpinning the illegality perpetrated by the detectives and spies through detailed close reading of narratives, this work contributes to the revised climate of detective fiction criticism.

Appendix:
Table of Statutes

1. **The Justices of the Peace Act, 1371.** Defines who is eligible to become a Justice of the Peace, their jurisdiction over offenders, including the right to imprison and punish offenders (Chapter 1).

2. **The Vagrancy Act, 1824.** Allowed for the punishment of idle and disorderly persons, rogues and vagabonds. It was enacted to cope with the increasing numbers of penniless and homeless urban poor following the Napoleonic Wars in 1815. Discharged military personnel and economic migrants from Ireland and Scotland arrived in London in large numbers, with no means of sustaining themselves (Richard Marsh's Hagar of the Pawn Shop).

3. **The Treason Felony Act, 1848.** Ensured the security of the Crown and the Government of the United Kingdom. The offenses in the act were originally high treason under The Seditions Act of 1661 and 1795 and the penalty was death (Arthur Conan Doyle's Sherlock Holmes in "The Adventure of the Second Stain").

4. **The Divorce and Matrimonial Causes Act, 1857.** Designed to allow moderately wealthy men to divorce their wives. A woman had to prove adultery, aggravated by desertion of two years, cruelty, rape, sodomy, incest or bigamy. This was law until 1923 (Arthur Conan Doyle's Sherlock Holmes in "The Adventure of the Abbey Grange").

5. **The Medical Act, 1858.** Enabled patients to distinguish between qualified and unqualified practitioners (Arthur Conan Doyle's Sherlock Holmes in "The Adventure of the Speckled Band").

6. **The Offences Against the Persons Act, 1861.** Consolidated many areas of law into a single piece of legislation and was used to prosecute those accused of committing crimes of personal injury, including a range of sexual crimes against women, and violent acts in general (Introduction, Arthur Conan Doyle's Sherlock Holmes in "The Adventure of Charles Augustus Milverton" and John Buchan's Richard Hannay in *The Thirty-Nine Steps*).

Appendix

7. **The Malicious Damage Act, 1861.** Imposed a penalty of two years imprisonment with hard labor on any "malicious spoliation," not otherwise provided for, if committed in the daytime. For acts committed between 9 p.m. and 6 a.m., the maximum penalty was five years (Arthur Conan Doyle's Sherlock Holmes in "The Adventure of Charles Augustus Milverton" and Arthur Morrison's Martin Hewitt in "The Case of Mr. Geldard's Elopement").

8. **The Pharmacy Act, 1868.** First piece of legislation to limit the sale of poisons and drugs to qualified pharmacists and druggists in Britain.

9. **The Railway Regulation Act, 1868.** Ensured a means of communication between passengers and the train guard on a non-stop journey of twenty miles or more following the first murder on the railways. It included a penalty for trespassing on the railways, fines for false alarms and provision for the removal of obstacles on the line (Richard Marsh's Judith Lee in "Conscience"). **Amended Regulation of Railways Act, 1889** introduced penalties for non-payment of fares.

10. **The Evidence Further Amendment Act—Breach of Promise, 1869.** Made provision for jilted brides, stipulating that a successful claim must be supported by proof of an engagement other than the word of the plaintiff. Proof had to be of a material standard, which was not defined (Arthur Conan Doyle's Sherlock Holmes in "A Case of Identity" and "The Adventure of Charles Augustus Milverton").

11. **The Habitual Criminals Act, 1869.** Stated that any person convicted of a felony and not serving a penal sentence was subject to police supervision for seven years to ensure that he or she was making an honest living (Arthur Conan Doyle's Sherlock Holmes in "The Adventure of the Blue Carbuncle").

12. **The Prevention of Crime Act, 1871 (Amended in 1908).** Stated that any person released on a Ticket-of-Leave (parole) could be brought before a magistrate and have his parole revoked if his behavior was deemed suspect. It enabled the judge to add a preventive detention order of between five and ten years to the original sentence if the prisoner had been proven to be a habitual criminal. Registers were kept of those convicted of crime (Arthur Conan Doyle's Sherlock Holmes in "The Adventure of the Blue Carbuncle" and Fergus Hume's Hagar Stanley in "The Seventh Customer and the Mandarin").

13. **The Licensing Act, 1872. (Amended in 1886).** Governed the licensing of premises and the sale of alcohol offenses. Drunken offenses against public order were also covered by the act (Arthur Morrison's Martin Hewitt in "The Affair of Mrs. Seton's Child").

14. **The Pawnbroker's Act, 1872.** Required registration of all pawnshops and the need for an annual license (Fergus Hume's *Hagar of the Pawn-Shop*).

15. **The Matrimonial Causes Act, 1878.** Allowed a less costly judicial separation, but without the possibility of remarriage. It was the first recognition that some wives were beaten by their husbands and needed protection. **Amended by The Summary Jurisdiction (Married Women Act), 1895.** The acts established grounds on which an abused or mistreated wife could obtain a legal separation at a local magistrates' court (Arthur Conan Doyle's Sherlock Holmes in "The Adventure of the Abbey Grange" and Arthur Morrison's Martin Hewitt in "The Case of Mr. Geldard's Elopement").

16. **The Married Women's Property Act, 1882.** Gave married women the same rights over property as unmarried women. It was the most important change in the legal status of women (Arthur Conan Doyle's Sherlock Holmes in "A Case of Identity" and "The Adventure of the Speckled Band").

17. **The Married Women's Property Act, 1884.** This act altered a woman's status from a chattel into an independent and separate individual. It was a landmark in the dismantling of patriarchy. (Arthur Conan Doyle's Sherlock Holmes in "The Adventure of the Speckled Band" and Arthur Morrison's Martin Hewitt in "The Case of Mr. Geldard's Elopement").

18. **The Criminal Law Amendment Act, 1885.** Raised the age of consent, set at twelve to thirteen in 1875, to sixteen, for the protection of both sexes following exposure by W.T. Stead in "The Maiden Tribute of Babylon" (Arthur Conan Doyle's Sherlock Holmes in "A Case of Identity").

19. **The Married Women (Maintenance in Case of Desertion) Act, 1886.** Allowed deserted wives to sue for maintenance for themselves and their children without first going to the Workhouse (Arthur Morrison's Martin Hewitt in "The Case of Mr. Geldard's Elopement").

20. **The Official Secrets Act, 1889.** Created offenses of disclosure of information and breach of official trust. It was replaced by **The Official Secrets Act, 1911,** which outlined the penalties for spying (Arthur Conan Doyle's Sherlock Holmes in "His Last Bow: The War Service of Sherlock Holmes").

21. **The Prevention of Cruelty to Children Act, 1889 (The Children's Charter).** Outlined the punishment for ill-treatment and neglect of children, placed restrictions on the employment of children and gave courts the power of search and removal of a child to a place of safety (Arthur Morrison's Martin Hewitt in "The Affair of Mrs. Seton's Child").

22. **The Lunacy Act, 1890.** Introduced reception orders authorizing mandatory detention of a person in an asylum (Catherine Louisa Pirkis's Loveday Brooke in "The Murder at Troyte's Hill").

23. **Summary Jurisdiction (Married Women) Act, 1895.** Extended magistrates' powers to order husbands to pay maintenance in the case of

desertion or neglect (Arthur Morrison's Martin Hewitt in "The Case of Mr. Geldard's Elopement").

24. **The Factory and Workshop Act, 1895.** Made provision as precautionary measures against the commission of crimes, such as the failure of factory-owners to fence off machinery or causing death or injury through neglect. It became part of the rapidly growing Criminal Law along with the Public Health Act. (Introduction).

25. **The Infant Life Protection Act, 1897.** Shifted control of overseeing paid children's nurses to the police for the protection of infants, particularly in baby-farms (Arthur Morrison's Martin Hewitt in "The Affair of Mrs. Seton's Child").

26. **The Criminal Evidence Act, 1898.** Allowed those accused of crime to testify under oath and be cross-examined (Arthur Conan Doyle's Sherlock Holmes in "The Adventure of the Abbey Grange" and Fergus Hume's Hagar Stanley in "The Eighth Customer and the Pair of Boots").

27. **The Prisons Act, 1898.** Reasserted reformation as the main role of prison regimes and led to the abolition of hard labor (Arthur Conan Doyle's Sherlock Holmes in "The Adventure of the Abbey Grange").

28. **The German Naval Act, 1900.** Augmented the strength of the German Navy (Erskine Childers's Carruthers and Davies in *The Riddle of the Sands*).

29. **The Moneylenders Act, 1900.** Was aimed primarily at small female moneylenders who lent money to neighbors at an exorbitant rate (Fergus Hume's *Hagar of the Pawn-Shop*).

30. **The Larceny Act, 1861.** Made provision for the punishment of theft and for crimes against the reputation (Arthur Conan Doyle's Sherlock Holmes in "The Adventure of the Blue Carbuncle," "The Adventure of Charles Augustus Milverton" and "The Adventure of the Second Stain"; Arthur Morrison's Martin Hewitt in "The Affair of Mrs. Seton's Child"; J.E.P. Muddock's Dick Donovan in "The Riddle of Beaver's Hill"; John Buchan's Richard Hannay in *The Thirty-Nine Steps*). **Amended in 1901.** One of the purposes of the amendment was to prevent the fraudulent conversion of property.

31. **The Poor Prisoners Defense Act, 1903.** Authorized the magistrates who committed a person to trial and the judge before whom he is tried to allow him legal aid (Arthur Conan Doyle's Sherlock Holmes in "The Adventure of the Abbey Grange").

32. **The Aliens Act, 1905.** Introduced immigration controls for the first time with "the power to prevent the landing of undesirable immigrants" and gave the Secretary of State the power to make an expulsion order (Introduction).

33. **The Court of Criminal Appeal Act, 1907.** Initiated the creation of the Criminal Appeals Court where the verdict of the courts could be challenged. The act superseded the jurisdiction of the Crown Court (Introduction to Arthur Conan Doyle and Sherlock Holmes in "The Adventure of the Abbey Grange").

34. **The Children Act, 1908.** Established juvenile courts and introduced the registration of foster parents. **The Punishment of Incest Act** made it a matter for state jurisdiction rather than the clergy (Arthur Morrison's Martin Hewitt in "The Affair of Mrs. Seton's Child").

35. **The Prevention of Crime Act, 1908.** Enabled the judge to add a preventive detention order of between five and ten years to the original sentence if the prisoner has proven to be a habitual criminal.

36. **The Official Secrets Act, 1911.** Outlined the penalties for spying as a felony and included harboring spies as a misdemeanor (Arthur Conan Doyle's Sherlock Holmes in "His Last Bow: The War Service of Sherlock Holmes").

37. **The Aliens Restriction Act, 1914.** Imposed restrictions on aliens. It was an act for operation in times of war or imminent national danger or emergency (Introduction).

38. **The Representation of the People Act, 1918.** Gave the vote to all men over twenty-one and to women over thirty who owned property to the value of five pounds or more, thus widening suffrage (Catherine Louisa Pirkis's Loveday Brooke in "The Murder at Troyte's Hill").

39. **The Sex Disqualification (Removal Act) 1919.** Removed the disqualification element of public service, meaning that women could enter the legal profession and serve on a jury (Catherine Louisa Pirkis's Loveday Brooke in "The Murder at Troyte's Hill").

40. **The Intelligence Services Act, 1994.** Made provision for the Secret Intelligence Services and the Government Communications Headquarters, including conditions for the issue of warrants and authorizations enabling certain actions to be taken (Preface).

Bibliography

Works Cited

Abel, Richard, editor. *Silent Film.* London: The Athlone Press, 1999.

"Alleged Kidnapping at Croydon." *The Morning Post.* 28 July 1894: 6. Issue 38106. *19th Century British Library Newspapers: Part ll.* www.bl.uk.

Andrew, Christopher. *The Defense of the Realm: The Authorised History of MI5.* Toronto: Penguin Canada, 2010.

Ascari, Maurizio. *A Counter-History of Crime Fiction, Supernatural, Gothic, Sensational.* London: Palgrave Macmillan, 2007.

Ashley, Mike. *Adventures in the Strand: Arthur Conan Doyle and the Strand Magazine.* London: The British Library, 2016.

The Athenaeum. Reviews from July, 1894 and June 1907 in Kathryn L. Forsberg. *Joyce Emmerson Preston Muddock: A Bio-Bibliography, 1943–1934: A Bio-Bibliography.* Graduate Paper (M. A. in L.S): University of Minnesota, 1977.

Baden-Powell, Robert. *My Adventure as a Spy.* London: Pearson, 1915.

Banks, Stephen. *Informal Justice in England and Wales. 1760–1914: The Courts of Popular Opinion.* Woodbridge, Suffolk: Boydell, 2014.

Baring-Gould, William S. *The Annotated Sherlock Holmes.* London: Clarkson Potter Publishers, 1998.

Bartlett, Ashmead. "Life on a Battleship." *The Strand Magazine.* vol. 54. July-December, 1917: 563–571. *The Strand Magazine: An Illustrated Monthly.* www.archive.org.

Barzun, Jacques. "Findings: Meditations on the Literature of Spying." *The American Scholar.* Spring 1965: 167–78.

Basbanes, Nicholas A. *A Gentle Madness: Bibliophiles, Bibliomanes and the Eternal Passion for Books.* New York: Henry Holt and Company, 1995.

Bates, Denise. *Breach of Promise to Marry: A History of How Jilted Brides Settled Scores.* Barnsley, Yorkshire: Pen and Sword, 2014.

Behlmer, George. "The Gypsy Problem in Victorian England." *Victorian Studies.* vol. 28. no. 2, Winter 1985: 231–253.

Bentham, Jeremy. "Critique of the Doctrine of Inalienable, Natural Rights." *Anarchical Fallacies.* Vol. 2 of *Works of Jeremy Bentham*, John Bowring, editor. New York: Russell and Russell, 1962.

_____. *An Introduction to the Principles of Morals and Legislation.* Oxford: Clarendon Press, 1907.

Bird, J. C. *Control of Enemy Alien Civilians in Great Britain, 1914–1918.* London: Routledge, 2015.

Bitton, Raphael. "The Legitimacy of Spying Among Nations." *American International Law Review* vol. 29 no. 5, 2014: 1009–1070.

Boone, Brian. *Ethics 101: A Crash Course in the Principles of Proper Conduct.* Boston: Adams Media, 2017.

Bourke, Charles F. "The Greatest Detective Agency in the World." *The Strand Magazine.* vol. 30, December, 1905: 694–705. *The Strand Magazine: An Illustrated Monthly.*

Brandon, David, and Alan Brooke. *Blood on the Tracks: A History of Railway Crime in Britain.* Stroud, Gloucestershire: The History Press, 2014.

Buchan, John. *The Complete Richard Hannay.* London: Penguin Books, 1993.

_____. *Memory Hold-the-Door.* London: Hodder and Stoughton, 1940.

Bibliography

_____. *The Novel and the Fairy Tale.* Oxford: University Press of John Johnston, 1931.

Buchton, Oliver S. *Espionage in British Fiction and Film Since 1900: The Changing Enemy.* London: Lexington Books, 2015.

Cavallaro, Rosanna. "Licensed to Kill: Spy Fiction and the Demise of the Law." *San Diego Law Review.* vol. 47, 2010: 641–647.

Cavanagh, Michael. *War and Morality: Citizens' Rights and Duties.* Jefferson, NC: McFarland, 2012.

Cawelti, John G. *Adventure, Mystery and Romance: Formula Stories as Art and Culture.* Chicago: University of Chicago Press, 1976.

_____. *Mystery, Violence and Popular Culture: Essays.* Milwaukee: University Press of Wisconsin, 2004.

Cawelti, John, and Bruce A. Rosenberg. *The Spy Story.* Chicago: University of Chicago Press, 1987.

Chesney, George. *The Battle of Dorking: Reminiscences of a Volunteer.* N.p., 1871.

Christ, Carol, and John J. Jordan, editors. *Victorian Literature and the Victorian Visual Imagination.* Berkeley: University of California Press, 1995.

Clarke, Ignatius F. *Voices Prophesying War: Future Wars 1763–3749.* Oxford: Oxford University Press, 1992.

Coates, Anthony J. *The Ethics of War.* New York: Manchester University Press, 1997.

Cobbe, Frances P. "Wife Torture in England." 1878, reprinted in "Making History with Frances Power Cobbe: Victorian Feminism, Domestic Violence and the Language of Imperialism." *Victorian Studies.* vol. 43, no. 3, Spring, 2001: 437–460.

Cole, Darrell. *Just War and the Ethics of Espionage.* London: Routledge, 2015.

Conan Doyle, Arthur. *The Complete Sherlock Holmes.* London: CRW Publishing, 2005.

_____. *Memories and Adventures.* London: Hodder and Stoughton, 1924.

_____. "What Reform Is Most Needed: A Symposium of Eminent Men and Women." *The Strand Magazine.* vol. 42, September 1911: 269–274. *The Strand Magazine: An Illustrated Monthly.*

Cox, Edward W. *Principles of Punishment.* London Law Times Office, 1877.

De Quincy, Thomas. "On Murder Considered as One of the Fine Arts." 1827, in *Thomas De Quincy: On Murder.* Oxford: Oxford University Press, 2009.

Derrida, Jacques. *Acts of Literature.* Derek Attridge, editor. London: Taylor and Francis, 1992.

_____. *Deconstruction in a Nutshell: A Conversation with Jacques Derrida.* John D. Caputo, editor. New York: Fordham University Press, 1997.

_____. "Force of Law: The Mystical Foundation of Authority." in Drucilla Cornell et al. *Deconstruction and the Possibility of Justice.* London: Routledge, 1992.

Diamond, Michael. *Lesser Breeds: Racial Attitudes in Popular British Fiction, 1890–1940.* New York: Anthem Press, 2006.

Dolin, Kieran. *Fiction and the Law: Legal Discourse in Victorian and Modernist Literature.* Cambridge: Cambridge University Press, 1999.

Dworkin. Ronald. *Law's Empire.* Oxford: Hart Publishing, 1998.

_____. *The Philosophy of Law: Oxford Readings in Philosophy.* Oxford: Oxford University Press, 1977.

Dyzenhaus, David. *The Constitution of Law: Legality in a Time of Emergency.* Cambridge: Cambridge University Press, 2006.

Edginton, May. "War Workers." *The Strand Magazine.* vol. 54. July-December 1917: 386–394. *The Strand Magazine: An Illustrated Monthly.*

Emsley, Clive *Crime and Society in England: 1750–1900.* Harlow: Pearson, 2005.

Emsley, Clive, et al. "Crime and Justice-Crimes Tried at the Old Bailey." *Old Bailey Proceedings Online.* www.oldbaileyonline. org, version 7.0, April 2015, January 2017.

_____. "Historical Background-Gender in the Proceedings," *Old Bailey Proceedings Online.* www.oldbaileyonline.org, version 7.

Encyclopedia Britannica. "Edward Marcus Despard: British Military Officer." www. britannica.com.

Forsberg, Kathryn L. *Joyce Emmerson Preston Muddock: A Bio-Bibliography, 1943–1934: A Bio-Bibliography.* Graduate Paper (M. A. in L.S): University of Minnesota, 1977.

Foucault, Michel. *Discipline and Punish: The Birth of the Prison.* New York: Random House, 1995.

_____. *The Foucault Reader.* 1984. Paul Rabinov, editor. Harmondsworth: Penguin, 1986.

Frost, Ginger S. *Promises Broken: Courtship, Class and Gender in Victorian England.* Charlottesville: University Press of Virginia, 1995.

Gardner, John. "Preventing Revolution: Cato Street, Bonnymuir, and Cathkin," *Studies in Scottish Literature*: Vol. 39: Iss. 1, 2013: 162–182. Available at: https://scholarcommons.sc.edu/ssl/vol39/iss1/14

Gardner, John C. *Punishment and Responsibility: Essays in the Philosophy of Law, H.L.A. Hart.* Oxford: Oxford University Press, 2008.

Gatrell, Vic. A. C, et al., editors. *Crime and the Law: The Social History of Crime in Western Europe Since 1500.* London: Europa Publications, 1980.

"The German Navy," *Black and White.* 1901 in Clarke, Ignatius F. *Voices Prophesying War: Future Wars 1763-3749.* Oxford: Oxford University Press, 1992:118–119.

"The German Navy and England." *The North American Review.* August 1909: 253.

Gibson, Colin S. *Dissolving Wedlock.* London: Routledge, 1994.

Gibson, Mary, and Nicole H. Rafter. *Criminal Man: Cesare Lombroso.* Durham, NC: Duke University Press, 2006.

Gilmour, David. *The Long Recessional: The Imperial Life of Rudyard Kipling.* London: Pimlico Edition, 2003.

Glazzard, Andrew. *Conrad's Popular Fictions: Secret Histories and Sensational Novels.* Basingstoke: Palgrave Macmillan, 2015.

Goldie, David. "Popular Fiction: Detective Novels from Holmes to Rebus" in Carruthers, Gerard, and Liam McIlvanney, editors. *The Cambridge Companion to Scottish Literature.* New York: Cambridge University Press, 2012: 188–202.

Goldman, Jan. *Ethics of Spying: A Reader for the Intelligence Professional.* Lanham, MD: Scarecrow, 2010.

Gray, Adrian. *Crime and Criminals of Victorian England.* Gloucestershire: The History Press, 2011.

Gregoriou, Christiana. *Deviance in Contemporary Crime Fiction.* London: Palgrave Macmillan, 2007.

Guest, Anthony. "The State of the Law Courts"

The Strand Magazine. vol. 1. January to June 1891: 402–409, 531–538, 638–647. *The Strand Magazine: An Illustrated Monthly.*

_____. "The State of the Law Courts: The Criminal Courts." *The Strand Magazine.* vol. 2. July-December 1891: 84–92. *The Strand Magazine: An Illustrated Monthly.*

Hamilton, Susan. "Making History with Frances Power Cobbe: Victorian Feminism, Domestic Violence and the Language of Imperialism." *Victorian Studies.* vol. 43, no.3, 2001: 437–460.

Hart, H.L.A. *Punishment and Responsibility: Essays in the Philosophy of Law.* Oxford: Oxford University Press, 2008.

Hepburn, Allan. *Intrigue, Espionage and Culture.* New Haven, CT: Yale University Press, 2014.

Hermes, Joke. *Re-reading Popular Culture.* Oxford: Blackwell Publishing, 2005.

Hide, Louise. *Gender and Class in English Asylums: 1890-1914.* Basingstoke: Palgrave Macmillan, 2014.

Hitchner, Thomas. "Edwardian Spy Literature and the Ethos of Sportsmanship: The Sport of Spying." *English Literature in Transition, 1880-1920.* vol. 53, no.4, 2010: 413–430.

Hitz, Frederick P. *The Great Game: The Myths and Reality of Espionage:* New York: Vintage Book, Random House, 2005.

Hollander, Bernard, M.D. "Can Criminals Be Cured by Surgical Operation?" *The Strand Magazine.* vol. 35, January, 1908: 94–96. *The Strand Magazine: An Illustrated Monthly.*

Hostettler, John. *A History of Criminal Justice in England and Wales.* Hampshire: Waterside Press, 2009.

Hudson, Barbara. *Understanding Justice: An Introduction to Ideas, Perspectives and Controversies in Modern Penal Theory.* Buckingham: Open University Press, 1996.

Hume, Fergus. *Hagar of the Pawn Shop.* New York: F. M. Buckles, 1898; reprinted London: Greenhill, 1985.

Hunt, Alan. *Governing Morals: A Social History of Moral Regulation.* Cambridge: Cambridge University Press, 1999.

Jenks, Edward. *The History of the Doctrine of Consideration in English Law.* London:

Bibliography

C. J. Clay and Sons, 1892, reprinted by BiblioLife, 2015.

Johnston, Helen, et al. *Victorian Convicts: 100 Criminal Lives*. Barnsley: Pen and Sword Books, 2016.

Johnston, Helen. *Crime in England 1815–1880: Experiencing the Criminal Justice System*. New York: Routledge, 2015.

Johnstone, T.E. "Judges Rules and Police Interrogation in England Today." *Journal of Law and Criminology*. vol. 57.1, article 12. 1966.

Jones, Michael. *The Byronic Hero and the Rhetoric of Masculinity in the 19th Century British Novel*. Jefferson, NC: McFarland, 2017.

Joyce, Simon. *Capital Offenses: Geographies of Class and Crime in Victorian London*. Charlottesville: University of Virginia Press, 2003.

Kant, Immanuel. Translated by Thomas K. Abbott. *Critique of Practical Reason*. New York: Prometheus Books, 1996.

Kemp, Sandra. *Edwardian Fiction: An Oxford Companion*. Oxford: Oxford University Press, 1997.

Kerr, Douglas. *Conan Doyle: Writing Profession and Practice*. Oxford: Oxford University Press, 2013.

_____. *Eastern Figures: Orient and Empire in British Writing*. Hong Kong: Hong Kong University Press, 2008.

Kertzer, Jonathan. *Poetic Justice and Legal Fictions*. Cambridge: Cambridge University Press, 2010.

Kestner, Joseph A. *The Edwardian Detective: 1901–1915*. UK: Ashgate Publishing, 1999.

_____, *Masculinities in British Adventure Fiction, 1880–1915*. Aldershot: Ashgate Publishing, 2010.

_____, *Sherlock's Sisters: The British Female Detective 1864–1913*. Aldershot: Ashgate Publishing, 2003.

Kilday, Anne M, and David Nash. *Histories of Crime: Britain 1600–2000*. England: Palgrave Macmillan, 2010.

Kingsbury, Celia M. *For Home and Country: World War I Propaganda on the Home Front*. Lincoln: University of Nebraska, 2010.

Kipling, Rudyard. *Kim*. London: Macmillan, 1901, reprinted in *Wordsworth Classics*. St. Ives: Clays Publishing, 2009.

Klein, Kathleen G. *The Woman Detective: Gender and Genre*. USA: University of Illinois Press, 1995.

Knight, Stephen T. *Continent of Mystery: A Thematic History of Australian Crime Fiction*. Melbourne: Melbourne University Press, 1997.

_____. *Crime Fiction: 1800–2000: Detection, Death, Diversity*. Basingstoke: Palgrave Macmillan, 2004.

_____. *Form and Ideology in Crime Fiction*. Bloomington: Indiana University Press, 1980.

_____. *Secrets of Crime Fiction Classics: Detecting the Delights of 21 Enduring Stories*. Jefferson, NC: McFarland Publishers, 2014.

Kukathas, Chandran, and Phillip Pettit. *Rawls: A Theory of Justice and its Critics*. Stanford, California: Stanford University Press, 1990.

Kungl, Carla T. *Creating the Fictional Female Detective: The Sleuth Heroines of British Writers, 1890–1940*. Jefferson, NC: McFarland Publishers, 2006.

Lambert, Andrew D. *War at Sea in the Age of Sail*. (Smithsonian History of Warfare): Orion, 2000.

Lankester, Sir Ray. "Culture and German Culture." *The Strand Magazine*. vol. 49, January, 1915: 31–39. *The Strand Magazine: An Illustrated Monthly*.

Ledger, Sally. *The New Woman: Fiction and Feminism at the fin de siècle*. Manchester: Manchester University Press, 1997.

Le Queux, William. *The Great War in England in 1897*. London: Tower Publishing. 1895.

_____. *Spies of the Kaiser: Plotting the Downfall of England*. 1909. Reprinted in London: Hurst and Blackett, 1918.

Lock, Joan. *Dreadful Deeds and Awful Murders: Scotland Yard's First Detectives*. Somerset: Barn Owl Books, 1990.

Malcolm, Joyce L. *Guns and Violence: The English Experience*. Cambridge, MA: Harvard University Press, 2004.

Mandel, Ernest. *Delightful Murder: A Social History of the Crime Story*. Minneapolis: University of Minnesota Press, 1984.

Marsh, Richard. *The Adventures of Judith Lee*. London: Methuen, 1916.

_____. (Richard Bernard Heldmann). *The Complete Adventures of Judith Lee*. California, USA: Black Coat Press, 2012.

Bibliography

_____. *Judith Lee: Some Pages from Her Life.* London: Methuen, 1912.

McLaren, Angus. *A Prescription for Murder: The Victorian Serial Killings of Thomas Neill Cream.* Chicago: University of Chicago Press, 1995.

_____. *Sexual Blackmail: A Modern History.* Cambridge, MA: Harvard University Press, 2002.

McNeile, Herman C. (Sapper). *Bulldog Drummond.* London: Hodder and Stoughton, 1920, reprinted by Hodder and Stoughton, 2007.

Miller, D. A. *The Novel and the Police.* Berkeley: University of California Press, 1988.

Milligan, Barry. *Pleasures and Pains: Opium and the Orient in 19th Century British Culture.* Charlottesville: University of Virginia Press, 1995.

Moretti, Franco. *Signs Taken For Wonders.* London: Verso, 1983.

Morning Post. Saturday 31 January 1891– "Supreme Court of Judicature, Court of Appeal." Case of Mr Leslie Fraser Duncan. *The British Library Nineteenth Century Newspapers.* Issue 37014:2.

Morrison, Arthur. "|The Case of Mr Foggatt." *The Strand Magazine.* vol. 7, May, 1894: 526–537.

_____. "The Case of the Dixon Torpedo." *The Strand Magazine.* vol. 7, June, 1894: 563–574.

_____. Introduced by E.F. Bleiler. *Best Martin Hewitt Detective Stories.* New York: Dover Publications, 1976.

Morrison, Robert. Introduction to *Thomas De Quincy* in *Thomas De Quincy: On Murder.* Oxford: Oxford University Press, 2009.

Muddock, Preston J. E. *Dick Donovan: The Glasgow Detective.* Edinburgh: Mercat Press, 2005.

_____. *Pages From an Adventurous Life.* New York: M. Kennerly, 1907.

_____ (Donovan, Dick). *Riddles Read.* London: Chatto & Windus, 1896.

Murphy, J.G. 'Retributive Justice.' Stanford Encyclopedia of Philosophy (www.plato.stanford.edu).

Newens, Stanley. *Arthur Morrison.* Loughton: The Alderton Press, 2008.

Nietzsche, Friedrich. *Beyond Good and Evil: Prelude to a Philosophy of the Future.* edited by Rolf Peter Horstmann and Judith Norman. Cambridge: Cambridge University Press, 2002.

_____. *On the Genealogy of Morality.* editor. T.R.N. Rogers. Translated by Horace B. Samuel. New York: Dover Publications, 2003.

Nord, Deborah E. *Gypsies and the British Imagination: 1807–1930.* New York: Columbia University Press, 2006

_____. *Walking the Victorian Streets: Women, Representation and the City.* Ithaca, NY: Cornell University Press, 1995.

Nordon, P. *Conan Doyle.* London: John Murray, 1996.

OBP. 20 April 1885, trial of James George Gilbert and Harry Burton (t18850420–532).

O'Connell, Daniel P. *The Influence of Law on Sea Power.* Manchester: Manchester University Press, 1975.

O'Connell, Sean, *Credit and Community: Working Class Debt in the UK since 1880.* Oxford: Oxford University Press, 2009.

Old Bailey Proceedings Online. 3 March 1890, trial of John Twyher (t18900303–234).

Ousby, Ian. *Bloodhounds of Heaven: The Detective in English Fiction from Godwin to Doyle.* London: Harvard University Press, 1976.

Panek, Leroy. L. *After Sherlock Holmes: The Evolution of British and American Detective Stories, 1891-1914.* Jefferson, NC: McFarland Publishers, 2014.

_____. *Before Sherlock Holmes: How Magazines and Newspapers Invented the Detective Story.* Jefferson, NC: McFarland Publishers, 2011.

_____. *Probable Cause: Crime Fiction in America.* Bowling Green, OH: Bowling Green State University Press, 1990.

_____. *The Special Branch: The British Spy Novel 1890-1980.* Bowling Green, OH: Bowling Green University Popular Press, 1981.

Parry, Edward A. *The Law and the Poor.* 1914. Clark, NJ: The Lawbook Exchange, www.gutenberg.org, eBook. 2004.

Perkin, Harold. *The Rise of Professional Society: England Since 1880.* London: Routledge, 1989.

Pinkerton, Allan. *The Gypsies and the Detectives.* New York: G.W. Gillingham Co. Publishers, 1879.

Bibliography

_____. *The Pinkerton Casebook: Adventures of the Original Private Eye*. Bruce Durie, editor. Edinburgh: Mercat Press, 2007.

Pinkerton Consulting and Investigations. "History of the Pinkerton Detective Agency." www.pinkerton.com, 2017.

Piper, Leonard. *The Tragedy of Leonard Piper: Dangerous Waters: The Life and Death of Erskine Childers*. New York: Hambledon, 2003.

Pittard, Christopher. "Cheap, Healthful Literature": *The Strand Magazine*. Fictions of Crime, and Purified Reading Communities." *Victorian Periodicals Review*. vol. 40, no.1, Spring, 2007: 1–23.

_____. *Purity and Contamination in Late Victorian Detective Fiction*. University of Portsmouth, UK: Ashgate Publishing Limited, 2011.

Pope, Jessie. Preface to *The Ragged-Trousered Philanthropists* by Robert Tressell. London: G. Richards, 1914.

Poplawski, Paul. *English Literature in Context*. Cambridge: Cambridge University Press, 2008.

Pound, Reginald. *The Strand Magazine: 1891–1950*. London: Heinemann, 1966.

Priestman, Martin. *The Cambridge Companion To Crime Fiction*. Cambridge: Cambridge University Press, 2003.

_____. *Crime Fiction: From Poe to the Present*. Plymouth: Northcote, 1998.

_____. *Detective Fiction and Literature: The Figure on the Carpet*. New York: St. Martin's Press, 1991

Proctor, Tammy M. *Female Intelligence: Women and Espionage in the First World War*. New York: New York University Press, 2003.

Putney, Charles R., Joseph A. Cutshall King and Sally Sugarman. *Sherlock Holmes: Victorian Sleuth to Modern Hero*. London: The Scarecrow Press, 1996.

Pykett, Lyn. *The Improper Feminine: The Women's Sensation Novel and the New Woman Writing*. London and New York: Routledge, 1992.

Radford, Andrew. "Victorian Detective Fiction." *Literature Compass*. vol.5, no.6, 2008: 1179–1196.

Rawls, John. *A Theory of Justice*. Oxford: Oxford University Press, 1999.

Reviews of J. E. P Muddock's fiction in *The Athenaeum*. July 7 1894 and June 22 1907, and *The Spectator*. June 1907, in Kathryn L. Forsberg. *Joyce Emmerson Preston Muddock: A Bio-Bibliography, 1943–1934: A Bio-Bibliography*. Graduate Paper (M. A. in L.S): University of Minnesota, 1977.

Rowbotham, Judith, and Kim Stevenson, editors. *Criminal Conversations: Victorian Crimes, Social Panic and Moral Outrage*. Ohio: The Ohio State University Press, 2005.

Ruston, Sharon. "Representations of Drugs in Nineteenth Century Literature." The British Library, May 2014. www.bl.uk

Rzepka, Charles K. *Detective Fiction: Cultural History of Literature*. Cambridge: Polity Press, 2005.

St. George, Andrew W. *The Descent of Manners: Etiquette, Rules and the Victorians*. London: Chatto and Windus, 1993.

Sarat, Austin, and Nasser Hussain, editors. *Forgiveness, Mercy and Clemency*. Stanford: Stanford University Press, 2007.

Schooling, J. Holt. "Nature's Danger Signals: A Study of the Faces of Murderers." *Harmsworth Magazine*. 1898 in Christopher Pittard. *Purity and Contamination in Late Victorian Detective Fiction*. University of Portsmouth, UK: Ashgate Publishing Limited, 2011: 109.

Schramm, Jan-Melissa. *Atonement and Self-Sacrifice in Nineteenth Century Narrative*. Cambridge: Cambridge University Press, 2012.

Searle, Geoffrey R. in Alan O'Day, editor. *The Edwardian Age: Conflict and Stability, 1900–1914*. London: Macmillan Press, 1979.

The Secret Barrister. *Stories of the Law and How It's Broken*. London: Macmillan, 2018.

Seitler, Dana. *Atavistic Tendencies: The Culture of Science in American Modernity*. Minneapolis: University of Minnesota Press, 2008.

Shanley, Mary L. *Feminism, Marriage and the Law in Victorian England*. Princeton, NJ: Princeton University Press, 1989.

Shapiro, Barbara. "Circumstantial Evidence: Of Law, Literature, and Culture." *Yale Journal of Law and the Humanities*. vol. 5, no.1, Mar. 2013: 219–241.

Shpayer-Makov, Haia. *The Ascent of the Detective: Police Sleuths in Victorian and*

Bibliography

Edwardian England. Oxford: Oxford University Press, 2011.

Sidgwick, Henry. *The Methods of Ethics.* Cambridge: Cambridge University Press, First Published in 1874. Digital Print, 2012.

Simmel, George. "The Sociology of Secrecy and Secret Societies." *The American Journal of Sociology.* vol. xi, no. 4, Jan.1906: 441–498.

Simon, William H. *Virtuous Lying: A Critique of Quasi–Categorical Moralism*, 12. Geo. Legal Ethics. 1999, 433.

Sims, George. *How the Poor Live, and Horrible London.* London: Chatto and Windus, 1889.

Slung, Michele B. *Crime on her Mind: Fifteen Stories of Female Sleuths from the Victorian Era to the Forties.* Middlesex: Penguin Books Ltd, 1975.

Smith, Phillip, and Kristin Natalier. *Understanding Criminal Justice: Sociological Perspectives.* London: Sage Publications, 2005.

Smith, Roger. *Trial By Medicine: Insanity and Responsibility in Victorian Trials.* Edinburgh: Edinburgh University Press, 1981.

Stafford, David. *The Silent Game: The Real World of Imaginary Spies.* Athens: The University of Georgia Press, 1991.

Stoddard, "The Martyrdom of Nurse Cavell." *The Manchester Guardian.* October 22, 1915.

"Supreme Court of Judicature, Court of Appeal." *The Morning Post.* Saturday 31 January 1891:2, Issue 37014. *19th Century British Library Newspapers: Part ll.* www.bl.uk.

Sussex, Lucy. *Women Writers and Detectives in Nineteenth Century Detective Fiction: The Mothers of the Mystery Genre.* London: Palgrave Macmillan, 2010.

Swinton, Col. E. D. "The Tanks." *The Strand Magazine.* vol. 54. July-December 1917: 270–277. *The Strand Magazine: An Illustrated Monthly.*

Symons, Julian. *Bloody Murder: From the Detective Story to the Crime Novel—A History.* Revised Second Edition. London: Pan, 1992.

Taylor, Anthony. *London's Burning: Pulp Fiction, the Politics of Terrorism and the Destruction of the Capital in British Popular Culture, 1840–2005.* London: Continuum, 2012.

Tonry, Michael, editor. *Why Punish? How Much? A Reader on Punishment.* New York: Oxford University Press, 2011.

Turner, Cecil J. W. *Kenny's Outlines of Criminal Law.* Cambridge: Cambridge University Press, 1964.

Uglow, Steven. *Criminal Justice.* London: Sweet and Maxwell Limited, 2002.

Usborne, Richard. *Clubland Heroes: A Nostalgic Study of Some Recurrent Characters in the Romantic Fiction of Dornford Yates, John Buchan and Sapper.* London: Hutchinson, 1983.

Vale, Allison. *The Woman Who Murdered Babies for Money: The Story of Amelia Dyer.* London: Andre Deutsch Publishers, 2011.

Vincent, David. *The Culture of Secrecy: Britain, 1832–1998.* Oxford: Oxford University Press, 1998.

_____. *I Hope I Don't Intrude: Privacy and its Dilemmas in Nineteenth Century Britain.* Oxford: Oxford University Press, 2015.

Vuohelainen, Minna. *Richard Marsh.* Cardiff: University of Wales Press, 2015.

Wacks, Raymond. *The Philosophy of Law: A Very Short Introduction.* Oxford: Oxford University Press, 2006.

_____. *Understanding Jurisprudence: An Introduction to Legal Theory.* Oxford: Oxford University Press, 2005.

Wade, Stephen. *Spies in the Empire: Victorian Military Intelligence.* London: Anthem Press, 2007.

Walkate, Sandra. "Courting Compassion: Victims, Policy and the Question of Justice." *The Howard Journal of Criminal Justice.* Vol. 51, no. 2, May 2012: 109–121.

Walkowitz, Judith R. *City of Dreadful Delight: Narratives of Sexual Danger in Late Victorian London.* Chicago: University of Chicago Press, 2013.

Wark, Wesley, editor. *Spy Fiction, Spy Films and Real Intelligence.* New York: Routledge, 1991.

Watt, Peter Ridgeway, and Joseph Green. *The Alternative Sherlock Holmes: Parodies and Copies.* Aldershot and Burlington: Ashgate, 2003.

Wawro, Geoffrey. *Warfare and Society in Europe.* New York: Routledge, 2000.

Bibliography

Welsh, Alexander. *Strong Representations: Narrative and Circumstantial Evidence in England.* Baltimore: The Johns Hopkins University Press, 1992.

White, Claude G. "The Aerial Menace: Why there is Danger in England's Apathy." *The Strand Magazine.* vol. 42, July, 1911: 3–8. *The Strand Magazine: An Illustrated Monthly.*

Wiener, Martin J. *Men of Blood: Violence, Manliness and Criminal Justice in Victorian England.* Cambridge: Cambridge University Press, 2004.

_____. *Reconstructing the Criminal: Culture, Law and Policy in England, 1830–1914.* Cambridge: Cambridge University Press, 1994.

Winder, W. H. D. "The Development of Blackmail." *The Modern Law Review.* vol. 5, no.1, July 1941.

Wojtczak, Helena. "British Women's Emancipation Since the Reformation." *History of Women.* www.historyofwomen.org.

Young, Sarah J. "Russian Literature, History and Culture." sarahjyoung.com.

Zedner, Lucia. *Women, Crime and Custody in Victorian England.* Oxford: Oxford University Press, 2004.

Other Sources

Ardis, Ann L. *New Women, New Novels: Feminism and Early Modernism.* New Brunswick, NJ: Rutgers University Press, 1990.

Aristodemou, Maria et al. *Crime Fiction and the Law.* Abingdon, Oxon: Birkbeck Law Press, 2017.

Barnes, Jonathan. *The Presocratic Philosophers: The Arguments of the Philosophers.* New York: Routledge, 1979.

Basbanes, Nicholas A. *A Gentle Madness: Bibliophiles, Bibliomanes and the Eternal Passion for Books.* New York: Henry Holt and Company, 1995.

Beattie, John M. "Looking Back at "Property, Authority and the Criminal Law." *Legal History.* vol. 10, 2006: 15–20.

_____. *Policing and Punishment in London: Urban Crime and the Limits of Terror, 1660–1750.* Oxford: Oxford University Press, 2001.

Bell, Ian, and Graham Daldry, editors. *Watching the Detectives.* London: Macmillan, 1920.

Bennett, Tony. *Popular Fiction: Technology, Ideology, Production, Reading.* London: Routledge, 1990.

Blackburn, Simon. *Ethics: A Very Short Introduction.* Oxford: Oxford University Press, 2003.

Blackstone, William. *Blackstone's Commentaries on the Laws of England.* London: Routledge-Cavendish, 2001.

Brandt, R. B. "Utilitarianism and the Rules of War." *Philosophy and Public Affairs.* vol.1, no. 2, Winter, 1972: 145–165.

Brantlinger, Patrick. *The Reading Lesson: The Threat of Mass Literacy in Nineteenth Century British Fiction.* Bloomington: University of Indiana Press, 1998.

_____. *Rule of Darkness: British Literature and Imperialism, 1830–1914.* Ithaca, NY: Cornell University Press, 1988.

_____. *The Spirit of Reform: British Literature and Politics, 1832–1867.* Cambridge, MA: Harvard University Press, 1977.

Brooks, Peter. *Reading for the Plot: Design and Intention in Narrative.* Cambridge, MA: Harvard University Press, 1992.

Carey, John. *The Intellectuals and the Masses: Pride and Prejudice among the Literary Intelligentsia, 1880–1939.* London: Faber & Faber, 1992.

Chandler, Raymond. "The Simple Art of Murder." *Atlantic Monthly.* December 1944, reprinted in *The Art of the Mystery Story.* Howard Haycraft, editor. New York: Carroll and Graf, 1992.

Chomsky, Noam. *Knowledge of Language: Its Nature, Origin and Use.* London: Praeger, 1986.

Cover, Robert. "The Folktales of Justice: Tales of Jurisdiction." *Faculty Scholarship Series.* Paper 2706.

Cross, Nigel. *The Common Writer: Life in Nineteenth Century Grub Street.* Cambridge: Cambridge University Press, 1985.

Doggett, Maeve E. *Marriage, Wife-Beating and the Law in Victorian England: Law in Context.* London: Weidenfeld and Nicolson, 1992.

Dresner, Lisa M. *The Female Investigator in Literature, Film and Popular Culture.* Jefferson, NC: McFarland, 1967.

Eco, Umberto, and Thomas Sebeok, editors. *The Sign of Three: Dupin, Holmes, Peirce.*

Bloomington: Indiana University Press, 1983.

Effron, Malcah, and Stephen Knight. *The Millennial Detective: Essays on Trends in Crime Fiction, Film and Television, 1990–2010*. Jefferson, NC: McFarland, 2011.

Eliot, Thomas S. *Selected Essays, 1917–1932*. London: Faber, 1932.

Emsley, Clive. *Hard Men: The English and Violence since 1750*. Cambridge: Cambridge University Press, 2005.

Emsley, Clive, and Haia Shpayer-Makov. *Police Detectives in History: 1750–1950*. Aldershot: Ashgate Publishing, 2006.

Evans, Mary. *The Imagination of Evil*. London: Continuum International, 2009.

Fitzjames, James S. *A History of the Criminal Law of England in Three Volumes*. First published 1883. Digitized by Google. *Harvard University*. www.archive.org.

Fox, Pamela. *Class Fictions: Shame and Resistance in the British Working Class Novel*. Durham, NC: Duke University Press, 1994.

Frank, Lawrence. *Victorian Detective Fiction and the Nature of Evidence: The Scientific Investigations of Poe, Dickens and Doyle*. London: Palgrave Macmillan, 2003.

Gardner, John C. *Law as a Leap of Faith*. Oxford: Oxford University Press, 2012.

_____. *On Moral Fiction*. New York: Basic Books, 1978.

Gilbert, Sandra, and Susan Gubar. *The Madwoman in the Attic: The Woman Writer and the Nineteenth Century Literary Imagination*. New Haven, CT: Yale University Press, 1979.

Gladfelder, Hal. *Criminality and Narrative in Eighteenth Century England: Beyond the Law*. Baltimore: The John Hopkins University Press, 2001.

Glover, Dorothy, and Graham Green, editors. *Victorian Detective Fiction*. London: Bodley Head, 1996.

Grossman, Jonathan H. *The Art of Alibi: English Law Courts and the Novel*. Baltimore: The Johns Hopkins University Press, 2002.

Hagan, John, and Ruth Peterson, editors. *Crime and Inequality*. Stanford, CA: Stanford University Press, 1995.

Harris, Susan C. "Pathological Possibilities: Contagion and Empire in Doyle's Sherlock Holmes Stories." *Victorian Literature and Culture*. vol. 31, no.2, 2003: 447–466.

Hay, Douglas, and Francis G. Snyder, editors. *Policing and Prosecution in Britain: 1750–1850*. Oxford: Oxford University Press, 1989.

Haycraft, Howard, editor. *The Art of the Mystery Story: A Collection of Critical Essays*. New York: Simon & Schuster, 1946.

Herbert, Rosemary, editor. *The Oxford Companion to Crime and Mystery*. Oxford: Oxford University Press, 1999.

Herring, Jonathan. *Criminal Law Statutes, 2012–2013*. London: Routledge, 2013.

Hiley, Nicholas. "Decoding German Spies: British Spy Fiction 1908–1918." *Intelligence and National Security*, vol. 5, no. 4, Oct. 1990: 55–79.

Himmelfarb, Gertrude. *Marriage and Morals among the Victorians*. Chicago: Ivan R. Dee Publishers, 1975.

Hoffmann, Josef. *Philosophies of Crime Fiction*. Harpenden, Hertfordshire: No Exit Press, 2013.

Hopkirk, Peter. *The Great Game: The Struggle for Empire in Central Asia*. New York: Kodansha International, 1994.

Jack, Adrian. *Detective Stories from The Strand*. London: Folio Society, 1995.

James, William. *Pragmatism: A New Name for Some Old Ways of Thinking*. Cambridge, MA: Harvard University Press, 2014.

Jann, Rosemary. *The Adventures of Sherlock Holmes: Detecting Social Order*. New York: Twayne Publishers, 1995.

Jonsen, Albert, and Stephen Toulman. *The Abuse of Casuistry: A History of Moral Reasoning*. Los Angeles: University of California Press, 1989.

Kalikoff, Beth. *Murder and Moral Decay in Victorian Popular Literature*. Ann Arbor: UMI Research Press, 1986.

Keating, H. R. F. *Whodunnit: A Guide to Crime, Suspense and Spy Fiction*. New York: Van Nostrand Reinhold, 1982.

King, Peter. *Crime and Law in England: 1750–1840*. Cambridge: Cambridge University Press, 2006.

Kleingeld, Pauline. "Kantian Patriotism." *Journal of Philosophy and Public Affairs*. vol. 29, no. 4, 2000: 313–341.

Knowles, Owen. *An Annotated Critical Biog-*

Bibliography

raphy of Joseph Conrad. New York: Harvester Wheatsheaf, 1990.

Kucich, John. *The Power of Lies: Transgression in Victorian Fiction.* Cornell, NY: Cornell University Press, 1994.

Langbein, John. *The Origins of Adversarial Criminal Trial.* Oxford: Oxford University Press, 2003.

Lavine, Sigmund A. *Allan Pinkerton.* London: Mayflower, 1970.

Lepps, Marie-Christine. *Apprehending the Criminal: The Production of Deviance in Nineteenth Century Discourse.* Durham, NC: Duke University Press, 1992.

Maunder, Andrew, and Grace Moore, editors. *Victorian Crime, Madness and Sensation.* Aldershot: Ashgate, 2004.

Mayhew, Henry. "Meeting of Ticket of Leave Men" in Vol III *London Labour and the London Poor: The London Street Folk.* London: Griffin, Bohn, and Company, 1861: 430–439.

McConnell, Frank. *The Science of Fiction and the Fiction of Science.* Jefferson, NC: McFarland, 2009.

_____, "Sherlock Holmes: Detecting Order Amid Disorder." *The Wilson Quarterly.* vol. 11. no. 2. Spring, 1987: 172–183.

McDonald, Peter D. *British Literary Culture and Publishing Practice, 1880–1914.* Cambridge: Cambridge University Press, 2002.

McGinn, Colin. *Ethics, Evil and Fiction.* Oxford: Clarendon Press, 1997.

Merrivale, Patricia, and Susan Sweeney, editors. *Detecting Texts: The Metaphysical Detective Story from Poe to Postmodernism.* Pennsylvania: University of Pennsylvania Press, 1999.

Morrison, Kevin, editor. *Companion to Victorian Popular Fiction.* Jefferson, NC: McFarland, 2014.

Morrison, Wayne. *Blackstone's Commentaries on the Laws of England.* London: Routledge-Cavendish, 2001.

Muddock, J. E. P. *For God and the Czar.* London: George Newnes, 1905.

Muller, John, and William Richardson, editors. *The Purloined Poe: Lacan, Derrida and Psychoanalytic Reading.* Baltimore: The Johns Hopkins University Press, 1998.

Plain, Gillian. *Twentieth Century Crime Fiction: Gender, Sexuality and the Body.* Chicago: Fitzroy Dearborn Publishers, 2001.

Plowright, John. *The Routledge Dictionary of Modern British History.* New York: Routledge, 2006.

Reddy. Maureen. *Sisters in Crime: Feminism and the Crime Novel.* 1988. New York: Continuum, 1988.

Reitz, Caroline. *Detecting the Nation: Fictions of Detection and the Imperial Venture.* Columbus: Ohio State University Press, 2004.

Richelson, Jeffrey T. *Intelligence and Spies: Intelligence in the Twentieth Century.* Oxford: Oxford University Press, 1995.

Rodensky, Lisa. *The Crime in Mind: Criminal Responsibility and the Victorian Novel.* Oxford: Oxford University Press, 2003.

Sampson, Robert. *Yesterday's Faces: A Study of Series Characters in The Early Pulp Magazines.* Bowling Green, OH: Bowling Green State University Popular Press, 1987.

Sarat, Austin. "Law and Literature Reconsidered" *Studies in Law, Politics and Society.* vol. 43. London: Emerald Group Publishing, 2008.

Seaton, James. "Law and Literature: Works, Criticism, and Theory." *Yale Journal of Law and the Humanities,* vol. 11, no. 2, art. 8. 1999: 479–507.

Showalter, Elaine. *A Literature of Their Own: British Women Novelists from Brontë to Lessing.* London: Virago, 2009.

_____. *Sexual Anarchy: Gender and Culture at the Fin de Siècle.* London: Bloomsbury. 1991.

A Solicitor. *The Pawnbrokers Act, 1872, Concisely and Clearly Explained for the Guidance of Both Pawnbrokers and Borrowers.* Google eBook, London: Wiley and Sons, 1872.

Stevens, Martin. *Four English Mystery Cycles: Textual, Contextual, and Critical Interpretations.* USA: Princeton University Press, 1987.

Storey, John. *Cultural Theory and Popular Culture: An Introduction.* New York: Routledge, 2015.

Symons, Julian. *Strange Tales from the Strand.* Oxford: Oxford University Press, 1992.

Thomas, Gordon. *Inside British Intelligence: 100 Years of MI5 and MI6.* London: J.R. Books, 2009.

Bibliography

Thomas, Ronald R. *Detective Fiction and the Rise of Forensic Science.* Cambridge: Cambridge University Press, 1999.

Thompson, Paul R. *The Edwardians: The Remaking of British Society.* London and New York: Routledge, 1975.

Thoms, Peter. *Detection and its Design.* Athens, OH: Athens University Press, 1998.

Tosh, John. *A Man's Place: Masculinity and the Middle Class Home in Victorian England.* New Haven, CT: Yale University Press, 2007.

Vaninskaya, Anna. "Russian Nihilists and the Prehistory of Spy Fiction." *BRANCH: Britain, Representation and Nineteenth Century History.* Edited by Dino Franco Felluga. Extension of *Romanticism and Victorianism on the Net.*

Varouxakis, Georgios. "Patriotism, Cosmopolitanism and Humanity in Victorian Political Thought." *European Journal of Political Theory.* vol. 5, no. 1, April 2006: 100–118.

Vuohelainen, Minna. "Contributing to Most Things: Richard Marsh, Literary Production, and the Fin de Siècle Periodicals Market." *Victorian Periodicals Review*, vol. 46, no. 3, Fall 2013: 401–422.

Ward, Ian. *Sex, Crime and Literature in Victorian England.* Portland, OR: Hart Publishing, 2014.

White, Rob, et al. *Crime and Criminology.* New York: Oxford University Press, 2004.

Winks, Robin, and Maureen Corrigan, editors. *Mystery and Suspense Writers: The Literature of Crime, Detection and Espionage.* New York: Charles Scribner's Sons, 1998.

Worthington, Heather. *The Rise of the Detective in Early Nineteenth Century Popular Fiction.* London: Palgrave Macmillan, 2005.

Zizek, Slavoj. *Looking Awry: An Introduction to Jacques Lacan Through Popular Culture.* Cambridge, MA: MIT Press, 1991.

Index

Index

"The British Campaign in France" 117
The British Raj 32
Britton, Wesley A. 136
Buchan, John 9, 15, 150, 164, 171, 174; *Memory Hold-the Door* 150, 158; "The Novel and the Fairy Tale" 150; *The Thirty-Nine Steps* 9, 15, 47, 49, 125, 143, 150-162
Bulawayo 153
Bulldog Drummond 15, 164
Bulwer-Lytton, Lady Rosina 112
burglary 23, 43, 51, 64, 68, 80

Calcutta 32
Camberwell 1
Campbell, Lady Gertrude and Lord Colin 23
"Can Criminals Be Cured by Surgical Operation?" 36
Carne, Simon 56
Carter, Nick 55
"A Case of Identity" 9, 21, 24-31, 42, 50, 172
"The Case of Mr. Geldard's Elopement" 11, 58, 60-66, 172
"The Case of the Dixon Torpedo" 130-132
"The Case of the Lever Key" 74
casebook tradition 11, 76
Casement, Roger 32
The Cathkin Rebellion 118
The Cato Street Conspiracy 118
Cavallaro, Rosanna 127, 150
Cavell, Edith 136
Cawelti, John G. 2, 147, 149, 151-158, 166
Cayley, Lois 95
Chancery Lane 131
Chandler, Raymond 3, 164
Chevalier, Auguste Dupin 58
Chicago 60, 127
A Child of the Jago 10, 57
Childers, Erskine: *The Riddle of the Sands* 9, 15, 118, 128, 142-150, 152, 155, 158, 162, 174
The Children's Charter 11, 67, 173
China-phobia 31
chivalry 65, 123, 134, 164
Christie, Agatha 16, 83, 109
The Chronicles of Addington Peace 82, 108, 169
The Chronicles of Martin Hewitt 59
The Chronicles of Michael Danevitch of the Russian Secret Service 133
cinema 15, 125, 136
Clarke, Ignatius 116, 143
Cleveland, Pres. Grover 36
The Cleveland Street Scandal 23
clubland hero 152
coining 130, 132
Cole, Darrell 125, 127, 137
Collins, Wilkie 20; *The Moonstone* 110; *No Name* 109
The Common Law 3
Conan Doyle, Arthur 1, 5-11, 19-22, 31-39, 53,

55, 56, 75, 79, 82, 116, 164, 171-174; "The Adventure of Charles Augustus Milverton" 48-52; "The Adventure of the Abbey Grange" 37-42; "The Adventure of the Blue Carbuncle" 42-48; "The Adventure of the Naval Treaty" 117-118; "The Adventure of the Second Stain" 117-123; "The Adventure of the Speckled Band" 31-37; *The Adventures of Sherlock Holmes* 5, 21, 32, 44; "The Boscombe Valley Mystery" 5, 49; "The British Campaign in France" 117; "A Case of Identity" 24-31; "The Final Problem" 10, 57; "His Last Bow: The War Service of Sherlock Holmes" 124-130; "The Man with the Twisted lip" 61; *Memories and Adventures* 33, 53; *The Return of Sherlock Holmes* 38, 48, 117, 118; "A Scandal in Bohemia" 6; *The Sign of the Four* 31, 79; *A Study in Scarlet* 6, 41, 49; "The Voice of Science" 75
Confessions of an English Opium-Eater 32
"Conscience" 12, 89-94, 172
Conrad, Joseph: *The Secret Agent: A Simple Tale* 95, 130, 162, 166
consequentialism 6, 168
The Continental School 36
Cooper, James Fennimore 14
The Court of Chancery 87
The Court of Criminal Appeal Act 2, 174
The Court of St. James's 134
Covent Garden 44, 46
coverture 26, 62
Cox, Edward W, "a searjant-at-law" *Principles of Punishment* 25
Dr. Cream, Thomas Neill 37, 101
Crimes Tried at the Old Bailey 44, 52
The Criminal 109
criminal anthropology 11, 35, 36, 47
The Criminal Evidence Act 2, 22, 104, 169, 174
Criminal Investigations Department (CID) 108
The Criminal Law Amendment Act 29, 53, 173
The Crimson Triangle (film) 125
Croft, Freeman Wills 11, 83, 169
"Culture and German Culture" 139

David Copperfield 44
decadence 51, 79
deceit 30, 40, 41, 110, 124, 140, 151, 154, 155, 157
deontology 6, 56, 78, 141, 168
De Quincy, Thomas *Confessions of an English Opium-Eater* 165
Derrida, Jacques 5
Despard, Col. Edward 117
Dickens, Charles 20, 87, 124, 151; *Bleak House* 48, 58, 87; ; *David Copperfield* 44 *The Mystery of Edwin Drood* 32, 110
dime novels 55, 56
The Diogenes Club 152

Index

Index

Index

Index

195